Life In Illisconsin

(1927-1951)

Patricia (Singletary) Phillips

Whispering Pines
Publications

3282 Yale Bridge Rd.
Rockton, IL 61072

Printed in the United States of America

ISBN 0-9647032-0-3

Cover Design: William Moore

Photo: Gene, Jackie, Tommy and Patsy Singletary—1936

Acknowledgements

My gratitude goes to the Beloit Daily News for in depth data, and to the Beloit College Library. Thanks to Rhonda Huber of the Beloit Historical Society for friendly help in locating various pictures. Appreciation also to Maurice Montgomery, curator-archivist, Rock County Historical Society.

Deep gratitude to my niece's husband, William Barth, editor of the Beloit Daily News for reviewing the book, and his suggestions. Special thanks to Marge Van Galder for encouragement, reviewing the book and her suggestions. Marge leads the memoir writing class through Society for Learning Unlimited, sponsored by Beloit College. This is an affiliation of Elderhostel Institute.

I am forever grateful to my beloved siblings: Thanks to Jacqueline H. Reynolds for her continual encouragement, great enthusiasm, and for allowing me to use contents from her picture albums, and scrapbooks. Thanks to Eugene M. Singletary, and Thomas W. Singletary. I am indebted to all of you for sharing memories, and being patient as I prodded you for information.

Special thanks to my dearest childhood friend, Barbara Kissling James. We lived in each other's pockets for a few treasured years. And thanks to all of the friends and family mentioned in this book. You have each helped me in unique ways.

This book would never have been published without the complete support and encouragement of my beloved husband, Richard A. Phillips. He trained me on the computer, overhauled the computer, spent endless hours helping with research, did some of the typing, cheerfully allowed me to awaken him in the wee hours for help on the computer, helped me wade through business forms, prodded me to meet deadlines, ran off hard copy and formatted the entire book on the computer. My deepest thanks, Richard!

Singletary
(Author's Grandparents)

	Children	Married
Joseph Charles Franklin Born 9-17-1879 Died 5-22-1944	1-Elton Eugene	Della Jenny Wessell
	2-Gordon Carlton	Cora Alice Vosburg
Married	3-Vera Irene	Henry E. Seils
	4-Ivan Curtis	1-Hazel E. Lewis 2-Mary Kathryn (Kay) Welsh
Abbie Stella Cooke Born 4-3-1874 Died 10-29-1936	5-Rollin Joseph	1-Mary Ullrich 2-Elizabeth (Wald) Fairbert
	6-Gaylord Penson	Helen S. Kimberk
	7-Ruby Stella	infant death
	8-Jeannette Elizabeth	1-Floyd Monroe 2-Richard Backberg

Wessell
(Author's Grandparents)

	Children	Married
Eli Pramer Born 9-11-1880 Died 10-7-1943	1-Leonard Clarence	Dorothy Mae Alexander
	2-Della Jenny	Elton Eugene Singletary
Married **Mary Ellen (Ella) Crouse** Born 9-11-1880 Died 11-17-51		

Singletary

	Children	
Elton Eugene Born 10-23-1900 Died 12-31-1993	1-Jacqueline Hilaire	12/10/27
	2-Eugene Maurice	01/15/30
	3-Thomas Warren	09/15/31
Married 4-15-27 **Della Jenny Wessell** Born 8-22-1907 Died 9-11-1992	4-Patricia Ann (Author)	11/05/35

Dedicated
in memory of
my beloved parents

Elton and Della Singletary

and my
beloved grandparents

Eli and Ella Wessell
JCF and Abbie Singletary

Your love and values
live in my heart

Contents

Illisconsin
Border People Enjoy Both States

Illisconsin - 1927-1951

Illisconsin, my beloved Illisconsin.
Romance of the border line people within.
Illinois workers drive north, what a quirk,
Passing Wisconsinites driving south to work.

Rockford boasts the magnificent Coronado theater,
Or vaudeville at the Palace, if you prefer.
Famous people dine at Rockton's Wagon Wheel,
Reunions in Illinois Parks have great appeal.

Beloit has its beautiful swimming pool,
While its library is the student's tool.
We pack a picnic for the Madison zoo,
Enroute dairy farms provide a scenic view.

What is this place I call Illisconsin?
Two states blending hearts of the people within.
Where lovers seek brides across the state border
And separate governments keep order.

An exchange of commerce and recreation,
Colleges and churches invite participation.
Back and forth we wine and dine,
Even pets tango over the invisible line.

Prologue

Suddenly I taste the sweet joy of my husband's retirement, and experience the realities of being the senior generation in our family. It seems like only yesterday that I embraced the beloved faces that I can see today only in portraits or cherished remembrance. How quickly it happens! Wasn't it yesterday that my siblings, neighborhood friends and classmates joined me in such childhood imagination and merry-making, such mischief and consequences?

It seems like yesterday, until I compare the results of technology, prices, wages, family structure, family activities, commitment in marriages and respect for God, life and country.

It is said that many people today seek old things - clothing, antiques, values. Why? For many reasons.

Life in Illisconsin (1927-1951) is a collection of snippets and vignettes of family life. Individual chapters are written chronologically, then put together topically. Time periods thus go forward, backward and take side trips as through the jumble of an exuberant, youthful mind. It is a special joy for busy readers who enjoy reading for brief periods of time.

Come along with me and experience adventures you may relate to, or find new. Laugh with us, cry with us, see our flaws and humanness, see how the families of our neighborhood touched one another's lives, find old family recipes, indulge in old fisherman's tales, rough it with us in primitive cabins in the north woods, and experience our beloved Illisconsin.

When I was growing up, sometimes I thought we were poor. In a sense we were; many people were in those years. But now I know how truly rich we were.

(1927-1951) Was it only yesterday? How many yesterdays? Today, even tomorrow, will be somebody's yesterday.

Chapter 1
A Family Established
(1927-1936)

Such tales my family has told through the years. I am both enlightened and puzzled in browsing through Grandma's and my parent's scrapbooks and photograph albums. Step with me into some scenes of yesteryear.

The headline in the Beloit Daily News, April 15, 1927: "Chinese Reject Demands of Powers." The United States will rush more cruisers to the Orient, in connection with the Nanking anti-foreign outrages. While tensions mount around the world, fear rages in America's Midwest as the mighty Mississippi rises rapidly from a week of heavy spring rain. States bordering the great river are threatened with the loss of lives, good farmland and possessions. Small cities are guarding against possible breaks in the levees. Railroad service is impaired around St. Louis.

Capital punishment is getting attention from all states. Some argue that the shadow of the gallows or the grim vision of the electric chair often influences juries to set free a guilty man who might otherwise have been sent to the penitentiary for life. In other states there is a plea for the return of capital punishment, on the ground that capital crimes have increased in the years since it was abolished.

A Beloit Realtor advertises in the classified ads: "New, 4 room house with electric lights, good east side location. Price $2200.00 Small payment down, balance monthly. J C F Singletary, 405 Goodwin Blk. Phone 547."

The Realtor, Joseph, sits in his living room on West Grand Avenue reading the paper. He looks up at his wife, "Abbie, there are some good grocery bargains in the paper tonight. Do we need anything else for Easter dinner?"

Abbie looks up from where she has been sitting gazing out the window "Oh, I don't know. I guess we have most everything. Joe, I can hardly think of Easter dinner with our son being married today in Chicago. The Wessells are fine neighbors, but Della didn't finish high school. Of course, she went to vocational school but she is only nineteen and Elton is twenty six. His achievements will take him far. When he quit high school and went to work, we never dreamed he could set you up in business and then put himself through college. Elton could have had his choice of more cultured girls."

"Abbie, Elton was our first child. He worked at your side

1

helping to raise our six other children. Our son is special in our eyes and perhaps no one would ever seem good enough for him. Della is intelligent and popular. She is a loving young woman and they will be happy," Joseph says. Going back to his paper, "are you sure you don't need any of these specials?"

At the International Grocery Co. and Meat Market at 202 State St. there are free deliveries. Sugar Cured, Cudahy's, Puritan, Plankington's Globe, Swift's Premium, Whole or Half Hams @ 28 cents a lb., Pork Loin Roast @ 19½ cents a lb., Pot Roast Beef @ 12 cents a lb., 10 lbs. Pure Granulated Sugar @ 65 cents, Qt. jar Dill Pickles @ 25 cents, Lb. pkg. of Prunes for 15 cents, and 4 lbs. good eating Apples for 25 cents, Bananas 3 lbs. for 25 cents, Large oranges 45 cents a doz., Lettuce 10 cents a head, large bunch of carrots 6 cents, and One lb. can of Maxwell House Coffee (Whole Bean or Steel Cut) 49 cents.

By endorsing officially the compromise farm relief movement, Republican President Calvin Coolidge has demonstrated he is ready to challenge the aspirations of the avowed presidential candidate of the agricultural belt, former governor Frank O. Lowden of Illinois, and thus open the road for a third term attempt.

In Indiana a final settlement of the coal strike in the strip mines appears near. The Beloit Daily News is also full of murders, suicides and accidents. There appears to be another murder, but a closer look reveals this ad: "*Constipation Murders Sleep*" Kellogg's ALL-BRAN brings prompt, safe, relief—guaranteed!

In Kenosha, for the first time in the history of the Wisconsin Congregational Church, a woman is ordained as pastor. Meanwhile, across the nation, states are battling over the justice system, with most states considered "dry." Some politicians, considered boozers, are working to overthrow Prohibition. Among the "wet" states favoring this trend are: New York, Massachusetts, New Jersey, Maryland, Pennsylvania, Illinois, Missouri and Wisconsin. Today a Beloit man, brought before Judge Chester H. Christensen in municipal court, pleaded guilty to violating the "Dry Law." The four counts are sale and possession of intoxicating liquor on April 7, and the possession of a still and possession of mash on April 14. He is fined $750.00 and costs, and sentenced to two months in the Milwaukee House of Correction.

At the Majestic Theater in Beloit, WI, Marion Davies is starring in, `The Red Mill.' The Rex Theater has a movie about a dog's devotion and a boy's love, `Hills of Kentucky,' starring Rin Tin Tin.

* — * — *

Elton Eugene Singletary is oblivious to any of the events that

2

are taking place across the country or around the world. It is April 15, 1927, Good Friday. In the Christian realm, people remember the suffering of our Lord Jesus Christ, as He took on the sins of all mankind; paying the price for the redemption of every human being that would accept Him as their Lord and Savior. But today Elton's heart is full of love and excitement. This is the day that he will marry the effervescent young woman next door. His younger brother, Ivan, had been engaged to her, but the relationship dissolved. Of the many suitors that have wooed Della Jenny Wessell, Elton has won her favor. He is about to embark on the longest adventure of his life.

Excitement nearly overcomes Della, as the train roars into the Northwestern depot in Beloit. But she feels the comfort of Elton's grip as he helps her board the Chicago bound train. As they settle into their seats she relaxes and smiles up at him. She ponders in her heart, her triumph over the variety of young women who have pursued this tall, dark, handsome man who graduated from Beloit College a year ago. She feels the current that passes from his hand to hers.

"Your Aunt Mary and Uncle Frank will be waiting for us in Chicago," Elton says. "They have made arrangements with Rev. Adkins in Crown Point, Indiana."

"I am happy they will be our attendants," Della smiles. "Aunt Mary's niece is planning a wedding supper for us after the ceremony."

"We couldn't ask for a more beautiful day, sunshine, blue skies, mild temperature. It's a good omen, Della."

Where are the cameras this day Della and Elton are married? They have many pictures of their frivolous activities before their marriage. But no one captures the lovely bride in her salmon pink, silk crepe dress or the groom in his dark blue suit. There will never be a wedding picture to look back on when they celebrate their sixty-fifth wedding anniversary.

Monday morning finds Elton back to work at Barber Colman Co. in Rockford, Illinois. While Elton is working at a job he is not happy with, Della is settling into their rented apartment in this city that seems quite strange to her. She will always be homesick.

3

Della J. Wessell shortly before her April 15, 1927 marriage.

Elton E. Singletary shortly before his April 15, 1927 marriage.

December ninth, on a blustery winter night, Della awakens with sharp pains. "Elton, wake up. We need to get to the hospital!"

Elton is on his feet in seconds, pulls on his pants and awakens Mrs. Dunlap in the neighboring apartment, requesting to use her telephone. He hurries back to assist Della.

"Dr. Anthony is on his way here. He will take us to the hospital in his car," Elton exclaims.

Della will always speak of this ride to the hospital. Elton wraps a blanket around her, and someone plunks a fancy hat on her head as she goes out the door.

On December tenth Della and Elton present the first grandchild to both of their parents, a darling baby girl. She will drive them nearly insane for weeks, crying night and day, with the colic. Della remains flat on her back in the hospital bed for ten days. Swedish American Hospital of Rockford presents her with the outlandish bill of $50.00. They charge her $4.00 per day room rate and $10.00 for the delivery room. Such a price when the average annual income is $936.00.

Elton proudly names the little lady Jacqueline Hilaire, although Della is convinced that such a long and unusual name will do serious harm to the infant. Baby Jackie is born tongue-tied. In February a specialist snips the membrane freeing the little tongue, and it has been wagging ever since. ☺

By September 1928 Elton and Della find a white, two story frame home at 125 S. Eighth Street, South Beloit, Illinois. Della is thrilled to leave Rockford and return to the area where their parents reside. The home is on the west side of Rock River. It is located on the corner of S. Eighth and Illinois Streets, and has two and a half city lots. They will now live just one block from the Wisconsin border.

Life in Illisconsin will be an adventure. The home has one closet, a coal furnace, dirt floor and limestone walls in the cellar, no electricity or inside plumbing. Still, Della exclaims, "Oh how wonderful, a big place of our own. Look at that beautiful stairway with the banister, Elton."

"Well, there are plenty of things we can do to improve the place, but it's a start," he responds.

On September 19, 1928 they place their down payment and mortgage with W. F. Silverthorne at the purchase price of $1,500.00. Spring finds Elton spading up the back lot for a large garden. By fall Della has a supply of home canned vegetables on the basement shelves. It is home.

October 24, 1929 Elton is reading the Beloit Daily News. "This doesn't look good, Della. It says, `Wave after wave of selling again mowed down prices on the stock exchange today and billions of dollars were clipped from values.' The same thing happened yesterday. This surely doesn't look good! It says here, 'President Hoover is resting after the most arduous trip since he was elected. He has outlined the most extensive engineering project ever contemplated by the federal government, to develop inland waterways. He hopes to get the $1,000,000,000 from savings in naval armaments.' I hope the economy doesn't go to pot. In a few weeks we will have another child to be responsible for."

"Oh Elton, don't be such a worry wart," Della says, as she picks up little Jackie. "You are going to have your second birthday in just six weeks, Sweetie Pie," she says, patting her.

"A truck ferry went down in a bad storm on Lake Michigan and they fear the whole crew of fifty men are drowned," he adds, in a gloomy voice.

January moves into its second week and Della calls her mother to come get Jackie, in preparation for Della's trip to the hospital. Grandma Wessell welcomes the opportunity. Della is concerned about the winter weather because the neighboring state of Indiana is battling the most devastating flood in the history of the state, and blizzards are menacing the West.

Elton glances up at Della, as he sits reading, and says, "They say Wisconsin is becoming the summer home of gangsters. The gangsters are buying off officials with beer and other bribes. They agree not to molest citizens in the vicinities where they encamp."

"That's disgusting. I read that tomorrow is the tenth anniversary of Prohibition. Four presidents have had to cope with it starting with Wilson; and to date it has cost the federal government $264,475,384.00 to enforce it," Della responds, looking up from the paper.

"Della, Strasburg Lumber and Fuel Company is advertising a coal sale. 6 x 3 Illinois Egg in 2 ton lots, at $5.75 per ton. It's guaranteed $7.25 grade of coal. It has good heat and no soot. They say their volume of business enables them to sell this coal so cheap. We'd better take advantage of this price and have the coal bin filled," Elton urges.

Della gets up and looks out the window, "It's snowing a little." She catches her breath and exclaims, "Ooh!"

Elton jerks his head up, "What's the matter?"

"I think we are going to have to get to the hospital," she answers. January 15, 1930 they are blessed with their first son, Eugene Maurice.

Elton's fear of an economic crisis in the country are becoming a reality. Farmers are having a rough time; mining, railroads and textiles are no better off. Many folks expect the economy to get brighter, but Elton continues to worry. Many more people are losing jobs and can't pay their creditors. Life savings and homes are being lost. The news indicates most European countries are even worse off.

By September 15, 1931 Beloit College is accepting farm produce in lieu of tuition. It takes a lot of food to feed the students, so it seems a sensible solution to the cost of education. Today there is also another mouth to feed for Elton and Della's household with the arrival of their second son, Thomas Warren.

Della sits up in her hospital bed to read the letter that has arrived from Elton's sister, Vera Seils, who is expecting her own child soon.

"We had a bad storm here this morning about five o'clock. Henry and I saw what appeared like a huge ball of fire go past our bedroom window. I put my hands up to my face in my fright and have been worrying ever since. I hope I didn't mark my baby.

"Sorry your Mother is ill. Hope she is better by now. Give her my regards. Bet the kiddies are crazy about their new brother. Have they seen him yet?"

At this time, many women are superstitious about causing their unborn baby physical harm, if they make the gesture of touching some part of their own body when alarmed by a condition. Della's brother was born with a hare-lip. Her mother says she knows exactly when she "marked" him. She claims to have seen a person with that condition, and with a gasp she jerked her hand up to cover her own mouth. Old wives' tales?

In 1931, "The Star Spangled Banner" becomes the national anthem of the United States. For those who are lucky enough to have jobs, the average annual income is $1,406.00 How does the saying go? "It is a recession when others are out of work and a depression when you are out of work."

At midday, midweek in the cool of spring 1932, four- year-old, Jackie warms herself over the dining room register. Little Gene is playing with baby Tommy. Della looks out the window and catches her breath. For the rest of her life this moment will be etched in her memory. Elton is walking up the sidewalk with his lunch pail in his hand. Her heart freezes with fear, she feels like an old, wet dish rag.

Elton comes through the back door looking like a ghost. Little Jackie can't understand what is happening, but she will always remember she senses something bad.

He utters the terrible words, "I've lost my job."

A time of fear . . . a time of pain . . . a time to pray . . . a time to receive . . . a time to trust . . .

Work comes in little spurts. Some government employment becomes available in South Beloit. He joins others on a major construction project for Blackhawk Boulevard. As winter approaches, Elton, his brother Rollin and Della's father clear trees off land for a farmer.

On a cold December evening in 1932, Elton parks the car in front of the white Broder mansion on Central Avenue, and gathers Gene into his arms. He opens the door for Della as she gets out with year old Tommy in her arms. Little Jackie grabs hold of her Mama's coat sleeve as they walk up the sidewalk to the house.

The Broder House (From the collection of the Beloit Historical Society)

"Mama, are we going to Grandpa's big house?" Jackie asks.

"Yes, Honey. Grandma invited us for the evening. We are privileged to visit such a grand home," Della replies.

"Why is there a little house on the roof?" Jackie questions.

"That's not a house, Honey. That's a cupola. It's just a lovely, decorative part of the architecture on this mansion."

The massive wood door swings open and Abbie Singletary smiles, "Come in. Come in. Jenny, help take the children's coats." Elton's beautiful little sister, with dark hair and snapping dark eyes, unbuttons Jackie's coat.

When the kisses and greetings subside all around, Joseph says, "Jenny, take the children in the other room and read to them for awhile."

The family enjoys an evening together in one of the most elegant homes in Beloit. J.C. Converse, an attorney from the east, built the home about 1867. He came here to establish a law practice with S.J. Todd. Mr. Gurley purchased the property when

9

Converse died and sold it to Alice Broder. The house located on the north two thirds of a plot of land between Wisconsin and Central Avenues, and bounded on each end by Chapin and Bushnell streets, had been mentioned as the possible site for a hospital at one time.

The elegant home has twenty three rooms and all the large rooms have fireplaces with marble mantles. Ceilings are ten feet high, and the rooms have tall arched windows. There are massive wood doors with heavy brass hardware. The living room has an impressive circular stairway leading to the second floor.

When Alice Broder bought this home, she brought exquisite furnishings from the east. With her sisters and brother, they made it a show place. Curious neighbors watched them ride up in elegant carriages. Dressed fashionably, they carried fancy black lace parasols to protect their complexions. The home became well known in the area as the Broder mansion.

Alice, Mary, Catherine, brother Paul Broder and sister Ann Mallen all died in the home. Rumors circulated that Paul had been murdered. The family mausoleum in Beloit's Oakwood Cemetery will hold an everlasting mystery.

When Alice Broder died and the estate came on the market, family history reveals that Will Webermeier and Joseph C.F. Singletary purchased it. They had plans for developing the land; building homes. But with the depression Will wanted out, so Joseph C.F. Singletary bought his share.

"This must be one of the most elegant homes in Beloit," says Della.

"Converting it into four apartments has made a few changes, but it is still an elegant home," Abbie responds.

"We thought it would be nice for Abbie to experience life in such a mansion, so we moved in. I will probably develop the land, when the time is right," says Joseph.

"I think it is a wonderful home to have in the family, Dad," says Della.

"We never expected to live in such a grand place after raising seven children," Abbie says. "Well, let's go enjoy the dining room. Jenny, bring the children. It's time we eat my homemade cream puffs."Amid happy chatter everyone gathers around the table. "I love your cream puffs, Grandma," says Jackie.

"Yum - yum," adds little Gene.

Tommy excitedly waves his patties from his Aunt Jenny's lap.

"There are a lot of birthdays coming up in the next few weeks," says Abbie. "Jackie will be five on the tenth of this month, and son Gaylord's is on the eighteenth. Your father, Eli's, is the twelfth, Della, and your brother Leonard's is the twenty

10

fifth. Then Jenny will be fifteen on the tenth of January, grand-son Freddie's on the eleventh, son Rollin's wife - Mary's on the twelfth and little Gene will be three on the fifteenth."

"I don't know how you can even remember all of those. It's time for us to go home and get the children to bed. Rollin, Pa Wessell and I are going to be cutting wood tomorrow," says Elton.

As they bundle up and leave the lovely Broder mansion, Jackie says, "I like Grandma and Grandpa's big house."

Elton says, "If the economy doesn't improve soon, I may never get my job back, and we could lose our home."

"Don't worry about it, Elton. You are earning a little money with these odd jobs. Let's just get home to bed. Morning will come soon and you get up so early to cut wood," says Della.

For Elton morning arrives too soon and cutting timber in the woods is hard work. The mind races with the body. "Where the hell is my pipe?" Elton asks in a frenzy, tossing a log in the trailer.

Eli laughs, "For Pete's sake, Elt, it's in your mouth!"

Family helps with groceries and gifts. Elton closes off the upstairs and they manage to live downstairs, to save heat. They hang sheets over the windows to help keep out the cold. Some-how they make it through the winter. Elton's father pays the delinquent sewer and state tax for 1931. Elton worries about providing for his family, and works hard when work is avail-able. This fear and the humility of accepting help from family leaves a lifelong effect on him. He develops a generous heart for the needs of others, but is an extremely conservative man.

March 3, 1933 - Beloit bankers today complied with the order of Gov. A. G. Schmedeman and Lt. Gov. T.J. O'Malley clos-ing all banks in Wisconsin for a two-week period, but declared emphatically that banking conditions in Beloit were in no wise responsible for the closing order.

Franklin D. Roosevelt is now President of the United States. March 15, 1933 Beloit holds a prosperity parade as banks reopen. Abroad, war talk and army activity stirs Europe to act. Today Della and Elton negotiate with Mr. W.F. Silverthorne, who holds the mortgage on their home. He is a kindly person who is a flagman for the railroad. Mr. Silverthorne sits in a tower at the tracks that cross the lower end of Shirland Ave. When a train comes, he holds up his sign to stop the traffic. He agrees to allow them to live up the equity they have in their home as rent. They sign a three-year lease with the option to repurchase.

On a perfect day in June, Elton embraces Della. They hug and kiss and dance around the dining room. He pats her fanny and the children join in the merrymaking.

11

Gene, Tommy & Jackie (1933)   *Tommy and Jackie (1933)*

"Oh happy day! Oh happy day! I've been called back to work, now we will be able to repurchase our home," Elton nearly explodes with joy.

They will pay an additional $700.00 for indoor plumbing, electricity and improvements made during the interval.

South side of 125 South Eighth Street in 1934.

"Thank God. Oh thanks to God," Della echoes the joy, and the children clap their hands as they all celebrate. People con-

12

tinue to struggle, but for those called back to work new hope blooms and people begin to dream again.

On Thursday, February 8, 1934, Elton has banked the furnace for the night. It is expected to drop down around zero degrees. The window shades are pulled down, and Elton, Della, Jackie, Gene and little Tommy are sleeping soundly in warm beds.

Della stirs, then sits up and listens. "What's the matter?" asks Elton rolling over.

Della jumps out of bed and grabs for her robe. "The telephone is ringing!" she says. She stumbles toward the hallway and flips on a light as she hurries down the stairway. At the head of the stairway, Elton hears her say, "Oh, no! Oh, Dad, I'm so sorry. We will be right there!"

"What is it, Della?" Elton hollers.

"The Broder mansion is on fire, and it's bad!"

Della races back up the stairs, and they both grab shoes and socks, and pull on the nearest warm clothes they can find. "We'll just bundle the children into their snowsuits over their pajamas. We'd better grab extra blankets off the closet shelf," yells Della.

"Mama, what's the matter?" asks six-year-old Jackie, as she is pulled from her warm bed.

"Oh, Honey, Grandpa's big house is on fire," Della says, close to tears.

The old car starts in spite of the frigid temperatures. "Della, did everyone get out of the house alright?" Elton suddenly asks in panic.

"Yes, but they had to run out in their night clothes."

When they reach the area, they can see flames leaping out the roof. Elton leaves Della in the car with the children and goes to investigate.

"Mama, who lives in the house besides Grandma and Grandpa?" Jackie asks.

"Your Daddy's brother Rollin and his wife, Mr. and Mrs. Charles Petit and Mrs. Myrtle Shaw," Della cries. Two and a half-year-old Tommy snuggles close on her lap.

They all peer through the windows, watching the multitude of people gathered as the firemen spray water. Jackie rubs her sleeve on the steamy window to see better, and four year old Gene squeezes up beside her. The entire area glows red with the upper half of the mansion engulfed in flames. Fire glows through the small attic windows, and the large arched windows enable everyone to see the interior of the house as it blazes.

Elton comes back and gets in the car for a few minutes. "They got very little out. A few personal effects and just a few

13

pieces of furniture. They are all in night clothes, wrapped in blankets. They're pretty upset, but thankful no one was hurt. They called the firemen at 10:35, and when they arrived at 10:55 they found a large section of the roof had already burned. They couldn't go up the circular stairway because the flames were too great. They think it started from a defective chimney. That cupola on the roof is old, and dry enough to provide fuel for the flames," he relates.

"This has got to be the most spectacular fire that Beloit has had in years. Look how high those flames are shooting. They light up the whole sky! And look how the water is freezing on the trees. Oh, my, I thank God, no one was hurt," Della exclaims.

Elton goes back to confer with the family, but there is little that can be done now. He comes back to the car shaking, partially from the cold, and from the emotion of the event. "They called for more equipment at 11:35. They have had five hoses running, but the water isn't fazing that ferocious blaze. There isn't going to be anything left but a shell. Della, look at the piano in the driveway that runs out toward Central Avenue. It is frozen solid in over two inches of ice from all that water! Some guy out there said to me, `J.C.F. Singletary, the Realtor owns this house.' I answered, Yes, that's my father. They lived in it."

"Did Dad have insurance on it?" Della asks.

"He had some, but not full coverage. This is a $12,000.00 loss. He says he'll have to tear the shell down, and divide the property into residential lots," Elton responds. "It's a good thing they have the furnished house on Prairie Avenue, over by the tracks. And no one is living there right now. Well, it's wee hours, and there is nothing we can do. The firemen will stick around a little longer, but we better go home."

As they head home, Della says, "Your Ma and Dad lost their dream to live in a mansion tonight, and Beloit lost a magnificent landmark. Those that witnessed this event will remember it for a lifetime."

On a golden day in late October 1935, Della steps out on the back porch observing her happy children at play. In a few weeks the little blond girl, Jackie, will be eight years old. Gene and Tommy are frolicking around with her. The three children are spaced approximately two years apart in age. It appeared that four year old Tommy would have completed the family circle.

Jackie smiles up at her from her tricycle, saying, "Hi, Mama."

"Hi, Sweetheart. Your mama is going away for a few days. I want you kids to be good while I'm gone. When I come home, I will bring something to you. Would you like something brown or white?"

Thinking it would be a little dog, the kids chorus, "Brown."

14

Jackie notices that mama's tummy is rather large, but she has no idea why.

Gene, Tommy and Jackie (fall 1935)

The stork is still making deliveries. The gift arrives on November fifth with an icy gale out of the West and the season's first snow flurries. Daddy has named the other three children, but Mama names me Patricia Ann. I am neither brown nor white, but ruddy red, weighing in at nine pounds, fourteen ounces, with an abundance of black hair.

On this winter day that I am born, if any of the family wishes to go to the Rex movie theater in Beloit they can see the last evening of "She Married Her Boss," starring Claudette Colbert. They could stay at home smoking their Chesterfield cigarettes, which are advertised as made of mild, ripe tobacco; while they read the news that Italy has bombed 500 Ethiopian soldiers, or that in the elections the Republicans win 82 seats and control of the Assembly.

While Jackie, Gene and Tommy are staying at Grandma and Grandpa Wessell's home at 2436 Riverside Dr. in Beloit. Mama writes letters to them daily. She says,

"You have a beautiful little baby sister with the cutest pug nose. (Reading these letters as an adult, I go into gales of laughter, never imagining my beak was ever pug!) *Now you are getting to be big boys and must not wet your pants; and don't fight. All of you are to mind Grandma, and I will soon bring your new baby sister home. Jackie, you are a good girl to help Grandma so much."*

These are hard times. There are still ten million people unemployed, but there is nothing but joy expressed throughout the family at the arrival of another mouth to feed. I will always be "the baby of this family."

"Hush, little Darlin. Hush baby, Patsy. Don't cry sweet baby," Jackie croons as she kisses my soft cheeks, and rocks me back and forth. It will be years before she confesses that she pinches me to make me cry, so she has an excuse to pick me up and love me.

* — * — *

In 1935, Roosevelt's administration enacts the WPA (Work Progress Administration) creating jobs for millions. The Social Security Act is signed into law. Benito Mussolini of Italy leads his nation to war with Ethiopia. Amelia Earhart is the first woman to fly over the Pacific Ocean. The first night baseball game is played in Cincinnati. Pan American Airlines begins flights to Manila on the "China Clipper."

The average income this year is $1,195.00. Bread costs 6 cents a loaf, coffee 24 cents a pound, an electric washing machine costs $47.75, and a portable phonograph costs $12.75. None of these things will be more important, to me, than the fact that I begin my journey through life.

January 3, 1936 when Patsy is two months old, eight year old Jackie writes this letter to Grandma and Grandpa Wessell.

Dear Grandma and Grandpa,
how are you today I hope you are all will.
I held the baby while you and Mother was gone. and what do you think she did she wet on the floor and on and on my dress and I said you naughty girl you.
Florence said oh oh. and then I had to change her pants. I changed her pants 3 times. You mow that tinker Tin book The little boy on the back why his pants are hanging down.
will guess I'll have to ring of

with love and kisses
Jackie   how is Grandpa?

16

My first winter will go down in history as the winter of the big blizzards and extended periods of sub-zero weather. Daddy experiences unbelievable winter conditions in his travels to and from work.

January nineteenth, just four days past Gene's sixth birthday, Daddy says, "It's a good thing we have just had the coal bin filled. That blizzard yesterday brought five inches of snow, with drifting that blocked roads shut. Some drifts are six feet deep and more snow is coming."

By the twenty third of January, the Beloit Daily News reports two hundred pupils marooned at a school in Genoa, Indiana. It is twenty four degrees below zero. Twenty nine people have died across the nation. International Falls has fifty six degrees below zero.

At the end of January a coal shortage is feared. By February fifth, all but the primary roads are blocked in the Midwest. On the eighth, a new storm jams roads. King Winter's toll to date is more than two hundred dead across the United States. Authorities say, "Rock County roads are blocked and we can't do anything about plowing them, because men operating the plows can't see a thing in this storm. Roads not yet cleared, from two previous storms, are buried anew."

The Chicago Weather Bureau predicts temperatures from ten to twenty five below zero in the Middle West, with no respite in sight until late next week.

Snow drifts near the Johnson farm south of Clinton, lack about three inches of touching the electric wires. In some areas, farmers are having trouble with cattle walking over the top of fences.

Mama is upset because Daddy has to spend a few nights at Barber Colman, in Rockford, due to bad weather. The men curl up on tables, in the cafeteria, for the night.

February tenth the Beloit Daily News runs a special bulletin: Illinois highway patrolmen are helping a couple of worried motorists look for two cars missing on the concrete highway between Rockton and Rockford. The cars were stranded in snow Saturday and are nowhere to be seen today. "They're probably covered by drifts," the patrolmen said. Neither car had been located by 3:00 p.m. This is the Gospel truth, not something just to be remembered on a hot August day. Snowplows stalled.

Through February, roads are cleared, new snow, much wind, cold waves, and fourteen foot drifts. Daddy will never forget traveling these roads all winter, going between snow walls towering many feet above the car on both sides.

Illinois begins to fear the worst floods in years. By March third it is twenty eight degrees and by March tenth it is sixty five degrees. Still, after such a winter, who would not want spring?

When I am eleven and one half months old, Grandma Singletary passes away. The time of grief for our family is lightened in the joy of seeing me take my first steps. I will never know her, but I will know Grandpa Singletary and experience much delight with Grandma and Grandpa Wessell. Come along and share the adventures...

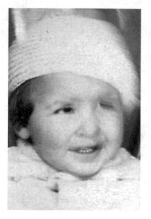
Patsy fall 1936

Abbie and J.C.F. Singletary

Chapter 2
Fun At Grandma and Grandpa Wessell's House
(1939-1943)

To Grandma and Grandpa's House We Go

To Grandma and Grandpa's house we go,
The four grandkiddies they love so.
We'll chase the chickens into the coop,
Trying to keep our feet out of the poop.

Dog "Blackie" will excitedly jump around,
Knocking little Patsy to the ground.
Jackie will pick up her little sister,
For she is always the great comforter.

To the top of the chicken coop roof,
The boys climb, then jump off.
Through raspberry brambles they'll squeeze,
Tommy howls as he steps on a nest of bees.

Into Grandma's kitchen the girls will fly.
Watching plump doughnuts in hot grease fry.
In a bag of powdered sugar she shakes "holes."
More joy or tastier treats, no one knows.

Gene and Tommy pull the cat's tail,
And wrestle each other, without fail.
They follow Grandpa down the cellar stair,
Admiring the woodworking he does there.

Here is laughter and squabbles to share,
Adventures to experience beyond compare.
Into treasure chests, memories we'll shove.
Created by Grandma and Grandpa Wessell's love.

Grandpa turns off Riverside Drive into his driveway, passing the green lawn and the two story green and white frame home that sits on the right side. The cinder-gravel crunches under the wheels as the car comes to a stop in front of the white, frame, single car garage. Grandma gets out of the front, with me in her arms. I am now three years old. Jackie, Gene and Tommy scramble out through the back door of the Oakland.

"Grandma, I will take Patsy for a walk around the front yard," offers eleven year old Jackie.

19

"Okay, Honey. Grandma has some cooking to do, so we will have good things to eat when your Mama and Daddy come for supper tonight," says Grandma. "Later, you can help Grandma clean the strawberries Mama sent along for our shortcake."

"Okay, Grandma, I'll be glad to help you," Jackie responds. She takes my hand and leads me to the front yard. When Grandma opens the door, their springer spaniel - Blackie, comes bounding out to join us. He wiggles and waggles, giving us kisses. We pass the front steps and walk out to Grandpa's fish pond on this warm, summer Saturday in 1939. It is a round pond about eight feet across and several inches deep. "Looky, Patsy. See the little gold fishies?" Jackie asks.

I bend forward and splash my hand in the water.

"Fishy - fishy," I say.

After a bit, Jackie attempts to lead me on to a new interest, but I like the fish. Pulling back, I stiffen my back, "Fishy, fishy!" I cry, puckering up.

"Oh, don't cry, Sweetie," Jackie says, patting my head. "Let's go look at Grandpa's wind mill."

"Mill?" I ask.

Jackie leads me slowly across the green grass. I totter along on my chubby little legs. My pudgy tummy bulges the seams of my pretty yellow dress. Jackie, in her motherly fashion, adjusts the yellow bow in my hair. "See the white and green windmill, Grandpa made?" asks Jackie.

I reach out to touch it. "Grandpa make it?" I ask.

Grandma & Grandpa Wessell's House On Riverside Dr.

20

Garage   *Chicken coop*   *House*

A friend, Gene, Jackie and Tommy -
June 1933

G, J, T, Hot Day at Grandmas -
July 1935

Grandpa
Wessell
in favorite
lawn chair.

Patsy 1936 →

Patsy, Jackie, Blackie   *Grandma & Grandpa Wessell*

In the back yard, nine year old Gene and six-year-old Tommy catch the two black and white spotted cats. They pet them and play with them awhile. Then Gene declares, "I've heard that any time a cat falls; it will always land on its feet."

"Let's try it," Tommy squeals. "We could climb up the open stairway to the upper apartment and drop them over the rail."

"Great idea. Let's do it," adds Gene.

They clamor up the stairs and look down. "It's a long way down. You go first, Gene."

Gene lifts the cat out over the rail and it twists and squirms scratching him. He lets go —- down, down, down!

"It did it! He landed on his feet!" Gene yells.

Tommy lifts his cat up, up and over the rail, the cat grabs hold with his claws. "Ouch, ouch," Tommy cries.

"Let go of him," yells Gene.

With a flip and pitch over the rail, the cat drops to the ground —- "Look, look —-He did it!" They scream.

Both cats leap off to hiding places; it will be awhile before they trust Gene and Tommy again. The boys race down the stairs jumping from the fourth step. They slow up at the chicken pen and cluck at the chickens.

Our family affectionately refers to the acreage between the back of the house and the river as "the park," and it is beautiful this morning. The green lawn slopes gently toward Rock River. Red squirrels scamper about, chasing each other from one oak

22

tree to another. The boys race each other through the park to the river's edge.

"Hey, Tommy, let's build a hut!" says Gene.

"Out of what?" asks Tommy.

"Grandpa has some orange crates and big, thin, packing crates up by the chicken coop," Gene states.

"Won't Grandpa care if we use them?" Tommy inquires.

"Naw, Grandpa doesn't care what we do," answers Gene.

"Come on! Let's go drag it down here. We can build it up against that big oak tree, near the neighbor's little old house where widow Mary lives."

After several trips of pulling, tugging and dragging, the boys construct their hut propped against the big oak tree.

"Let's build a fireplace in it," suggests Tommy.

"Yeah, that's a great idea. Here, we have one orange crate left, let's use it," replies Gene.

When the fireplace is situated, the boys observe their hut and decide it's a neat cabin.

"It's cool, let's build a fire in the fireplace," says Gene.

Tommy gathers sticks and old oak leaves, while Gene runs up to the house to get some of Grandpa's matches.

They place the collection in the orange crate; after striking several matches Gene says, "The dang thing isn't going to start."

Tommy takes a candy wrapper from his pocket and sticks it in the leaves. This time as Gene puts the lighted match to it, a little flame flickers.

"Oh boy. It's gonna go," Tommy exclaims.

They put their hands close, to feel the warmth, but now smoke fills the hut and they are forced to vacate it. The flames begin to leap and spread to devour their hut.

"Oh, oh," yells Tommy, in fright.

"What should we do?" screams Gene.

"What are you doing?" shouts Grandpa, as he comes running toward them. "Land sakes! You'll burn down the tree and the neighbor's house!"

The boys look at Grandpa and then to their flaming hut with wide eyes and pounding hearts. Grandpa jerks out a couple pieces of crate that hasn't caught fire, and beats at the flames. Gene spies an old bucket near the river and races to dip it in. Tommy runs to help and they race to the fire with the water. Grandpa grabs it and douses the smoldering remains.

The boys have never seen Grandpa look so upset, and they know they have done a dangerous and stupid thing. No tongue lashing is needed because each little heart knows they have hurt Grandpa and broke some of his trust in them. Grandpa, with wisdom, can see frightened and repentant boys. "Don't ever

23

play with fire again," is all he says. The boys hang their heads. Are these tears escaping?

Mama and Daddy arrive about five thirty, and Mama goes in to the kitchen to help Grandma. Grandpa is outside.

"Hey, Elton, come on out to the chicken-coop, and I'll show you my new lawn mower. Firestone Auto Supply had a sale on them," Grandpa says.

Daddy follows Grandpa into the storage area of the chicken-coop. "That looks like a nice one," says Daddy.

"It has five self-sharpening and adjusting blades on it," says Grandpa.

"Are those ten inch rubber tires?" Daddy asks.

"Yup. And it has roller bearings, too. It ought to be easier to push. The reel turns easily. It had been $7.95. They had a close-out sale for $6.50. Seemed like a good buy. The boys are eager to try it out," Grandpa says.

Tommy comes into the shed, "Grandma says supper is ready."

Supper is a happy event. There is succulent roast chicken, mashed potatoes and gravy, fruit salad, candied carrots and bread and butter.

"I'm stuffed," says Jackie, finishing a drumstick.

"Lou called to say they're coming out for the evening, so we'll have dessert later," says Grandma.

"Is Dick bringing his guitar, Ma?" asks Mama.

"Yes. We'll make music and have fun."

I know we will have an evening of merrymaking when Mama's cousins, the Stebbins family, arrive. The small living room joins the dining room with almost no wall between. Soon, everyone settles into a chair or on the davenport. Grandma, Grandpa and Lou have their harmonicas. Dick Stebbins tunes up his guitar and adjusts the rack that holds his harmonica. Gene gets a couple spoons, and to the rest of us, Mama passes out combs with a piece of waxed paper folded over the teeth of each one. We try our ability at humming through the waxed paper covered combs, to see how well we can vibrate that special sound. Already Blackie is looking around in perplexity.

Once everyone is tuned up, the fun begins. "Take Me Out To The Ball Game" —- "The Lady In Red" —- Such joyful noise. Blackie is howling. Feet are tapping, combs are vibrating, spoons are clacking —- "Let Me Call You Sweetheart" —- This is Grandma's favorite song. Over and over the music plays, louder and louder Blackie howls. Mama requests "The Beer Barrel Polka." Some set aside the combs to sing. Music is bouncing off the walls. We frolic and rollick, hands a clapping. Then comes "Goodnight Sweetheart" and we know that it's time to enjoy

24

Grandma's delicious strawberry shortcake, which Jackie helped to prepare.

*　—　*　—　*

The wonderful interaction of three generations is a way of life in our family. The sharing of fun, learning experiences and helping each other is a normal, continual process. Seasons' dissolve into one another as this family celebrates the joy of life, in our Illisconsin.

I burst through the school door at four o'clock Friday afternoon May 23, 1941. There sits the old, black, six cylinder Oakland, in front of Riverview School. Tugging on the door handle, I climb into the back. It's difficult for me to pull the big door shut.

"Hi, Sweetie Pie. Give Grandma a kiss," Grandma smiles.

I willingly supply the desired hug and kiss, and bounce around in excited anticipation of spending the weekend with Grandma and Grandpa. Standing up behind the front seat I hang on to the thick, satin, rolled cord that is attached to the seat backs. Peeking into the huge pockets on the sides of the doors, I find a map, a flashlight and a pencil.

"Grandma, are we gonna pick Grandpa up?" I ask.

"Yes, Honey. We'll park awhile and wait for him," she answers.

Grandma drives the big old car through downtown Beloit and heads to Riverside Drive. We reach the intersection of Riverside and Lawton Streets, where one gate of Fairbanks Morse Company is located. She maneuvers the car to face south, parking in front of the old homes west of the shop. We roll the windows down.

In the front yard of one home is a fire pit, a foot deep and about two feet across. A metal rack with a grill is arranged over a wood fire. Wafting toward us is the delicious aroma of ribs roasting. A rotund, Negro man brushes the meat with barbecue sauce. He leaves the meat and goes into the house.

All of a sudden Grandma exclaims, "Oh! Oh, look Patsy! Look what's happening."

A black and white spotted cat appears from somewhere. It stretches up to the edge of the pit, and licks the ribs. Grandma and I chuckle in disbelief. The man opens the door. Upon seeing the cat, he springs toward it swinging his arms and it takes off.

Grandpa climbs into the car saying, "Hi there, Patsy, Grandpa's little girl." He gives Grandma an affectionate kiss.

Soon after we enter their home, Grandma's cooking fills the house with a delicious aroma. Blackie jumps around us. We take turns petting him. Grandpa tousles my hair and says, "It's pay day Patsy. I'll bet you can find something in Grandpa's coat pocket."

Running to the small entry way above the cellar steps, I see Grandpa's work coat hanging on a hook. I can barely reach it as I stand on tiptoe. Reaching deep into the old jacket, I pull out a candy bar in a blue and white wrapper and run to Grandpa. "What kind is it, Grandpa?" I ask.

"Why, it's a `PayDay', of course," says Grandpa.

"Keep it for later, Patsy. It's nearly supper time," cautions Grandma.

Grandpa is resting in his favorite overstuffed chair, in the corner of the living room, listening to the radio.

I join Grandma in the kitchen. Blackie lays nearby. Grandma says, "Blackie, go tell Pa supper is ready." The dog jumps to his feet and races to Grandpa. He nudges Grandpa's leg with his nose, wiggles and waggles around and then races back to the kitchen table. Grandpa doesn't respond right away, so Blackie repeats his ritual. By the third time, Grandpa comes to supper. Grandpa loves to tease everyone, even Blackie. Blackie knows Grandpa loves him, as much as he loves Grandpa.

When supper is over Grandma says, "Patsy, would you like to feed Blackie?"

"Yes, Yes, Grandma. Where's the food?"

Grandma takes a can of Rival dog food from the cupboard and opens it. She hands me the can and a tablespoon.

"Blackie likes to eat from a spoon," Grandma smiles.

The canned meat smells good enough to eat. I sit and feed Blackie one spoonful of pink meat at a time until it is gone.

Grandma rocks in her rocking chair as she stitches tiny colorful pieces of material together in a sunburst quilt pattern. Grandpa sits in his corner chair listening to the radio between dozes.

"Grandma, look at my black house. It has white dots," I say, getting up. "Oops," I shout as I accidentally knock the structure over. The playing cards that had been a roof scatter with the Dominoes.

"Let's have a bedtime snack, Patsy," Grandpa says.

We all go to the kitchen table and enjoy bowls of broken white soda crackers in milk.

At bedtime they push two large upholstered chairs together, front to front. Presto, a soft bed with soft arm rails. After helping me prepare for the night Grandma hears the little prayer that she and Mama have taught me.

"Now I lay me down to sleep,
I pray the Lord my soul to keep.
If I should die before I wake,
I pray the Lord my soul to take."

I don't fully understand the words I recite, but I have a sense that there is a Greater Presence that cares for me.

Blackie is kissing me. I sit up rubbing the sandman out of my eyes. The sun shines through the windows.

"Come on sleepy head. Breakfast is almost ready," Grandma calls.

Grandma is short with dark hair. Her glasses accent her cheery face. She is wearing a red and white cotton, floral print, house dress and black shoes with wide one and a half inch heels. "You've gotta get up so Grandpa can have his easy chair," she adds.

Grandpa comes into the living room. Blackie is excitedly seeking his attention. Grandpa's slender frame is clothed in grey slacks, and a white stripe shirt that is mostly covered with his favorite grey, zippered, cardigan sweater. A narrow face is complimented with blue eyes behind his metal rimmed glasses. His thin white hair is parted on the left and combed back. He looks serious. How does he hide his mischievous nature?

When I get to the kitchen, I watch with wide eyes, as Grandma removes a glass syringe and a needle in a metal fitting from a small grey, granite pan of boiling water. With clean pliers she fits the two together. She sticks the needle through a small rubber tipped bottle and draws out insulin. After rubbing the upper part of her leg, with alcohol dipped cotton, she pinches up flesh between her thumb and index finger. Then jams the needle into her leg and pushes the plunger.

"Oh, Grandma, doesn't it hurt?" I cry.

"Not too much, Honey. Grandma is used to it," she says. "But I miss not being able to eat sweets. That's one bad part of having diabetes."

After breakfast Grandpa takes my hand, and we follow the long green front lawn along the dirt and cinder driveway. As we reach the three lane highway 51, Grandpa takes a firmer grip on my hand. When traffic clears, we walk across to the Texaco station. Grandpa buys a pack of Twenty Grand cigarettes, with the horse head on the front of the package. He and Mr. Rose exchange chatter.

"How is little Patsy today?" he asks, offering me a piece of candy.

I smile, shyly accepting the gift and add Mr. Rose to my list of boyfriends.

When we return to the house, Grandma is on the north side of the lawn smelling and surveying the beautiful peony bushes. Huge fuchsia, pink and white blooms are weighing down the long stems. Grandma comes across the lawn to the edge of the driveway where colorful irises are blooming. Blackie runs up to meet us.

"Blackie, the kids are coming," she announces, "The kids are coming."

Blackie goes into a frenzy, racing up and down the driveway.

"Is Della bringing Jackie, Gene and Tommy out, Ella?" Grandpa asks.

"Yup, Eli. Then Della and Elton will come back for supper," she smiles.

She hardly has the words out of her mouth when the car rolls in. Such pandemonium! Hugs and kisses for everyone, Blackie jumps around and wags his tail, and the boys turn cartwheels as Mama heads back home.

At thirteen, Jackie enjoys helping Grandma in the kitchen, preparing chicken with homemade noodles, and baking cakes. Grandma rolls the egg and flour mixture out on a floured board to a large circle about an eighth inch thick. She lets these large circles dry for several hours. Then she cuts them in six sections, stacks them, then rolls them up and slices them in less than quarter inch slices. This creates noodles that she fluffs up and scatters around the board to continue drying until time to cook them.

Grandma turns over a couple of dining room chairs and spreads her old Indian design blanket over them. I crawl under the table, in my make believe house, where I will play until the table is needed for dinner. My large doll with the cloth body and composition head, legs, and arms plays with me. She wears a long housecoat with a wide zipper from the waist to the neck. It is blue and white cotton print, with wine color cabbage roses. Grandma made it with scraps left from making her own.

"With Aunt Dorothy and Uncle Leonard living in the upstairs apartment, we can see them more often," says Jackie.

"Yes, Honey, they will join us for dinner this evening. You know how Uncle Leonard loves chicken and noodles," Grandma says.

Grandpa goes down in the cellar to work on the large, wood, cartoon characters he is making. He has Jiggs and Mutt done and is working on Jeff. The boys will see what they can learn from Grandpa. He lets them use hand saws, hammers and nails.

The hours fly by. Everyone is seated around the dining room table enjoying delicious food and conversation. Grandpa has the pitcher of ice water that sits beside him at every meal. The rosy pink ceramic pitcher is a winking man with a high collar, bow tie and sailor-like cap.

"I have eaten too much, I'm stuffed," says Jackie.

"You'll put on pounds," says Tommy.

"Well, don't worry about it. I was just reading an article of comments by a famous Hollywood designer. He's been measur-

28

ing and making clothes for stars for many years and he says that the female stars are roughly twelve pounds heavier than they were in 1935. In less than five years they have gone from painfully thin and shapeless to having shapely curves. So, I guess, you can eat some extra noodles, once in awhile. Grandma makes such good noodles," says Aunt Dorothy.

"Mother, why don't you get Grandma's recipe for this apple sauce cake? It is so good!" says Gene.

Grandma gets a pencil and paper and gives it to Gene with the recipe. "Here, you can copy it off for her," she says.

Gene takes the paper and pencil and starts writing:

1 cup sugar — 2 eggs — 1 cup shortening — 1 1/2 cup apple sauce — 2 teaspoons soda, in apple sauce — 1 teaspoon vanilla — 1/2 teaspoon cinnamon — 1/4 teaspoon cloves — 1/4 teaspoon allspice — 2 cups flour — 1 cup raisins — 3/4 cups chopped walnuts—Soften raisins in hot water, but don't add any hot water to cake. Cream sugar and shortening, add eggs, then alternate apple sauce and dry ingredients, blending well. Pour into greased loaf pan. Bake in oven at 350 degrees. About 45 minutes, or until inserted toothpick comes out clean.

As the women clear the table and do dishes, the men converse in the living room. Mama's brother, Uncle Leonard, gets himself in trouble raising a ruckus tickling and rough housing with the boys and me. He puts his mouth tight against my bare skin and blows hard, making a loud noise. We all laugh, yell and squeal, pulling away, yet, begging for more.

"Leonard, stop that. Behave yourself," Aunt Dorothy jovially reprimands.

I climb up on Grandpa's shoulders, straddling his neck, as he sits in his big chair. I comb his hair, snapping a metal curler over a section of hair, I roll it up, then fasten the wire loop over the end. He sits patiently and lets me play.

"Did you see that picture in the paper of people going to work in London with all the terrible bomb destruction?" asks Daddy.

"It's terrible. I don't know where all of this is going to lead to," answers Grandpa. "They estimate that the Nazis have lost ten thousand planes in the twenty one months of the war. Britain is really getting pounded and has had so many ships sunk. It's terrible, think of all the people who have been killed. I hope we don't end up in it."

"I hope we don't either. Did you listen to the fight between Joe Louis and Buddy Baer last night, Pa?" Daddy asks.

"I sure did. It was a wild fight. Lots of people are claiming that Louis hit that final blow after the bell had rung. I guess Baer's manager is going to appeal," answers Grandpa.

"Have you guys solved all of the world's problems?" Mama asks, as the women come into the living room.

"I wish we could," says Uncle Leonard.

"Well, I don't think you can, and we should get these kids home to bed," says Mama.

* — * — *

Summer finds us spending more time than ever at Grandma and Grandpa's on the river. Often, nighttime will find me curled up in my bed of two overstuffed chairs in the living room, with Jackie on the roll-a-way bed. Gene at eleven years, and Tommy at nine years, are sleeping on the old buffalo robe on the screened in front porch.

Before I drop off to sleep, I can hear the boys talking.

"Listen to the train going by, down across the river," says Gene.

"Yeah, hear the whistle? Ooooh - ooooh -" says Tommy. "It sounds lonesome, doesn't it?"

"Yeah, it's kinda eerie. Do you want to take the boat across the river again tomorrow? You can row tomorrow."

"Yeah, but I don't want to catch another one of those things. When I pulled that thing into the boat today, I nearly wet my pants," says Tommy. "It scared the liver out of me!"

"You were so funny. I thought you were going to jump in the river. You turned white and were shaking all over. It's a good thing when you raised your pole it flopped off into the water. We didn't have to touch it."

"What did Grandpa say it was?" asks Tommy.

"An eel. I guess, it's a fish, but it's long. You can't see any fins and it's so slimy, yuk. It gives me the creeps, too. Maybe tomorrow we'll catch some catfish."

I hear Jackie turning over. "How come the boys don't have to wear life jackets when they go out in the boat? I always have to wear one," I say.

"Well, the boys were lucky to get in on that free program they had at the YMCA, and they learned how to swim. We'd better get to sleep now. Grandma's china clock on the shelf just struck eleven times," Jackie answers.

"I like that pink clock with the roses on it. I hope it lasts forever. Maybe Uncle Leonard will take me to the Hamburger Limited, for one of those double dip, orange pineapple ice cream cones again. He paid five cents for the one he bought the other day."

"Uncle Leonard has to work tomorrow. Now go to sleep."

The day dawns sunny and warm. Jackie and Grandma are in the raspberry patch, out behind the garage.

"Grandma, I think Mother and Dad are going to take

Mother's cousin, Arlene Puttkemery, up north on vacation this summer," Jackie says with enthusiasm.

"I'm glad to hear that, because your Mother needs help with the work," says Grandma.

"Yes. After all it's Mama's vacation, too."

While Jackie and Grandma pick berries and enjoy each other, I am busy in the house. I wander through the dining room and kitchen, to Grandma and Grandpa's bedroom at the back of the house.

I step down three inches into a room that had once been a back porch. The floor slopes slightly from the doorway to the back wall. At the far right side of the back wall is a small walk-in closet with a clothes bar and overhead shelf on one side. As I enter the room I glance at the bronze, iron, double bed that sits in front of the double windows to my right. The head of the bed is a tubular arched iron rail, with spindles and ornate trim about three and one half feet higher than the bed. The foot of the bed has a matching rail about half the height.

To my left is a low dresser and above it hangs a vertical rectangular mirror with ornate composition frame in a dull bronze color. I pick up Grandma's yard stick and take my place in front of the mirror. I am a majorette and the yard stick is my baton. I lead the parade and twirl the baton marching in style, while time marches quickly.

Gene and Tommy in their blue bib overalls, short sleeve blue shirts and straw hats take their fishing poles and a can of worms to Grandpa's T shaped pier.

"It's too windy to take the boat out now. I get the bench on the right side," states Gene.

"Who cares? Grandpa puts brush in the river on both sides of the pier to attract fish." As soon as Tommy drops his line in the water there is a tug on it. The cork sinks under water and pulls away from him. Tommy gives a little jerk on his line.

"Look, I've got one," he yells, lifting a nice crappie onto the pier. He pulls a fish stringer out of his overalls. Runs the clip in the fish's mouth and through the gill then snaps it shut, like a huge safety pin. Tommy lowers the fish into the water and fastens the stringer to a hook on the pier. By lunch time Tommy has two more crappies and Gene has a catfish and a bluegill, all keepers.

* — * — *

One day I am at Grandma's without my siblings. I played with my doll all morning. We had lunch, and now Grandma and I are walking down through the park.

"Let's sit on the bench and rest a minute, Patsy," says Grandma. "We can watch the squirrels."

I climb up on the park bench beside her. The squirrels leap from limb to limb, and scamper about in the lofty oak trees. The green leaves and the green grass contrast with the bright blue sky and fluffy, white clouds. Shade provides relief from the heat of the sun. But I have been here long enough. "Come on, Grandma. Let's go back up to the house," I say. I grab her arm and tug on it.

"We just got here, Patsy. Don't you want to watch the river for a while?"

"No! Let's go!" I cry.

I tug at Grandma as we walk back toward the house.

"It's time for you and me to take a little nap, Patsy." Grandma says. "We can have a tea party first."

"No! I don't want a nap! I don't want a tea party, either!"

"Don't you want a treat with Grandma?"

"No! I'm not going to take a nap!"

"Well, don't get sassy. That's not nice."

"I don't care! I'm not going to take a nap!"

"Well, don't get naughty. You have to mind Grandma."

"You're not my boss. I'm not going to take a nap."

"Patsy, if you aren't nice to Grandma, I'm going to take you home."

"I don't care!" I lie and stick my tongue out at Grandma.

"Alright, young lady, gather up your things. I'm going to take you home." Grandma picks up the phone and calls Mama. She tells her how naughty I am, and that we are on the way home.

Suddenly, I am terribly ashamed of myself. What have I done? Why did I treat Grandma like this? I begin to cry. Grandma marches me to the car. I cry all the way home.

Mama says, "Patsy, I'm ashamed of you. Go to your bedroom and take a nap." I go to my bedroom and cry myself to sleep.

When I come downstairs, later in the afternoon, Mama says, "Are you feeling better?"

"I'm sorry, Mama."

"Do you want to tell Grandma you are sorry?"

I shake my head yes, and she calls Grandma.

"I'm sorry I was naughty, Grandma. I love you."

"I forgive you, Honey. I love you, too."

* — * — *

The summer continues and one Saturday morning when we are at Grandma's, we follow Grandpa across the back yard to the chicken coop.

"Pe kwak, kwak, kwak kwak. Cock-a-doodle-dooo," say the chickens in the outdoor pen.

Grandpa lifts the latch and the big door squeaks open. We step into the warm coop. Tommy sneezes as we stir up dust with our feet and as the chickens flutter around.

"Cheep, cheep, cheep," say the little chicks. Little balls of golden yellow fluff fall over each other as they try to get water from the round tray at the base of the galvanized metal watering fountain. White Leghorns, Plymouth Rocks and Rhode Island Red hens are in their setting boxes. They cock their heads and eye us as Grandpa fills the feeding troughs with mash and crushed oyster shell. My nose twitches from a mixture of dust and the scent of chicken manure. In the sunlight filtering through the small, square window panes we can see the varied dust particles floating in the air.

"We are going to butcher four chickens this morning. Gene and Tommy, you can go out in the pen and catch two red hens and two white hens," says Grandpa.

"Grandpa, what are hens?" I ask.

"They are the lady chickens, Patsy. They are the ones that lay eggs, like the chickens here in the setting boxes. Look at their heads. The female has a small comb. The rooster has a large comb. He is the male; he thinks he is boss. That's why he struts around crowing - cock-a-doodle-do."

There is a terrible ruckus in the pen outside. The boys shout, the chickens cluck and feathers fly.

Jackie and I follow Grandpa outside. Gene has two white hens by the legs, holding them upside down. Tommy is struggling with a red one that is squawking and flapping its wings rapidly. Grandpa takes the hen by the legs and wraps a cord around them. Tommy darts into the pen after another red hen.

When the hens have been caught and their legs bound, Grandpa gets a hatchet from the chicken coop. The blade's sharp edge glistens in the sun. He carries a chicken to the chopping block. The block is a two-foot log standing up on end. Grandpa has notched a groove in one side. It has a piece of metal which pivots over the groove. Grandpa puts the head in place, and fastens the metal band over the neck. He pulls the feet, stretching the neck out. With one swift blow with the hatchet, the head is off. The chicken is released and put on the ground where it flops around for a while.

"Patsy, do you want to chop a head off?" Grandpa asks. To his surprise and mine, too, I say, "Yes."

He prepares the chicken and holds its feet. He shows me how to hold the hatchet with both hands. My blow nearly severs the neck. With one swift blow, Grandpa finishes it. It also ends forever my desire to want to do it again.

The chickens flop around on the ground with blood splattering here and there. It is a terrible sight, and makes my stomach feel funny. Finally they are still.

33

Grandma calls from the back door. "Eli, the water is ready." Grandpa goes to the kitchen and returns with a pail of boiling water. One at a time, he plunges the dead chickens into the hot water for a few minutes. This enables him to pull the feathers out easily.

When Grandma comes to get the plucked chickens, Jackie and I follow her into the house. The kitchen table is covered with newspapers. One by one Grandma carries the chickens to the gas stove, where she has a burner lit. She holds the chicken over the flame and singes off any remaining pinfeathers. It smells like hair burning. Jackie and I pinch our noses shut. Grandma lays the chickens on the table and with a sharp butcher knife, cuts the chicken open between the legs. With wide eyes fixed on the chicken I watch Grandma butcher it.

"I wish I had a nickel for every chicken I have dressed," she says.

It certainly doesn't look to me as though the chicken is dressed. It is as "undressed" as I have ever seen one. Grandma reaches her hand inside the chicken and pulls out the innards. Pointing to the gall, she says, "I must be careful not to break this or it will spoil the chicken." She sets the heart and the liver aside. Taking the knife, she slices open the gizzard, emptying the gritty meal content.

"See this girls. It is undigested food the chicken ate." She removes from the innards a partially formed egg with a soft semi-transparent shell, and a couple yolks.

"I'll cook these in the gravy when I roast the chickens tomorrow. I can't cook and eat chicken the same day I clean it," Grandma says.

When Grandma cuts the chicken up, she does not cut through the breastbone, so there will be a "V" shaped bone with a stem at the base. It is called a "wishbone." This is considered a magical bone. They say that two people should make a wish. Each is to take hold of one end of the "V" shaped bone and pull. When the bone breaks, one person will usually get a full side with the stem on it. The person who gets the side with the stem will have his wish come true. I have collected a dozen or more wish bones and have them tied on a ribbon of variegated pastel colors. Someday I will have many wishes come true.

Grandma fixes some hot dogs for our lunch. As we sit at the table preparing our sandwiches Grandpa says, "Tommy, try some of this horseradish. It's good on hot dogs. Put a big spoonful on."

"Really, Grandpa?" Tommy says. He piles the horseradish on and takes a big bite. Suddenly he howls and the tears roll down his cheeks. "Ugh, that's hot!" Tommy wails.

Grandpa and Gene explode with laughter at Tommy when he falls for Grandpa's trick. "Patsy, do you want some gutama-growlie? I'll share mine with you," Grandpa says.

"No, Grandpa. I don't want any," I answer.

Tommy has gulped his water and is curious again. "What is gutamagrowlie? There is no such thing. I don't trust you, Grandpa. Is it hot?"

"Naw. Gene has some in his sandwich," Grandpa says.

"I do? What is it?" asks Gene.

"Here, Tommy, try some," Grandpa says. He pushes the jar of pickle relish toward him.

* — * — *

Besides the wonderful meals provided by raising chickens, Grandma and Grandpa make a profit by selling them. To help Gene and Tommy earn some money, they allow them to raise one hundred and twenty-five chickens to sell.

One day a friend of Grandma and Grandpa's buys a chicken from the boys.

"Would you like us to clean the chicken?" asks Gene.

"No, no. We can do it," replies Irma. So they take the live chicken home in a gunny bag.

A week later, the friend returns and says to Grandma. "Ella, you'll never believe what happened to that chicken."

"What happened?"

"I took the chicken home and Carl killed it and removed the feathers. I washed it and prepared it for roasting, put good seasoning on it and put it in the oven before we went to church. When we came home and opened the door there was a horrible smell. Carl said, 'Irma, what stinks'?"

Grandma looks puzzled for a moment, then she bursts into laughter. "Irma, don't tell me . . . don't tell me you didn't remove the innards?" Irma dabs at her eyes with a handkerchief and holds her stomach. Between hilarious gasps of laughter she says, "I didn't . . . the chick . . . en was . . . green."

* — * — *

Among the winged and feathered creatures of the chicken coop is a blind chicken that decides he likes Tommy. Tommy is delighted to have the chicken for a pet and carries him everywhere on his shoulder. Gene becomes jealous because Tommy has a pet among their feathered friends and he doesn't.

"Tommy, guess what I'm gonna do?" says Gene.

"I don't know."

Gene chases a white chicken and snatches him up. "I'm going to mark this bird and make a pet of him," he says.

"How are you going to mark him?" asks Tommy.

"See, here, I'm gonna wrap some of this black electrical tape

35

around his leg," says Gene.

"Good idea," says Tommy.

Shortly after that, our family goes for our annual two-week vacation in the north woods of Wisconsin. Upon returning, the boys run to the chicken yard to find their pets. Tommy soon has the blind chicken riding on his shoulder. Gene searches the chickens' legs for the black tape.

"Oh, no!" Gene exclaims.

In the corner of the pen flopping about is his chicken, marked with the black tape. He sees only a small piece of tape on the stub, where there used to be a leg! The tape had been too tight, and the chicken's leg fell off. Picking up the chicken, he hugs it to him.

"Poor chicken, I'm sorry. I didn't mean you any harm," he says.

Gene goes into the house and asks Grandma for a popsicle stick, and gets the electrical tape again. This time he is careful not to wrap the tape too tight. When he is finished, his pet chicken has a wooden leg. He sets "Peg Leg" down and the chicken walks around quite well. He no longer falls over and flops around. The two chickens are happy and so are the boys. They take them home and the chickens are their constant companions. Every time they get on their bikes to go somewhere, the chickens go along. Here a peck, there a cluck, such fun with the feathered friends!

One day Gene and Tommy are watching the chickens in Grandpa's chicken pen.

"Look, Gene. What is the matter with the chickens? That white one is flopping around and several are lying on their sides," says Tommy.

"The red ones, too," says Gene. "They are pecking at some yellow orange stuff over there on the ground. Most of them are staggering around."

"We'd better tell Grandma," says Tommy.

"Yeah."

The boys run in through the back door yelling, "Grandma, come quick. Something is wrong with the chickens."

Grandma follows them outside and looks in the pen. "Oh my," she says. "I had some home canned peaches that had fermented, and I told Grandpa to throw them out. He threw them in the chicken coop and these chickens have been eating them."

"Are they sick, Grandma?" Gene asks.

"Are they going to die, Grandma?" Tommy asks.

"I don't think so, boys. I believe those silly chickens are drunk."

The boys clap their hands over their opened mouths. With

widened eyes they snicker. "Wait 'til we tell Grandpa," they say. The next day the chickens are fully re-"coop"-erated. Walking about the pens scratching and crowing, they appear to have no hangover.

* __ * __ *

Often I play with Grandma and Grandpa's neighbor children, especially Joanie who lives a few houses to the north. We like to get into the large, wooden, double glider swing that sits in their side yard. We can make it sway back and forth. Their goldfish pond is also an attraction to us.

Sometimes, her Mama has us come into their living room and sit together in a big overstuffed chair. She turns the radio on to a children's story hour, and we are spellbound by tales of witches and children in dangerous situations.

In the spring of 1942, Joanie's Mama gives us each a hard-boiled Easter egg. She has decorated the white shell with many different colored dots made with crayons. They are such pretty speckled eggs. When I get back to Grandma's, she says, "Patsy, would you like to help Grandma color some Easter eggs?"

"Yes. Can we, please, Grandma?" I beg.

Grandma boils a dozen eggs. She gets out two pans. Into one she puts some onion skins, from yellow onions, and adds water. Into the other she pours the juice from a can of beets. She puts the fire under each and brings them to a boil. Then she adds a spoon of vinegar to each. She brings them to the table and shows me how to lower the eggs into them with a spoon. We get different shades of yellow-tan, and rosy-pinks by the length of time we leave the eggs in the liquid. "Oh, Grandma, they are so pretty."

I play with the little boy, Larry, who lives next door to the south. Their home is much closer to the river, and it is all fenced in. One day his Mama invites me in to see his tiny new baby sister. In the house just north of Grandma is a little grandson, Jackie. He shares his horse with me. It is on a long, curved, strip of iron that springs. I can bounce half way to the sky.

Sometimes my brothers will play with me. One day we set up a telephone company on the screened in front porch. We have ropes strung around the porch with tin cans and clothes pins hanging on the ends. We make phone calls all afternoon.

The porch swing is a favorite place for Grandma or Jackie to cuddle up with me and read. When I spend time with Grandma, she wants us to take a nap together. She brings a little half circle table up close to the davenport and we have a tea party first. She fixes Ritz crackers with Pimento cream cheese on them. We drink milk from little cheese glasses that have pretty designs painted on the sides. Then we lay down at opposite ends of the davenport, and I smell Grandma's toes!

37

Sometimes Mama and her cousin Madeline Ennis go on a special outing. Then Grandma keeps Madeline's children Mary (about Tommy's age) and Danny (about my age), so there are six of us kids.

One afternoon as Gene and Tommy are having one of their frequent wrestling matches in the front yard, Tommy's neck gets wrenched a bit. He screams at Gene, "Oh! You broke my neck! You broke my neck!" Tommy continues to wrestle with his broken neck!

The rest of us root and boo them on, laughing all the while.

When winter arrives, I spend more time playing indoors. Grandma makes large fat sugar cookies cut in different shapes and sprinkles them with colored sugar or tiny colored candy balls. Sometimes Aunt Dorothy comes downstairs to help her. Grandma now uses the window box outside the kitchen window as an additional refrigerator.

Grandpa helps the boys make skis out of old barrel stays and they ski in the back yard toward the river. When the river is well frozen the boys ice skate on it.

In the summer of 1942, my brothers have come back from one of their fishing trips in Grandpa's row boat. I run down to the pier to meet them.

"Where did you go?" I ask.

"Across the river. We have a special point we like," answers Tommy. He pulls up a stringer of fish to show me.

The boys aren't leaving the pier, so I go out to investigate what they are doing. "Oh, oh. I'm gonna tell Grandma," I say. Gene has lit a cigarette and is puffing on it. He hands it to ten year old Tommy, who puffs on it.

"Do you want to try it?" asks Tommy.

I've had a lot of experiences in my six years, but this isn't one of them. "Can I, Tommy. Can I?" I ask.

"Sure. Come here," he says. He holds the cigarette down for me. "Just put your lips on it and draw in like a straw."

I try, but don't draw hard enough at first. Then I draw harder and get a big mouth full of smoke. I cough and sputter, and nearly fall off the pier.

In his great wisdom, being the eldest, Gene says, "Now you mustn't tell anyone, or we will `all' get in trouble."

* — * — *

Such happy days at Grandma and Grandpa Wessell's home on Rock River. Sometimes we are naughty and do stupid things. We are taught right from wrong, but always we are loved. Grandma rocks us in her rocking chair, even when we grow too big. There is always room on Grandma or Grandpa's lap, and room in their hearts. Blackie enters all of the happy activities.

In September 1943, a great, dark cloud hangs over our lives. Grandpa is confined to bed with a serious heart condition. Thursday, October seventh he passes away. Our family is engulfed in deep grief. His body is brought home in the casket. It sits in the living room, and people come to pay their respect.

Grandma talks to God, "I feel numb, like I just can't function. He has been my beloved companion for nearly forty-four years. Our relationship has always been one of joy. We never bickered or said unkind words to one another. I know my family loves me. I will go to live with Della, Elton and the kids. But how will I live without him? I feel so alone, like half my soul is gone. What will I do? Oh, what will I do without him? Oh, Lord, if you are there, I need you now."

Since Grandpa went into the hospital, Blackie has been moping around. Now he lies near the casket and cries. He is not eating well. He acts as though he has lost his best friend, which, indeed, he has.

I survey the living room, all rearranged to accommodate this strange box. It is an odd bed, grey with handles on the sides. The covers are satin. Why is it so fancy? And Grandpa, he doesn't look right. Why is he in bed with his good suit on? He never wears his glasses when he is sleeping. Why does he have them on now? Something is wrong. Something is very, very wrong! I reach up and touch Grandpa's arm. It is not warm and soft, it feels like a block of wood. They say Grandpa has gone to live with God. Why has he left us, and if he has left us, why is he so still in this strange bed? I feel warm and funny, like I could be sick. Mama comes up and puts her arm around me. She is crying; we both cry. Then she says, "We must trust God. We will see him again someday." I don't understand. I want Grandpa to hold me, now. Yet, something deep inside me flickers with hope. Thinking of the bedtime prayer that I say, . . . If I should die before I wake, I pray the Lord my soul to take . . . I'm not sure what my soul is, but I am, somehow, aware that God loves me. I will trust.

Among those coming to pay respect is a close family friend, Walter Anthony. Tony, his nickname, is about to leave Grandma's when he sees Blackie walking toward the highway. Blackie never goes to the highway. Tony follows him, calling to him. Blackie is walking along looking forlorn, but determined. A large truck is coming. Tony calls, "Blackie! Come boy. Blackie come back!" Blackie looks back at Tony, then he looks up at the truck and walks determinedly into its path.

"My God, he has committed suicide!" Tony cries. Through his tears, Tony gathers him up, and takes him to his own house on Vernon Avenue, where he buries him.

Our grief is compound. Our lives will never be the same. But the sun continues to shine. Grandma comes to live with us. The happy days spent at 2436 Riverside Drive, with Grandma and Grandpa Wessell, will be a legacy forever etched in our hearts.

* — * — *

Jackie, Mama, Daddy, Gene and Tommy at Grandma and Grandpa's home (1940)

Chapter 3
The Magnificent Maple Tree
-1940-

Legend of The Maple

I think that we shall never agree,
On exactly who owns the old Maple tree.
A tree that grows on the corner lot line,
Margie and I battle, is it yours or mine?

A lovely tree, magnificent black trunk,
Climbing its height takes real spunk.
Gene or Tom could break his neck,
If discovered, Mama will give him heck.

It's lofty limbs spread far and wide.
The huge knot hole hides elves inside.
I often wonder what they are about,
And try to see when they'll come out.

They wear green jackets and blue pants,
Their red hats tilt as they do their dance.
They chase the squirrels from limb to limb,
As the birds swoop in to share their gym.

Winter's icy branches, a giant wind chime,
Winged seeds; helicopter toys of springtime.
Summer brings her lacy green leaf attire,
Which in fall feeds the fragrant bonfire.

Whipped violently, she survives each storm,
Leafy boughs shelter us when the sun is warm.
I think that I shall never see,
A more magnificent Maple Tree.

Our home is on the northwest corner of South Eighth and Illinois Streets. Our land borders Milner's on the east and Nicolls' on the south. The magnificent old maple tree grows primarily on our land with roots and limbs extending over the Milner property. We have congenial relationships with these neighbors that will grow to deep friendship through the years. But always there will be a love-hate situation concerning the magnificent old maple tree.

Of course, "I" own the old maple tree. I am nearly five years old, and this has a strong influence on this decision. Perhaps my perpetual love for all trees is rooted in the legend of this beloved tree. I dream fantasies of it as a child and envision it long after its demise.

On a warm spring evening I sit on the top step of our back porch. My parents sit in lawn chairs in their favorite spots on the back sidewalk or dirt - gravel driveway. My brothers and sister have scattered.

"Listen Patsy, you can hear the lonesome whistle of the train somewhere below the hill," says Mama. Blocks away we can hear crashing sounds.

"What is that? Are the trains crashing?" I ask.

"No, Patsy, they are just recoupling cars and changing tracks," answers Daddy.

"Do they go far away?" I ask.

"Some do. Maybe some day you can take a train ride," Mama says.

I look up, beyond the edge of the garage I can see the sprawling limbs of the huge old silver maple. I envision myself climbing from limb to limb like the squirrels do. It's a long way up to the treetops. Suddenly there is a loud squawking and a robin swoops down from a lofty height in the maple tree with another robin in hot pursuit. The birds and squirrels call this tree home. I'm happy to share it with them, but I'm glad it's "my" tree.

Can you imagine my surprise when I come out to "my" tree in the morning and there hangs a wonderful swing? It has a nice board seat suspended from a limb, high overhead, by two hefty ropes. I'm thrilled. One of the little elves that live high up the trunk in a knot hole must have hung the swing. I know my father didn't put it there, but the elves would know I'd like a swing.

I climb into the swing and try it out. Back and forth I work it with my body. Up, up, up, this is wonderful! I can see Nicolls' chicken coop and the little red banty hens, also our cherry trees and the apple tree next to our garage. There is the pine tree, the rhubarb and asparagus patch and some of Daddy's flower beds, where the yellow and red tulips, purple, yellow and white iris and pink and fuchsia peonies smile at each other. I can smell the heady fragrance of our lavender and white lilac bushes. This is exhilarating. I can almost touch the fluffy white clouds in the bright blue sky.

"Patsy. Patsy," Mama calls from the back porch. I run to see what Mama wants.

Later I come back to the magnificent old maple tree, and what do you think I see? Here is my little neighbor friend, Margie, swinging in "my" swing in "my" tree.

She is sitting in the swing facing the opposite direction. As she goes up, up, up, back and forth, she can see the little house that sits so close to the Maple tree. She looks upon her mother's clotheslines and the back of her folks' garage.

"Margie," I call.

She quits pumping the swing, drags her feet and twirls to a stop.

"Hi Patsy. How do you like my new swing?"

"Wha - what do you mean - your swing?" I ask.

"Daddy just put it up for me."

"But Margie, this is my tree," I challenge.

"Your tree? It's our tree, too."

"Look at it Margie. You can see it's in our yard," I say.

"Patsy, try the swing. Daddy says we can all have fun in it."

Well, it is "my" tree, but if the elves didn't put the swing here for me, maybe I'd better share it or Mr. Milner might take it down, I reason.

"Well, it's `my' tree," I say pouting, "but you can keep the swing in it, as long as I can use it too." I have a strong sense for the need to guard my tree, yet I know the swing will be fun.

* — * — *

My Swedish friend Alice lives two-thirds down the north side of Illinois Street. I stand in the yard in front of her back porch calling, "Alice. Alice."

Mrs. Anderson opens the door, and looks at me with a smile as big as the sturdy frame that is covered with her clean crisp rose print house dress and apron. Her graying light brown hair is pulled back loosely into a bun.

"Good morning Potsy. Olice just finished her breakfast," she says in her heavy Swedish brogue.

"Can she come to my house to play?" I ask. Just then Alice squeezes through the doorway past her mother. Her golden hair is neatly combed into two long braids, with a blue plaid bow on the end of each one. She is wearing a pretty blue print cotton dress.

"Can I Ma, please?" Alice begs.

"Yos, yos, but no racin and tearin," she cautions.

Alice and I never play with dolls because Alice enjoys more rugged things. Today we sit on the linoleum floor at one end of our dining room and play with jacks and a rubber ball. We go through our babies, ladies, ups, downs, up-cast-quicks and down-cast-quicks. As each of us misses the correct procedure the other gets a turn. After an hour or so we are tired of playing this game.

"Let's go outside and look at Daddy's flowers," I suggest.

"Okay," Alice responds.

We walk along the flower beds, stopping to smell certain ones.

"Smell this purple iris, Alice. It smells like sweet grapes."

"Um, It smells good."

As we reach the backyard, Alice spies the swing.

"When did you get a swing?" Alice asks.

I shrug my shoulders, "I've had it awhile."

"Can we swing in it?" Alice asks.

"Sure we can, climb in; I'll push you," I offer.

Alice is having a great time, and I'm working hard pushing her.

"Hang on," I caution, "is this high enough?"

"No, no. Push harder," Alice squeals, "I want to touch the sky."

I push harder, jumping a little to reach the seat, as Alice flies back and forth, up and down.

Suddenly, there is a ripping sound and Alice is sailing through the air. Is it Alice or I that screams? I dodge the board as the swing sails back toward me. On its return I grab the rope. Alice lands on the grass in one piece, unhurt. There is something in the swing. I pick it up. With unbelieving eyes, I look at it and then at Alice. Momentarily we both stare at it and then at Alice's back side. Simultaneously, we burst into laughter; rib tickling laughter that has us holding our sides. I hand Alice the entire back half of the skirt of her dress.

She puts the skirt half where it belongs and holds it in place. Skipping along in fits of laughter, we head down the street to Alice's huge red insul-brick house. As we approach the back porch, Alice's mother comes out the door. One look at her expression sobers us right up. She grabs the back half of the skirt of Alice's dress.

"Olice, Olice! What have you done? Look at this new dress. Shame on you! I just bought this dress," she says, shaking the piece of material.

I really want to support my friend, but I decide it is time to leave. I turn and run home!

* — * — *

My brothers enjoy tormenting me. Gene is eleven and Tommy nearly nine, and they will torment me for years. They find ways to climb my tree. They go up beyond the knot hole where the elves live. Sometimes they take the swing up with them and set the board in the crotch of a limb so I can't reach it. I stand at the base of the tree hollering up at them.

"Let it down, Gene. Put it down!" I yell.

"Did you say something, Pete-Turd-Eye?" Gene hollers down from his lofty limb.

"You Snot, Poop, Brat," I scream, "Put my swing down."

"Why, Pete-Turd-Eye?" Tommy mimics, like a parrot.

"I'm gonna tell Mama, Snot-Poop-Brat," I yell back.

"You'd better not or we'll never put it down," Gene threatens.

Feeling naughty and defeated, I decide to pursue something else, and leave the boys to their climbing adventure. They continue to climb around like monkeys, but they have not overcome their mischievous dispositions. They see Mr. Nicolls come out to work in his back yard. Gene and Tommy perch on a limb and decide to serenade him. With a few trials and errors they put together this little ditty, and sing with gusto.

"Grampa Grump was a great old man,
He fried his rump in a frying pan.
Picked his teeth with a carving knife,
Turned a somersault and let some dice."

Mr. Nicolls takes offense, not finding anything so pretty in the boys' singing of this ditty. He goes directly to our father and complains about the boys' offensive serenade.

"We'd better get out of this tree," Tommy exclaims.

"Yeah, better put the swing down, too," says Gene.

"Oh, oh. Dad's coming," whispers Tommy.

"We're gonna get it," whispers Gene.

Dad walks into the back yard and says, "All right boys, get to your beds!" The boys quickly skirt around him and run for the house, bounding up the back steps through the house like a shot and up the stairs to their room.

"Quick, Tommy, let's put our pillows under the covers to look like us," orders Gene.

They quickly arrange blankets over the pillows and then crawl under the bed.

In spite of his anger, Daddy has to stifle a chuckle when he sees these fake bodies in the bed. These two little rascals are naive to think they can accomplish such deception, he muses. He says, "Come out from under the bed, right now." Defeated, the two mischievous boys crawl out and accept the tanning.

45

Jackie poses for a glamour shot. Behind her— mystery at the Maple Tree.

In a future year, far beyond the time span of this book, when I am grown and have a family of my own, my magnificent maple tree will meet its demise. My parents and Howard and Delores Milner share the cost of having the tree removed. It is the sensible thing to do since it is old and is a threat to the little house Milners own that stands a few feet from it. Why am I shedding tears? Where will the elves go? My old friend has been slain. Walking to the pile of logs and limbs that is the remains of my fallen friend, I wipe away tears and smile. I pick up a thin half circle wedge; I will always have a remnant of "my" Magnificent Maple Tree.

Chapter 4
The Spirit of Illisconsin
(1939-1950)

Life in Illisconsin is unique. We are the borderline people, living in South Beloit, Illinois, on the west side of Rock River. Daddy works in Rockford, Illinois. My siblings and I go to Riverview School, and South Beloit High School in Illinois. We do most of our shopping in Beloit, Wisconsin, and go to the doctor and hospital there. For many years we will vacation in northern Wisconsin. We will take the Beloit Daily News and listen, often, to Beloit radio stations. Some of our family lives in Illinois and some live in Wisconsin. We seek entertainment in both states.

Most unique of all, is Shirland Avenue which is one block from our home. The north half of Shirland Avenue is in Wisconsin and the south half is in Illinois. If I straddle the centerline, I can stand in Illinois and Wisconsin at the same time!

Daddy pays to ride to work with Tom Anderson. He transports a car full of people to Barber Colman Co. in Rockford. He and his wife, Fern, live several blocks west of us on Shirland Avenue. and eventually own and operate Andmar Grocery in that area. Tom drops Daddy off at the corner of Shirland Ave. and So. Eighth Street. From age five, when it is time for him to arrive, I often skip down to the end of the block and walk home, hand-in-hand, with him.

Mama is always waiting for him, in the kitchen, with a welcome home kiss and hug. She is five feet four inches tall, her dark hair fashionably permed, her makeup artfully applied, and she wears a colorful crisp cotton house dress with an apron over it. Supper is ready, the preparations finished at the sink before Daddy arrives, because that is where he washes up for supper. Our average meal is meat with gravy, boiled potatoes, vegetable, bread, salad and dessert. Mama and Daddy drink coffee and we all have ice water.

Before I arrive in 1935, Daddy has dug the entire basement a foot deeper by hand and cemented it. The house has had electricity and inside plumbing added, including a claw foot bathtub that will be there, yet, in 1995. This house echoes laughter, painful cries, and whispers of love, as the Singletary - Wessell families experience many changes in their lives in Illisconsin.

About 1939 Mama has a green stove that stands on legs. It sets in the southeast corner of the kitchen near the pantry door. It is a gasoline stove, and has a rod with a knob on top similar to a tire pump. Before Mama can light the burners, she has to

47

pump it several times. There are three burners. The oven is a separate box that goes over two burners. Mama makes that old stove produce some delicious meals, even cakes and pies.

The pantry is a small unfinished room on the back of the house, really an extension of the entry shed with a partition between. It has a narrow shelf across the end that goes around the right side. The thin wood walls are full of nails for hanging pans and kitchen articles. The end has one tiny window.

Mama has a utility table, with a small drawer in it, along one side. The room is not heated. It is hot in summer, and can be used as a deep freeze in winter when the weather cooperates.

Mama often says, "I don't know what I'd do without that pantry."

Mama and Daddy now have an old '32 Chevy that had belonged to Grandpa Singletary. It is great to drive to go grocery shopping, but Daddy cautions Mama that if the car doesn't start, she will have to rock it. "I hope that won't happen," she says. But it does.

For years Mama will speak of the embarrassment this car causes her. Mama has the car loaded with groceries ready to come home, but it won't start. Her face glows red as she gets out and rocks the car back and forth. She sees people watching her, and she wants to crawl under the car! Finally it starts. Hurrying into the car, she heads home. The flywheel has a tooth missing, and when the starter gear lands on that spot; the car will not start. Then the car must be rocked to rotate the flywheel to a new position to enable it to start. To Daddy this is only a minor nuisance, but to Mama it is a constant source of embarrassment.

When we go on a trip, and come to the Baraboo hills, the car doesn't have enough power to make it up the hill.

"Danged if this isn't a heck of a note," says Daddy. "Well, we'll just have to try something else." He turns the car around and backs up the hill!

* — * — *

With the might of a sonic boom thunder raps our ears, and the trees sway and twist in the ferocious wind. The rain pounds the roof, and streams down the windows like the gigantic tears that accompany a family's tragedies and heartaches. The old house shakes and creaks, but stands as firm as the marriage that will survive within its walls for over sixty five years. Eventually the sunbeams brightly shine through the windows, echoing the fun and laughter that resounds from room to room in the gaiety of an active family. We scamper out to the porch, like woodland animals emerging out of their hiding places after a storm. "Look at the brilliant rainbow," Mama exclaims. We all look up to the rainbow. It proclaims hope for blessings yet to experience.

Della and Elton Singletary home for sixty-five years.
(Estate 1994)

Grandma and Grandpa Wessell come to visit often. One summer afternoon Grandpa and Uncle Leonard are sitting in the multi-color, striped canvas lawn chairs on the driveway. In the kitchen the womenfolk finish supper preparations, and Daddy is upstairs. The men visit as they smoke. Grandpa finishes a cigarette and throws the butt in the driveway. Quicker than scat, eight year old Tommy picks it up and puts it to his mouth. The men laugh at him. He takes a puff, and just then the screen door opens, and Mama comes out on the back porch. Knowing that he is in trouble, Tommy quickly tries to throw the cigarette butt down, but it sticks to his lip. "Ow ow," he howls. He dances around howling while the cigarette burns his lip.

* — * — *

"Mama, where are you going tonight?" twelve year old Jackie asks. "Are you going to card club or dancing?"

"We are going dancing at Waverly Beach tonight. Grandpa Singletary loves to dance, and he is going with us. He dances until the perspiration rolls from him. After sitting, when he gets up it looks as though he has wet his pants," she answers.

"Oh, Mama, does it really?"

"It sure does!"

"Which neighbor girl is going to stay with us tonight?"

"Dorothy Rosenthal will be here soon. You help with getting Patsy to bed, Honey. At four she is going through a rebellious stage."

"Alright. Mama, you look beautiful in your black dress and rhinestone jewelry. You are wearing the artificial white, gardenia flower, in your hair, which Aunt Dorothy brought you last week. I think you both look pretty with those flowers in your dark hair. What makes them glow in the dark?"

*Mama loves black dresses
yet in 1948.*

*Daddy's picture from
Barber Colman.*

"I'm not sure, Honey, I guess, they are specially treated. There is some chocolate cake you can all have, but clean up the dishes."

Daddy comes into the kitchen. At six feet, he has no trouble reaching his comb in the little box on top of the refrigerator. He sticks it under the water faucet and slicks down his thin, straight, dark hair. He sings, "First couple down center, and there you divide. The ladies go right, and the gents to the other side. Now honor your partner, your corner, the same, and waltz down the center, with the waltz promenade." He does a little waltz around the kitchen.

"Hi, Dorothy, I'm so glad you could come tonight. I appreciate it. We will be home about eleven thirty. Elton will walk you down the street to your house, when we get home," Mama says, as Dorothy comes to the door.

50

"I'm happy to do it. Have a good time," Dorothy responds.

When Mama and Daddy leave, the kids tell stories and we eat the cake. When it is time for me to go to bed, I don't like the idea. I throw a little tantrum, refusing to go upstairs. Jackie takes my arms and Gene takes my feet. They tote me upstairs, and I rebel all the way. Jackie is able to calm me down. She tucks me in, and recites a little prayer with me.

Daddy continues to spade his large garden by hand. He has a beautiful berry patch with ten long rows of strawberries. There are lots of strawberries for our family and many are sold to supplement the income. Jackie, Gene and Tommy are expected to help pick them. I am only four at this time so most of my pickings are devoured. Eight year old Tommy does not like picking all these berries. His continual lament is, "When I get married, I am going to have four rows of strawberries and ten kids!"

* — * — *

Our neighbor, Howard Milner, is our milkman; he is also a South Beloit policeman. He drives the truck for Dougan Guernsey Farm. Every morning he leaves two or three quart bottles of milk beside our front door, even on Sunday. We bring the milk in and shake it up before we use it. Usually Mama will pour some cream off the top into a little jar, to use for Daddy's coffee. In the summer we must get it into the refrigerator quickly, so it won't sour. In the winter if we leave it out, too long, it will freeze. If it freezes, the milk will push the cardboard bottle top up, and rise like a solid white popsicle above the bottle. People with cats have to get the frozen milk in before the cats lick it.

Mama has cereal bowls for us that have pictures of little children riding tricycles, scooters or wagons around inside the bowl. Sometimes I have Kix poured out of long, narrow, waxed boxes that come inside the big cereal box. Mama adds a spoonful of sugar and pours on the milk. "Look, Mama," I say. I rapidly stir the cereal around and around in my bowl. "See? The children are riding around the bowl on their toys."

"Patsy, eat your cereal, and quit playing with it," Mama responds.

When I am five, Dougan Dairy sponsors a photography special to advertise their milk in the Beloit Daily News. I am selected for an ad.

I wear a pretty, pink print dress with dark blue trim and hair bow. The photographer lets me hold a light blue and white stuffed bunny. The ad states that I have been a Dougan milk fan since birth. That I arrived weighing nine and a half pounds and that I now weigh forty-three pounds. Many people comment about the cute picture in the paper, with the ad for "The Babie's Milkman."

51

How can I know what this picture at five years old will lead to? In my eighth year of grade school, the Dougan ad promoters call my parents offering another photography special. Mother and Dad agree that it would be nice to take advantage of the photo offer. To my dismay, the ad comes out in the paper October 17, 1949, when I am a Freshman in high school. No one has given much thought about when it would come out in the paper. Meanwhile, I have gained weight, and I am teased unmercifully about drinking rich, creamy milk and doing so well on it.

Patsy's first picture for Dougan Dairy ad.

"Saw your picture, Pat." "You're sure doing well on creamy milk." "Just eighteen cents for a quart, glass bottle, no wonder you're doing well." "Still taking from the babies' milk man?"

I am five when Mama says, "Patsy, do you want to walk to Field's Grocery Store with me? I need to pick up a few things." The neighborhood store is just a block north, and the third place around the corner, to the east on Shirland Ave.

"Sure, Mama," I say, and skip along beside her.

As we enter the store, Kenny Brooks greets us with his jovial banter. He is medium height, with blue eyes and sandy red hair. He is always laughing and teasing someone. In 1941 he has just married the widow, Gladys Field. His wife wears a long white apron over her house dress, dark shoes and thin white anklets. Her casually styled dark hair, frames her kindly face. She looks through her glasses at us, and says, "What can I help you with, today?"

"I would like a chunk of big bologna," Mama says.

We go over to the glassed in refrigerated case, and look at the large chunks of lunch meat and cheese. The cheese looks so good. I would love to take a big bite out of the center of that huge chunk of cheese.

Mr. Brooks waits on another customer who wants a large box of cereal. I watch with mouth open and wide eyes, as he takes pincher tongs on the end of a long pole and stretches as high as he can to reach a box on the top shelf. He gets it off the shelf and then does a little juggling act to catch it and set it on the counter.

"I'll have a pound of that American cheese, and slice it please, Gladys," Mama says.

I watch, captivated, as she lays the cheese against the slicer. She takes the slices as they drop off and stacks them up. She wraps the cheese, as she did the bologna, in pink paper pulled from a long roll in an iron holder on the counter, and ties it with a string pulled from a huge spool.

"I'll have this loaf of Colonial Bread and that will be it," Mama says. We head home with our brown paper bag of groceries.

Field's Grocery on Shirland Avenue.

Grandpa Singletary comes to our house for supper regularly. He comes from his real estate office in the Goodwin Building in downtown Beloit. Grandpa most always dresses in a business suit, and has a watch with a gold chain hanging from his pocket. Dark hair with a receding hairline accents his square face. He has full lips. Dark eyes twinkle through his gold rimmed glasses, overshadowed by heavy, dark eyebrows. He is medium height with a rather rotund belly and a jolly disposition. Joseph Charles Franklin Singletary, I always wonder what it would be like to write that name. It has more letters than the entire alphabet! I'm glad I just call him Grandpa.

As he lifts his coffee cup to take a drink, I watch. His hand trembles, and I wonder if there will be any coffee in the cup by the time he gets it to his mouth. This hereditary tremor will afflict Daddy, some of his brothers and several offspring for generations to come. By high school, I will have it. Well, as one friend says, "You can make a great milk shake!"

On a November evening in 1941 Grandpa is at our house.

"Della, did you read in the Beloit Daily News about the Dutch Mill Dance Hall, over at Lake Delavan? It burned on the fourteenth," he says.

"Yes, I did. The guy that owned it, said he was threatened a year ago that he wouldn't be running the place at this time, because he didn't pay extortion," Mama answers.

"Well, it was bombed on June 26th. Now this. Those crooks get what they want, I guess," Grandpa says with disgust.

"The paper said souvenir hunters were burning their fingers in the hot ashes the next morning, searching for coins. Besides losing the building, they lost about $2,000 worth of liquor."

"I guess, people will have to find another place to dance," concludes Grandpa.

* — * — *

One evening when Jimmy Nicolls and I are about six years old, his mother invites our family to their house, next door, for the evening. Jimmy and I go upstairs to his bedroom and play hospital. He has a beautiful, cloth, stuffed drummer boy doll, about twenty inches tall. It has a red jacket, blue pants and a black hat all trimmed with gold braid. Drummer Boy becomes very ill, and we decide he needs surgery. We lay him on the bed and assemble all the medications and bandages. We wipe Jimmy's jackknife with a cloth to be sure it is clean. I hold Drummer Boy down, while Jimmy cuts him open to remove his appendix. He is tightly packed with sawdust which erupts all over everything. We look at each other in alarm as we hear Mrs. Nicolls coming up the stairs. There is nowhere to hide, either ourselves or Drummer Boy.

"What are you two doing? What have you done? Look what you have done to Drummer Boy! You have ruined him! James Nicolls, you ought to be ashamed of yourself!" she scolds.

We really didn't mean to be destructive. We just got carried away with our operating procedure. Realizing we have made a big mistake, we hang our heads, as a big cloud settles over our evening of fun.

* — * — *

I am down cellar with Daddy, while he putters around at his work bench. He has an old radio on. Suddenly, he says, "Oh my God, no - no."

"What's the"

"Shh - Listen!" He turns the radio up louder. "President

Roosevelt announced this morning, December 7, 1941; the Japanese have attacked Pearl Harbor from the air. Coming in from the southwest the planes attacked Oahu at 7:55 as the city was at rest on a quiet Sabbath morning. Wave after wave of bombers swarmed the clouded sky. WE ARE AT WAR!"

I follow Daddy up the stairs. He is extremely upset. "Della, the Japs have bombed Pearl Harbor. Our country is at war!"

"Oh, no. I was hoping it would never come to this," Mama cries.

We spend the afternoon and evening glued to the big console radio in our living room. In the hours to come, we learn that about 1,500 of our men and boys have been killed. The nation mourns, as it prepares to do battle.

Life goes on at home and families try to achieve some sense of normalcy. Our dear friends and next door neighbors, Erla and Floyd Nicolls, decide to host a sleigh ride party for Jackie. Now that she is in high school she has some new friends.

It is a moderate night, perfect for a sleigh ride. The country-side is hidden below a deep mantle of winter ermine. Like millions of diamonds, the snow sparkles in the moonlight.

Vapor rises, like little wisps of fog, from the horses' nostrils as they snort and toss their heads.

"Everybody on?" asks the driver.

"Yep, yeah, yes," comes a mixture of voices.

The driver snaps the reins and clucks to the team. The draft horses trot along, as though they know they are out for an evening of fun. Sleigh bells jingle, as the team goes forward on the snow packed roads.

Teenagers squirm and wiggle in the hay to get a comfortable spot, on the big farm wagon on runners. Someone starts singing Jingle Bells, and most join in. They go from one song to another. Laughter rings merrily, boys tease the girls, and some boys jump off to throw a few snowballs. They race up and clamor back on.

The team approaches an area of deep snow close on both sides of the sleigh. Some kids jump off. Jackie jumps and sinks in snow to her waist. She tries to run, but the snow holds her prisoner.

"Help, help!" she yells. "I can't get out!"

The driver stops the team. Mr. Nicolls and a couple of the boys get off the sleigh and pull her out of the snow drift. They struggle back onto the sleigh with everyone laughing.

The party draws to a climax at Nicolls house, where the group chatters excitedly about their adventures in the snow. The crisp winter air, and lively activity have created healthy appetites. Erla's delicious barbecues, potato chips, cookies and hot chocolate add the grand finale to a winter evening, which will live on in the delights of winter memories. Jackie will always love and appreciate Mr. and Mrs. Nicolls.

* — * — *

Tuesday, September 29, 1942, Beloit, Wisconsin and South Beloit, Illinois cooperate to have the first dim-out in the residential areas. South Beloit synchronizes its fire whistle with Beloit's factory whistle. The whistles blow two minute short blasts to start the dim-out at eight o'clock. The dim-out is a trial run, in preparation for a total county black-out. People driving cars must turn off lights, park, and seek shelter. All lights are to be out and no one should use telephones during this period of time. Two long whistle blasts end the dim-out at eight thirty. It is scary thinking that we could be trying to hide from enemy planes, which might be overhead to bomb us.

By October 1, 1942 the whole nation is called to sacrifice for the war effort. A great campaign begins, to gather rubber, sheet metal, rags, scrap iron and scrap metals such as copper, brass, zinc and lead. People are urged to form family treasure hunts to find these items. All forty-eight states cooperate to reduce speed limits to thirty-five miles per hour to conserve rubber in every way possible. People are asked to drive less. Gasoline rationing is expected to take place by November twenty second.

Officials estimate that it takes twenty pounds of steel to manufacture a Garland rifle, bayonet, helmet and mess kit for an infantry private. It takes eight tons of scrap for a light tank, nineteen tons of scrap for a medium tank and thirty-nine tons of scrap for a heavy tank.

The old cannon that has been displayed in Field Park on West Grand Avenue, next to Beloit High School, since 1934 is dismantled. The cannon was used by American soldiers in the front lines in World War I. Now the scrap from it will aid our soldiers in another World War.

People are being urged to buy War Bonds and Stamps. Daddy signs up to have money deducted from his paycheck every week toward the purchase of the bonds. He will continue this procedure for many years to come, no matter how tight the budget gets. Daddy believes the slogan, "A penny saved, is a penny earned." The government is predicting that by 1943 taxes will take one third of everyone's income.

In the first week of October 1942 the nation's farmers are begging for people to help harvest the crops. They are appealing to office workers, students, prisoners, Mexican workers, Japanese in evacuee camps, Indians on reservations, women and city dwellers. The loss of manpower because of the war is creating a critical situation.

Life marches along; our family is busy with the daily activi-

56

ties of school, birthday parties, family gatherings, holidays, summer vacation, but over all is the weight of a country at war. There is news of loved ones called in the draft, wounded in action, friends mourning losses. The songs and movies take up the cause of the war. In school we are singing, "The Battle Hymn of the Republic," "Over There," "The Caissons Go Rolling Along," "God Bless America," and at home we sing "Don't Sit Under the Apple Tree," and "You're In the Army Now."

Mid summer 1943, Mama says, "Come on, Patsy, let's walk up to Patrick's Grocery Store, on the corner. I need some margarine and some bread."

I scamper along beside Mama the short block to the south west corner of So. Eighth and Center Streets.

"Hi, Francis," Mama says, to the lady behind the counter. They exchange pleasantries, and Mama gets what she needs.

"Mama, may I please have an ice cream cone?" I ask.

"Oh, I guess so. Strawberry or vanilla?"

"Strawberry."

"We'll each have strawberry," says Mama putting down a dime. I watch as Mrs. Patrick dips up two big scoops onto each cone. She dips the ice cream scoop in a glass of water between scoops. We walk toward home licking steadily.

Patrick's grocery on So. Eighth Street.

October 7, 1943, the Beloit Daily News sponsors a campaign to raise money to buy cigarettes to send to our boys in service. In the heart of rationing, it mentions how we have all "squawked" for not having enough gas to drive somewhere we have wanted to go, or we didn't have enough points to buy the cut of meat we might want. It brings our attention to the boys who are fighting, some dying for us. The paper route carriers will distribute envelopes for donations and collect them. They claim it's a small thing we can do to "keep 'em smoking" over there by sending them FREE cigarettes. Five cents buys a pack, ten cents buys two packs, and a half dollar buys a carton. It is also a contest among the carrier boys, with prizes for the largest collections - twenty five-dollar war bond for largest city collection. Ten dollars in War Stamps for largest East Side collection; ten dollars in War Stamps for largest West Side collection; all intended to give the boys a merrier Christmas.

By the end of the first week in October, Wisconsin is harvesting the best corn crop in its history. It is great to have good news sandwiched in with all of the heavy activities of the times.

In Europe, allied forces on the attack by land, sea and air, plow through Adolf Hitler's shattered Russian winter line. The battle fury mounts.

Our family is in the middle of its own crisis as Eli Wessell dies October 7, 1943. Our terrible grief of losing our beloved grandfather and the adventures we have known at their home on Riverside Drive in Beloit, is overwhelming. It will be a new adjustment to have Grandma come to live in our home, but we welcome her with open arms and hearts full of love. She and Jackie will share a bedroom.

How privileged I am to have my very own room, right off Grandma and Jackie's room. The single spring cot is a wonderful bed if I don't use too much space in rolling over. I have about a foot and a half between the bed and my other furnishings. The single, dark brown wardrobe holds my clothes and shoes. I decorate the exterior with my favorite pictures and pin-up girls. Grandpa made the marvelous, narrow, dressing table on tall legs, with drawers and mirror. It is painted deep rosy pink. The matching bench has a lid that opens, revealing some of my favorite treasures, and it slides under the dresser.

This room is my hide-a-way. It doesn't matter how ugly the world gets; I can always escape to this wonderful room. My old doll, the stuffed panda and monkey are waiting here to welcome me. My friends: Joyce Field, Marjorie Milner, Alice Anderson, Barbara Kissling, Bertha Busker and others, plus cousins Marilyn and Myrna Singletary will spend hours playing in my room with me. Here I can be transported to enchanting events and distant lands. I can escape even the things that go bump in the night, well, usually. It doesn't matter, that someday this room will be used for a closet.

These rooms are upstairs on the front of the house. Directly in back of them across the hall is Mama and Daddy's room and to the right of their room is the boys' room. The small bath is at the end of the hall.

One small bath for seven people can be a real problem at times. I race up the stairs. I have to go so bad. Oh, no, someone is in the bathroom. "Hurry up in there," I yell. "I have to go bad."

"I'll be out soon," answers Tom.

I am racing around the upstairs, into my room, back to the hallway. I cross my legs; it doesn't help. I grab myself. Some things can't be held back; no matter what you grab. "Hurry up," I scream. Just when I think I can't possibly hold it another moment, the door is unlocked and opened. We fly past one another.

I am never very brave about coming upstairs to the bathroom at night, though there is a light in the hall ceiling. The doorways along the hall are always dark. I fly nervously past them. As I sit on the stool, I look at the wall a few feet ahead of me. In the plaster are some rather crude grooves. Is it a man's head with an eye that I see up there? Is he looking at me? I think it's a good idea to hurry and go back downstairs to the safety of my family.

When everyone settles into their own beds at night, I call out from my bed, "Goodnight, Mama dear. Goodnight, Mama dear." I hear a snicker from my parents' room.

"Goodnight, Patsy," Mama answers.

Now I am giggling. "Goodnight, Papa bear. Goodnight, Papa bear," I giggle. I hear laughter from their room, but this time the voice is rather stern.

"Goodnight, Patsy. Now get yourself to sleep!" answers Daddy.

Grandpa Wessell's sisters - Hattie, Lucy, Sue, Eva, Alice.
A group of musical and jolly good sports.

It's 1943, Grandpa Wessell's sister, Aunt Sue Rambolt is visiting us from Maybelle, Colorado. Aunt Sue and her husband

George Ramboldt left Sharon, Wisconsin to become shepherds in Colorado. Uncle George has since passed away. Every winter Aunt Sue comes to visit us.

"Tell us about your train ride, Aunt Sue," I beg.

"The train climbs up into the mountains, snaking through blue green spruce and pine forests. Through the window, I can see the land fall away only a few feet from the edge of the tracks, dropping into vast canyons. A stream, resembling a narrow silver ribbon, winds its way on the canyon floor. Woooo it's way - way down below."

"Doesn't it scare you, Aunt Sue?" asks Gene.

"It makes your tummy tingle! The train descends around curves and switchbacks, and then we are down in the bottom looking up at sheer rock walls, towering above us. You must get your Dad to bring you to Colorado sometime. You would love it. My son Frank and his family would help show you a great time."

"I'd sure like to come," I say, and Gene, Tom and Jackie agree.

"If I can ever pry Elton out of Wisconsin's northwoods, I'd love to come," says Mama.

"Mama you look pretty. Why are all of your good dresses black?" I ask.

"Because black is always so dressy," says Mama.

"Where are you going tonight?" asks Jackie.

"We are going to a card party at the home of Bud and Madeline Ennis. Aunt Sue is going to stay with you kids. See that you all behave yourselves," she adds.

"Aunt Sue, are you going to behave yourself?" asks Jackie.

With that mischievous twinkle in the eye that resembles Grandpa Wessell, Aunt Sue says, "Who, me?"

While Mama and Daddy are away enjoying their evening out, Aunt Sue tells us tales of the mountains of Colorado. She talks of wild horses, sagebrush and the antics of her grandkids.

"Aunt Sue, we like to smoke when Mom and Dad aren't here," says Tommy. "Do you smoke?"

"Sure. We can smoke, but if we let your folks find out, we'll all get our rears kicked."

We all go to the kitchen, and the boys light up. We take turns puffing until the kitchen is filled with smoke.

"Okay, kids. If we don't want to get caught we'd better get this smoke out of here," says Aunt Sue.

We open all the doors and windows. Waving flour sack dish towels, we chase the smoke out! In this era, no one is issuing health warnings against smoking. We think we are just pursuing a habit limited to adults. Because Mama and Daddy are smokers,

60

they detect nothing unusual. It will be years before the truth is laughingly revealed.

* — * — *

My leg won't stretch high enough to get it over the bar of my brother's bike, so I stick it through the opening below the bar. Gripping the handlebars and hanging out one side, I attempt riding. It doesn't work well; I get scraped and bruised.

I wheel the big bike to the back porch steps, climb on and wobble down the street. If nothing is in my way, I make a large circle returning to the steps to dismount. If I am where the steps aren't available, I fall over, adding more bruises and abrasions to my body.

Gene and Tommy make bike riding look so easy. They sit backward on their handlebars and ride, practicing stunt riding for a Boy Scout-Arama. They use their bikes like horses and ride without touching the handlebars, while they twirl a lariat in circles. It isn't fair, I can't ride straight forward, and the boys can do stunt riding.

* — * — *

Mid May 1944, Grandpa Singletary is in Beloit Municipal Hospital. He suffers from a severe heart condition. I know it is serious when I see how upset Daddy is. Only seven months ago, Grandpa Wessell died. I am seized with fear. "Mama, Grandpa Singletary isn't going to die, too, is he?" I cry.

"We just don't know, Honey. He is very sick. We just don't know," she cries.

Grandma Wessell comforts me by playing games with me. I sense she is concerned, too.

Mama and Daddy return from a visit to the hospital. I am surprised to see Daddy cry. Mama puts her arms around him and they both cry. Mama turns to Grandma, "They had to put Dad in restraints. He is delirious. He doesn't know us. He got out of bed and tried to throw a nurse through the window."

"Oh, dear!" cries Grandma.

Monday, May 22nd, Mama and Daddy return from the hospital. I can see they have been crying. Mama says, "Grandpa Singletary died at 7:30 tonight."

"Is he in heaven with Grandma Singletary?" I ask.

"Yes, Honey. They are together now," Mama answers.

A few days after the funeral some of the family is gathered, at Grandpa's house, at 640 Central Ave. Uncle Rollin's family and Uncle Gay's family are here. The children and teenagers are milling around outside. This scene etches itself in my memory. I am discovering new cousins, as we rarely see them. Why is it that families sometimes distance themselves from one another, even when there is a bond of love, and they reside in the same area?

Jackie says, "Grandpa built and sold many houses in and around the Beloit area."

"Yes, responds one of the older cousins, "He was a Realtor here for 25 years.

"Dad has been in business with Grandpa for some time," says one of Uncle Gay's children. "He will continue to run the office."

* — * — *

With a war still raging, our nation is grieved at the death of President Franklin Roosevelt on April 11, 1945. Vice-President Harry Truman becomes the new President of the United States.

Our next door neighbor friends, Mr. and Mrs. Nicolls, often take me places with them and Jimmy. This afternoon we are stopping at Jimmy's father's parents. Mrs. Nicolls says, "Patsy, Jimmy's grandparents are deaf mutes. They can't hear or speak, but they talk with their hands." I am spellbound as I watch the adults communicating on their hands. Even Jimmy can say a few things to them. This is quite a new experience for me. I wish I could talk like that!

When I come home, I find my family out on the back porch crying. I am frightened. "What's the matter, Mama?" I ask.

"We are grinding horseradish," says Mama.

"Why do you grind it, if it makes you sad?" I ask.

Mama laughs, "It doesn't make us sad, Honey. It has such strong fumes when it's being ground it makes our eyes water."

I walk into the kitchen, turn, and run back to the porch. I understand. It makes my nose tingle and my eyes burn.

The summer evening is warm. Daddy says, "Let's go for a ride to cool off." We all climb into the car, and Daddy takes us out in the country. We roll the windows down and let the fresh air blow through the car, cooling us down. When our ride is nearly over, Grandma says, "Elton, if you want to drive down to the Barrel, I'll treat."

A chorus of "Oh, Boy!" goes up from us kids. "The root beer stand!"

When Daddy stops at the Barrel on Blackhawk Boulevard in South Beloit, a car hop comes up to our car.

"Can I help you?" asks the pretty young girl.

Grandma gives her the order. We can smell the wonderful hamburgers, before they arrive.

When the girl returns she is carrying a tray. "Roll your window up just a bit, please," she says. Then she places the brackets on the tray over the window, and adjusts the rod on the bottom of the tray to fit snug against the side of the car.

Daddy starts handing the wrapped burgers back to us.

"Um, they smell so good. Pickle, mustard and ketchup. Um

62

um," says Tommy.

Carefully, Daddy begins to hand the cold, frosty, glass mugs of foamy root beer back to us. We take them by the side handle.

"Thank you, Grandma," we say, one-by-one, "This is so good!"

* — * — *

We are close friends with the Nicolls family. Mrs. Nicolls is always so good to help our family at times of grief, needs or parties. She and Mama become like sisters for a long period of time; the couples belong to card clubs, and entertain each other.

Early Sunday evening Mrs. Nicolls invites us to come out in the yard with our lawn chairs. She has gone to the York farm on South Bluff Road, and bought two quarts of fresh cream. Using fresh strawberries, she has made homemade strawberry ice cream. When the last few difficult turns on the ice cream churn are done, Mrs. Nicolls calls, "Come and get it!" She begins dishing up the rich, pink, creamy delight. Surely, this must be a taste of Heaven! We hear music.

The Pentecostal church, which is pastored by Rev. Brooks, sits kitty - corner across Illinois Street from our house. A service is in progress; they sing and clap their hands. It is truly lively, joyful music. We feel like dancing.

Pentecostal church on Illinois Street. Uncle Leonard and Aunt Dorothy Wessell.

Grandma and Mother are listening to "Ma Perkins" on the radio, when I come in for lunch. I know they have already listened to "Our Gal Sunday." They never miss these programs.

"Mother, are we going to listen to "Fibber McGee and Molly" and "Henry Aldrich" tonight? When Mama and Daddy bought a

63

new parlor set, the old couch was put in the dining room. Now we gather in the dining room to listen to our favorite programs.

"Yes. We probably will," Mother answers.

"You and I can walk up to the liquor store on Shirland Avenue and get some beer, pop and chips. Then we can tap a keg of nails when the programs are over," smiles Grandma.

* — * — *

I can't believe the day has arrived! It is mid June 1945. Mother turns the car off West Grand Avenue, around the end of the Northwestern Depot toward the south, and pulls into a parking place along the depot platform. Jackie has started working as receptionist for Doctor R. H. Gunderson, so she can't see us off. Gene and Tom hop out of the car and carry Grandma's and my bags as the five of us walk up onto the platform and into the depot. Inside, the depot is light mint green, and the bare floor is narrow boards. Grandma goes to the office window and purchases the tickets to Chicago. Grandma and I have been invited to spend a couple of weeks with Aunt Dorothy and Uncle Leonard in their apartment at 1262 Argyle Ave.

Northwestern depot, Beloit, Wi. From the collection of the Beloit Historical Society.

"It's nearly time for the train to be pulling in from the north. We should go out on the platform," says Mother. She hugs Grandma and kisses her, then wraps me in a bear hug and kisses me. "You be sure to mind Grandma. Be careful, have fun, and don't forget to write." The boys hardly have time to give us goodbye hugs, when I hear a tremendous roar.

"Stand back! Everyone back!" yells an attendant with the railroad. I look up the track and see the huge iron horse heading toward us. The red lights begin swinging back and forth at the road crossing, and the ding-donging adds to the noise.

I shudder with a mixture of fear and excitement, as the great cyclops roars into the station, slowing to a chug-chug, chug-chug, as it belches forth a burst of steam. A railroad man pushes an iron wheeled, red cart down the platform, where they start to unload cartons and baggage.

All of a sudden, I see someone in a handsome blue uniform give Mother a hug. Then he turns and says, "Hi Patsy!" It is Uncle Ivan, Daddy's brother, in his conductor's uniform.

Grandma and I board the train, take our seats and wave, as the big locomotive chug-chug, chug-chugs out of town. When we reach the country, it starts picking up speed.

Through the train windows, we see a new world appear as

we enter the suburbs of Chicago. Clustered close together, some only a foot or two apart, we see tall, red or tan brick buildings. Some look dirty. Clothes lines stretch between a few of the buildings, often three or four stories up. "Grandma, how do they get their clothes up there?" I ask.

"The rope is circular and runs through a pulley. They can pull the rope and move the clothes toward or away from them," answers Grandma.

"Wouldn't it be funny if the wind blew them off?" I ask. "They would surely have to go a long way after them."

"Yeah. Someone might run off with them before they could get there," chuckles Grandma.

Aunt Dorothy and Uncle Leonard are waiting for us at the depot. It looks like a big barn full of train engines. It is all so massive and noisy. It makes me feel very small, but we are soon whisked away to their apartment.

We climb stairs to the second floor and there is another flight that goes beyond. When Uncle Leonard opens the door, I hear a sharp, "Yip, yip, yip."

"I didn't know you had another dog, where is it?" I ask. I know they no longer have the small husky they once had.

"We haven't had her very long. Uncle Leonard wanted to surprise you," says Aunt Dorothy. Out of the kitchen comes the tiniest dog I have ever seen. She is tawny like a deer, with a white vest. She isn't much bigger than a kitten.

"I got her from my butcher," says Aunt Dorothy. "When we first got her, Uncle Leonard carried her around in his pocket."

"What kind is she?" asks Grandma.

"She is a Mexican Chihuahua," says Uncle Leonard. "We call her `Tootser'."

At night Uncle Leonard pulls out the sofa, in the living room, and makes it into a bed for Grandma and me.

It seems strange up here; all night we hear sirens screaming through the streets. Far below, people laugh, slam, car doors and some yell. I snuggle up close to Grandma, and wonder if people ever sleep.

Aunt Dorothy and Uncle Leonard work, so Grandma and I spend the days roaming the shopping areas near by. We stop at a market and Grandma buys some fruit and asks for the rectangular, cardboard fruit basket with a handle over the middle. While we are in a dime store she buys a yard or so of pink floral print, cotton material and a small rubber doll. When we get back to the apartment she covers the basket with the material, makes a little pillow, and a dress for the doll. Presto, I have a doll and doll bed.

Another day we are out walking and watch a man pedaling a

bicycle-like cart. He has various tools hanging on it. A bell tinkles as he pedals along. He sharpens shears and knives for people.

We stop at a drug store, go to the soda fountain, and climb up on tall stools at the counter. "Patsy, would you like a fresh limeade?" asks Grandma. "I'm thirsty,"

"Yes, please," I answer. I watch as the girl takes a couple of fresh, green limes, puts them in a metal device and pulls the handles together to squeeze the juice into a tall glass. She adds ice, sugar and water. "Um, Gram. It's good!"

Late one afternoon Aunt Dorothy takes us to the butcher shop with her, and introduces us to Herman, the butcher. He wears white pants, coat, apron, hat and has a large meat cleaver in his hand. The floor is covered with sawdust and there is a huge butcher block, on legs, standing in the middle of the floor. Back in one corner, a large German shepherd gnaws on a big bone. Herman notices me watching the dog. "No one tries any funny stuff with him here," he says. He wraps Aunt Dorothy's selections in white paper and ties it with string.

One afternoon Grandma and I go to a movie theater to see, "The Story of Dr. Wassell." It is good, but a war picture with some sad parts. Grandma and I both cry.

Grandma's brother and his wife live in Chicago, also. Aunt Mary calls and wants Grandma and me to spend a couple of days with them in their apartment at 3603 Jannsen. Uncle Leonard takes us over. Aunt Mary's house sparkles.

"I just painted my kitchen floor," says Aunt Mary.

"You painted the linoleum?" asks Gram. "How did you get such a pattern?"

"I painted it beige and let it dry. Then I stippled it with red, let it dry, then stippled it with green," says Aunt Mary.

"It's really pretty, Mary," says Gram. I agree.

In the late afternoon, Uncle Frank arrives from his job at an office with the Chicago transit system. "Hello, Ella. And this is Patsy. My gosh it's hot! You got some iced tea, Mary? People are dropping dead in this heat."

Aunt Mary fixes iced tea for them and gives me lemonade. Uncle Frank is a large man with glasses. A gold chain loops down from the watch in his pocket. His booming voice intimidates me.

I look at the antique picture over the davenport. In a round, black, wood frame, with an ornate edge, under glass, three wild, white horse heads look at me with wild eyes. I wonder what they are running from? They appear to be racing with the wind. They intrigue me. I can not know that fifty years from now the picture will hang in my own home.

When it is time to go to bed, Aunt Mary opens two full length doors, with beautiful, beveled edge mirrors. She pulls down a fold-a-way bed, into the center of the living room.

This neighborhood is quieter, but we still hear distant sirens in the night. The city talks.

One afternoon Gram, Aunt Mary and I walk to a shopping area. Aunt Mary decides to stop at her church. The large, brick building has a tall steeple. She wants us to go in with her, but we must be wearing hat's, and I have none. She rummages in her purse, finds a white lace handkerchief and places it on my head. The pews with kneeling benches, the genuflecting, dipping in Holy water, and crossing of one's self is something I have seen only in movies. Gram says this is a Catholic church, and I realize there are some differences in churches. I see a cross, but the sagging, wounded body of Jesus on it makes me want to cry.

Aunt Mary and Uncle Frank Crouse, leaving Aunt Mary's church.

We go back to Aunt Dorothy and Uncle Leonard's. They take us sight-seeing around the city often. Soon it is time to take the train home again. I am full of happy memories. This is one of many visits we will make to Chicago.

* — * — *

It is good to be home again. I missed Mama, Daddy and the rest of the family. Gram is stirring up a double batch of cake, but she seldom uses a recipe. She puts all of the ingredients together, at the table, then she sits down with the large mixing bowl in her lap. Beating the batter with a large spoon, she stops to rest, and then beats it more before dividing the batter between two enameled, loaf pans. Gram sprinkles the top with a cinnamon and sugar mixture, because Daddy doesn't like frosting on cake.

With the oven going, it becomes too warm in the kitchen. The kitchen window and the back shed door are open. Tommy comes in through the screen door, and somehow a sparrow darts in, too. Mama shrieks and tries to shoo it back out the door. The bird is as frightened as we are. Everyone is frantically trying to shoo the bird back outdoors.

Mama yells, "Shut the dining room door. I don't want it to get in the rest of the house." In the dining room, Gene gives the door a flip shut. Just then the bird darts toward this open doorway. "Oh, no!" Mama screams.

We all look in time to see the bird flying through the opening, just as the door slams shut. It never could have happened if we'd planned it that way. The sparrow is caught directly in the middle. SPLAT. He is truly a mugwump bird. His mug is on one side, his wump on the other! His demise.

* — * — *

Monday, August 6, 1945 Daddy picks up the Beloit Daily News and reads the headlines. "Della, have you seen the paper?"

"No, I haven't had time to look at it, yet," says Mama.

"Unleash Powerful Atomic Bomb. Explosive has might of 20,000 tons of TNT. President Truman revealed this great scientific achievement today and warned the Japanese that they now face "a rain of ruin from the air the like of which has never been seen on this earth." The new atomic bomb was used for the first time yesterday. An American plane dropped one on the Japanese army base at Hiroshima," Daddy reads.

"I hope this puts an end to their terrible efforts to conquer the world by killing everyone that gets in their way," Mama says. "This war has gone on far too long!"

THE WAR IS OVER! The evening of August 14th, we join other war weary Beloit area people downtown. President Truman has announced that Japan has accepted the surrender terms of the allied nations. The town has exploded with people, whooping, and hollering. People laugh, cry, yell, clap, wave flags and blare car horns. The crowd is orderly though exceedingly joyous.

August 15th, rationing ends on gasoline, canned fruits and vegetables, fuel oil and oil stoves. It will remain indefinitely on meats, fats, oils, butter, sugar, shoes, tires and other commodities.

September 1, 1945 - Japs sign on dotted line today!!!

Having graduated from South Beloit High School in 1945,

69

Jackie has been working as receptionist for our family doctor. It is a beautiful day toward the end of April 1948 when she walks into Baird's Pharmacy near Beloit's Power and Light office. She smiles her friendly greeting and sits down to order lunch. She glances toward the tall, slender man with dark wavy hair, sitting nearby. He smiles and nods. "You eat lunch here quite often, don't you?" he smiles.

"Yes, I do. You do too, I've noticed," she smiles back.

"You are attractive in your white uniform and cap, with your blond hair and dark eyes. Do you work for a doctor?" he asks.

"Yes, I work for Dr. Robert Gunderson. You must work near here, too," she smiles.

"I work at the employment office. My name is Bob Reynolds."

"I'm Jackie Singletary."

The conversation resumes over the lunch counter at Bairds for several days, and the dating begins. At the doctor's office another tall, handsome man with dark hair, delivers fresh towels, from Ideal. He, too, asks Jackie for a date. When he persists, she tells him she has a close friend she will introduce him to.

Thus, Jackie and Bob, Corrine Strand and Bill Mayo begin whirlwind courtships. The two couples double date, sharing movies, picnics and dancing with joy and laughter. When our family goes north on vacation, Corrine comes to stay with Jackie. After evenings out the girls say goodbye to the guys, then get out the cake. Amid chatter and laughter they devour it. Many years later they explode with laughter wondering why they never offered the guys anything to eat. Each couple goes to the altar in a matter of weeks.

I come into the dining room to find Mama visiting with Grandpa Wessell's brother, Uncle Rube. He is slender like Grandpa was, and he always has funny stories to tell. I greet him, and he responds, then launches into his current story. "Pearl (his wife) and I, and another couple were returning from our vacation in Florida. The women were riding in the back seat and I was driving. We had driven all day and I was tired. Wouldn't you know it, when we came through downtown Beloit I turned a little short in the intersection of West Grand and State streets, and clipped the edge of that cement pedestrian island.

An officer immediately came up to the car. I rolled down the window and said `That's alright, officer, you go right ahead and arrest them! We are just getting back from a trip to Florida, and those women in the back seat have been driving ever since we left home! Go right ahead and arrest them!'

The officer burst out laughing and said, "Oh go on, and be careful."

70

Jackie & Bob's wedding
8/1/48

Bill & Corrine's wedding
8/28/48

We burst out laughing, too. We always enjoy Uncle Rube.

* — * — *

Loud, lively music ascends to greet me as I start downstairs for breakfast this spring morning of 1949. I open the dining room door, and see Tom standing in front of the long buffet where the little radio sits. Using the buffet as a combination drum and keyboard he thumps staccato, rhythmic beats on the top. Tom accompanies the radio's music, expressing the joy that fills his heart. He is in love with high school classmate, Mildred Fulton.

"Tom, quit that! You are going to wear out my buffet," scolds Mother.

Tom will graduate from high school in a few weeks, and I will graduate from grade school.

Pat & 2 week old Dougie

May 30, 1950, our nation observes Memorial Day, paying tribute to those who sacrificed their lives to keep America free. While folks march in parades, attend ceremonies, and picnic, Jackie goes through pain and joy to deliver her first child. Douglas Robert Reynolds makes his debut as the first grandchild for Elton and Della Singletary! Grandma is now Great Grandma, Gene and Tom become uncles, I am AUNT PAT! JOY - JOY -

Gene has completed high school amid a swirl of popularity with the girls. He is active in theater, dancing, dance roller skating, and is jovial and out-going.

Tom & Gene clowning around prior to their marriages.

Gene has chosen a beautiful farm girl, Ruth Clowes, from Clinton, Wisconsin for his bride, and they plan an August 1950 wedding. The invitations are printed, but Gene belongs to the Marine Reserve and the Korean war is expanding.

It appears evident that his unit may be called up. Gene and Ruth decide to scrap their wedding plans. Ruth's mother and Dad and Mother Singletary agree to accompany them to Dubuque, Iowa, July 24th to get married. They travel one hundred miles and discover they need Dad's signature because Gene is only 20 years old. What to do? What to do? They travel the hundred miles back to South Beloit. But now Mother and Dad Clowes have farm animals that need attention and chores

72

won't wait. Cows don't care who is getting married, they have "udder" problems, so Ruth's parents go home. Dad and Tom get home from work and accompany Mother, Gene and Ruth the hundred miles back to Dubuque. By the time they round up the minister it is nine in the evening before they are married.

Bob, Tom, Millie, Gene, - Jackie, Gram Wessell, Pat and Ruth (Gene and Ruth's wedding reception.)

Tom takes pictures throughout the ceremony. After the wedding he says, "Oh no! The film hasn't been advancing!" No pictures. They adjust the film and capture a few poses, before they travel the hundred miles back to South Beloit.

They return from their honeymoon in northern Wisconsin and stay with Mother and Dad. Gene returns from work to find Ruth sitting on the bed crying. He doesn't have to ask, he knows his unit has been called to active duty.

August twenty first, Mother, Dad, Ruth, Grandma, and I go to Rockford to see the troop train depart for California and parts unknown.

Gene embraces each of us, then mother and his new wife. Sweethearts, sons, brothers, husbands all caught in a tearing apart of the human heart. I shall never forget walking along railroad tracks at the south side of Rockford, as the troop train moves slowly away from the Central Illinois depot. A cry of war, fear and separation wrestles with those feigning courage. We slowly wade through the tears, back to the car. With tears flowing and hearts heavy, we head home.

Gene is assigned duty with the cooks. By September, Ruth joins him in California. A knee that was injured in a roller skating accident begins presenting major problems. By November, Gene is discharged and they return home. Within weeks, Gene mourns the death of his closest friend, who is hit by mortar fire in his foxhole. He dies in his brother's arms in transit.

73

Tom & Millie's wedding (1950)

In a lovely formal wedding, Tom marries his high school sweetheart, Mildred Fulton, October 1, 1950, in the Methodist Church, Rockton Illinois.

With all of my siblings married, our home seems strangely quiet. Yet the excitement of new experiences fill my high school years.

Chapter 5
A Day At The Farm
-1943-

What a treat it is to visit Aunt Alice's farm in the forties! Daddy pulls the car to a stop on the edge of the green, front lawn. Mama, Daddy and we four kids tumble out. The aroma of home baked bread and roasting chickens floats across the lawn to greet us.

Uncle Hank comes toward us from across the yard. Ivory teeth flash through his broad grin. He wears his legendary bib overalls. In his left hand he carries the cigar that is usually clenched in his teeth. His right hand is extended toward us in welcome.

The old frame home is perched behind a green lawn only a few feet in front of a railroad track. As we reach the door, Aunt Alice welcomes us with her cheery smile, "Hello Dearies, come right in." I am struck by how much Aunt Alice resembles Grandpa Wessell, with her white hair and slender face. Grandpa's sister has his twinkling eyes and pleasant personality, too. As we enter the house, there is a roar and the house begins to rattle. I look up startled and grab Mama's hand. The roar gets louder and I move closer against Mama. "It's all right, Honey. It's just a train going by."

"Della, I'm busy in the kitchen. You and the girls can come out and chat if you'd like to," says Aunt Alice.

We start into the kitchen and a voice says, "Shut up, shut up." We look at each other startled. The voice continues with a blast of cuss words.

"Oh hush, mind your manners, Polly. Don't show off when we have company," says Aunt Alice. "I'm sorry, that parrot picks up Hank's vocabulary." We see the cage that holds a beautiful red and blue macaw.

"He is pretty for such a naughty bird," says Mama.

"I'm sorry," says the parrot.

I am in awe of the great black iron cook stove. My eyes grow wide and fixed on it as Aunt Alice adds a chunk of wood in one side of the stove. Then to my puzzlement she lifts a lid on the other side and dips out a kettle of hot water. Opening the door of the lower center, she removes a huge roasting pan filled with huge chickens. In the small warming oven, up above, set bowls of squash and green beans. A sideboard holds large loaves of freshly baked white bread with golden brown crusts, apple and custard pies. I am accustomed to seeing abundant amounts of tasty food, but this array seems adequate for a restaurant. A huge kettle of mashed potatoes and a steaming coffee pot complete the results of Aunt Alice's hard work at the great black iron cook stove.

With Mama's cousins - Hank Jr., Arlene and Don - there are eleven of us gathered at the overladen kitchen table. Our small town eyes pop wide open when we see the mounds of potatoes piled on these farm boys' plates. Either individual serving would serve our entire family. When the abundance of delicious food is devoured, the stack of dishes waiting to be washed is staggering. However, many hands make light work. The women folk soon have the kitchen work done.

The four boys had gone outdoors, when they finished their pie, and now they are in the barn.

"Wow!" says Tommy, "I have never seen such a huge animal."

"Look at the bull's nose; it has a large ring," says Gene.

"Is that jewelry?" asks Tommy.

"No" laughs Don. "See this," he says, holding a long pole with a hook on the end. "This fastens onto that ring. It's the way Dad leads that ornery beast around. It's the only way to control him. The bull's nose is sensitive. If he doesn't want to move along or starts to act up, Dad twists the pole and it hurts his nose, so he obeys."

"He's the biggest bull I've ever seen," says Gene, eyeing the creature through the sturdy stall. "Come on," says Junior, "We've got to bring the steer up from the other field."

Gene and Tom climb up on the wood fence. They watch as Don and Junior jump on the back of steers and ride them to the barn.

We girls walk around some farm buildings with Mama and Aunt Alice. Aunt Alice has a basket and collects eggs in various spots, and in the chicken coop. We round the corner of a building and suddenly a huge, black bird swoops out of the sky and lands on Aunt Alice's shoulder.

"Hi, Blackie, how are you today?" she asks the big crow.

I draw closer to Mama. "This is Aunt Alice's pet crow," she says.

Aunt Alice walks around with the crow on her shoulder.

"Do you know what this naughty bird does on wash day?" she asks.

"Makes a mess on your clean clothes?" I ask.

Aunt Alice laughs, "No Patsy. He swoops down and perches on the clothesline as I'm hanging up the wet clothes. When I put the clothespins on the clothes, he comes along and pulls them out so the clothes drop to the ground."

Mama gasps, and we all laugh. We follow Aunt Alice back to the house.

"What a pretty kerosene lamp you have on the wall, Aunt Alice," Jackie says. "It looks like a pin-up lamp. What is the shiny plate behind the globe for?"

"That is to reflect the light when the wick is burning," answers Aunt Alice. "It makes more light."

"That's a pretty dress you have on Jackie," says cousin Arlene.

"Thank you. It's one of my school dresses."

"Boy, when I went to school, I had only one dress I could wear to school. I had to come home every day and put on an old dress. Then I had to wash my school dress and hang it up to dry. Before I could go to bed, I had to heat the flat iron on the cook stove and iron that dress so that it was ready for morning. Boy, we were poor! I sure didn't have any trouble deciding what I was going to wear," exclaims Aunt Alice.

At milking time we go to the barn. A strange blend of sweet smelling hay and fresh cow manure greets our nostrils. The barn is clean, but the cows do their thing when the urge strikes. Uncle Hank sits on a stool beside a large cow. Its udder bulges with the weight of milk it has produced.

With wide eyes I ask, "Will the cow explode?"

"Not if I milk her," Uncle Hank laughs.

He pulls and squeezes the teats making warm milk sound like raindrops on a tin roof, as streams splash into the pail. Kittens come by for a sample. I scream and jump back when he aims a spray at me.

Wandering into the pig pen, Jackie screams as a pig charges toward her. Chunking the pig with an ear of corn, Don chases it away.

We learn many things at the farm that is different from our way of life. We hate to leave.

A few weeks later, the boys return to help with the corn harvest. "Look, this horse has a moustache," exclaims Tommy.

"It surely looks like one, doesn't it? That's Jimmy. The other draft horse is Jessie," says Gene.

The boys walk along cutting corn and throwing it into the wagon pulled by the horses. Tommy sneezes uncontrollably, and by the end of the day, his eyes water; and swell nearly shut. This is his first discovery of hay fever. It will plague him for years.

*Gene, Jackie and Tommy gather at the bird bath in the side yard.
The outhouse is behind them to the left.(1933)*

Chapter 6

Long Paths and Crescents
(1936-1949)

Endless tellings have kept this story alive through the years. Grandpa Wessell's sister, Mama's Aunt Hattie, entertains the family and friends for a gala birthday celebration. Her little house rocks on its foundation with music and laughter. The dining room table sports Aunt Hattie's best lace table cloth. A vase of fresh phlox, in varying shades of rosy pink and white, sits in the center of the table. In the kitchen, mounds of sandwiches hide under a towel cover waiting until serving time. Pickles, fruit salad and baked beans will accompany the sandwiches. A tall angel food cake with whipped cream and strawberry garnishes, a layered chocolate cake, and a sunshine orange cake tempt all who pass by. Everyone enjoys tall glasses of fresh lemonade.

Grandpa stands in the backyard smoking a cigarette. Mama opens the back door and comes out in her pink party dress. Aunt Dorothy is right behind her in her lovely light blue dress.

"You girls look mighty pretty tonight," he says. "August twenty first is Dorothy's birthday. Isn't it nice that my daughter-in-law's birthday is just the day before my daughter's birthday? I'm glad you girls are giving us something to celebrate tonight. Hope you both enjoy the party," he adds.

"Thanks, Pa," Mama says.

"Come on Della, I've got to go," Aunt Dorothy says.

"Yeah, me too. It's all that lemonade wanting out," Mama responds, leading the way.

As they reach the outhouse, Mama steps back and says, "Go ahead, Dorothy. I'll wait."

"Thanks," Aunt Dorothy responds. She opens the old door and steps in. A loud crash with the horrible sound of splintering wood, combines with Aunt Dorothy's loud shrieks!

"Dorothy! Oh, my God! Help! Help!" Mama screams in horror as she sees Aunt Dorothy. The floor has given way and Aunt Dorothy is submerged up to her armpits in the putrid, foul waste.

At the screams people swarm out of the house, like wasps from a disturbed nest. When they see the situation some grab their noses and flee back to the house.

"Oh, no!" cries Uncle Leonard. "Dorothy, are you hurt?"

Aunt Dorothy, in a state of shock, cries "No, just get me out of here. I'm going to be sick!"

Onlookers stand in disbelief. One says, "That outhouse was in need of repair. She probably couldn't afford to have it fixed. Some of us could have helped her, if we had known."

Grandpa and Uncle Leonard try to hold their breath while they brace themselves on the framework of the privy. They pull a couple of boards back to avoid scraping Aunt Dorothy, and then taking her arms they pull her up and out.

"Oh, Dorothy, you poor, poor dear! Your beautiful dress is ruined. How will you get cleaned up? You look like - like—" and then despite the pitiful situation Mama convulses in laughter.

"Bring pails of water. I will clean her up," commands Aunt Hattie.

Men pump water and those toting it take a deep breath and don't exhale until they are away from the stench. As Aunt Hattie pours the water Aunt Dorothy cries out, "Oh! Oh! It's so cold!"

Mama, Grandpa and Uncle Leonard hold blankets as a curtain, while Aunt Hattie works with soap and water, wash cloth and towel. Refreshed and clothed in Aunt Hattie's housecoat, Aunt Dorothy returns to the party, amid a buzzing crowd.

Aunt Dorothy will always be grateful to those who helped her. Mama will always be thankful that she showed Aunt Dorothy that little act of courtesy by letting her go first! Neither of them will ever forget this birthday party.

* — * — *

Before our home in Illisconsin has indoor plumbing, our family is accustomed to the long path and familiar crescent. For anyone owning an outhouse, Halloween is always a time of concern. In the dark, coolness before daybreak Mama and Daddy are often struggling to set the outhouse back up before the neighbors see them.

We enjoy the story our Swedish neighbors tell about some farm friends who get extremely upset to find their outhouse tipped over every Halloween. Mr. Farmer decides he will fix these rascals who come to do such devilment. He hides in some nearby bushes so he can observe the event. It is too dark to see much, but finally he hears voices.

"Come on guys, this is the one that is so sturdy. We will all have to push at the same time," says one of the three figures.

"Let's push it so it falls on the door like we always do. Lean your shoulder into it and give it all you've got on the count of three," says another voice.

"One, two, three . . . "

The three push with all their might. The outhouse (that has been put on large rollers) rolls forward and the three boys pitch into the putrid pit.

The screams emitting from the pit are enough to wake the

80

dead! Scrambling and tugging at one another, they extract themselves with words that describe the mire from which they struggle. Mr. Farmer goes to bed thoroughly amused, confident that he will never have to set his outhouse up again.

Our home has indoor plumbing before I need to be concerned with it. I get acquainted with the long path and crescent as we vacation at primitive resorts in the northwoods of Wisconsin. Perhaps it is because these places are spooky that they are designed with two or three holes in the seat so no one has to use it alone. The holes are often different sizes, some so large that I could fall right through them. You never know when grandaddy long legs or mice might come to greet you. One resort has a big old dog that has access to the pit and comes to lap up waste when the place is in use. Sometimes we hold the door open and snap a picture of the protesting victim. It provides a little moral support to have someone with you. But what an affront, to have others watching you grunt!

One day, when I'm about five, the family is enjoying a drive along rustic roads, visiting various lakes in the area. I really need to use a toilet, but I know that there is nothing but those terrible outhouses. We stop to take a little walk near one lake. "Oh, dear, I've got to tell Mama," I think.

"Mama, I've got to go . . . Oh, oh," I cry. It is such a desperate feeling, but the dike has broken and there is no holding it back. Warm liquid is running down my legs and squishing in my shoes. Almost immediately my slacks feel cold and mighty uncomfortable. They don't smell too great, either.

"Patsy, what have you done?" Mama asks. "Your little pink slacks are all wet. We don't have a change of clothes with us."

I am so embarrassed. I hang my head and now big tears are running down my face and getting my little pink top wet too.

"Don't cry, Honey. I'll find something," Mama soothes.

I finish out the journey in my father's long, blue overall jacket. The sleeves are rolled up and it comes to my feet, but it works. Mama rinses my clothes out in the lake and we all get back in the car and continue our outing.

As I grow old enough to read the messages written and carved into the walls of the outhouses it becomes a bit entertaining. Many folks find it desirable to leave their name and address. Others like to draw hearts with initials, and some have a yearning to share their poetic talent. One such poem lingers in memory: "This little palace is all I own, I try to keep it clean and neat. So please be kind, with your behind, and don't poop on the seat!"

Aunt Dorothy always has her "biffy" papered with inspirational poetry and pin-up girls. Most of them are cute, but some are risque and some are nude. An acquaintance visits their log home, and when he uses the biffy he is offended by the decor. He plays "fireman" and sprays some of the pictures. Do two wrongs make a right?

Chapter 7

Adventures In The Northwoods
(1929-1950)

Northern Wisconsin is more than a vacationland. Its spruce, hemlock and pine scent permeates the clear air. The heady fragrance fills your being like the essence of romance. On the forest floor is a unique display of lichen, evergreen needles and decaying logs with seedlings squeezing up from within. Various shades of browns, grays, yellows, blacks and greens weave intricate designs in the under growth. Ferns grace the needled carpet, while striped chipmunks and red squirrels dart in and out of leafy boughs, and scamper up the tall trees. Sunshine filters through the umbrellas of green overhead, as colorful songbirds serenade us, and call to one another. Pause a moment in the forest, and hear God's symphony of nature.

A walk on trails or country roads often provides the sighting of whitetail deer. The buck lifts his proud head and sniffs the air for a scent of the two-legged tribe. The doe keeps ever watchful eyes upon her little, spotted, twin fawns as they frolic nearby.

A night drive sometimes reveals the beautiful black and white striped skunk, waddling down the road with a trail of little ones following. They are oblivious of their sickening odor, but they know exactly when to use it for their own protection. Woe to the family pet that chooses to tangle with them!

In the cabin, you may hear a ruckus by the back door. Investigation reveals the clever antics of masked bandits. Raccoons use their little hand-like paws to take apart the garbage can, cooler or any food container that will yield them a midnight snack.

Slip into the rowboat and explore the lakes with me. Such a variety! We find darkened, deep waters with strangling, tangling weeds that can tie a person up. Waters graced with lily pads yield small, yellow, cup-like lilies, or lovely white, tropical looking lilies. Also, find crystal clear waters with golden sand beaches and areas delightful for swimming. Don't forget to bring your camera, the shoreline reveals beauty that fills your breast with joy and lifts your spirit unto heaven. Black and white loons on the lake create the sound of laughter. Occasionally glimpse playful otters, as they do their acrobatics in the water.

Northern Wisconsin is home to the American Indians, the lumberjacks and old legends that live on through the telling. It is an experience, something you must savor for yourself. This is a time of sightseeing, fishing, swimming, hiking, roughing it in primitive cabins, sharing with family and close friends. We can satisfy enormous appetites whetted by activity and healthy air, find time for browsing in souvenir shops that hold cedar wood crafts, pine sachets and birch bark canoes. We must not forget special treats in the local ice cream shop, where a coin will bring unique music from the mandolodian.

The early years in primitive cabins, means carrying water from an outside pump. Some cabins have a sink and pump in the kitchen. Find the outhouse at the end of a path, and the thunder mugs under the bed. No one wants to go outdoors in the middle of the night. Sometimes the cabin isn't as clean as it should be, and when the roof leaks we have to set kettles around to catch the water. Mama works with less convenience than she has at home; she is a wonderful sport. Her spontaneous laughter carries us through difficult situations. For many years she accepts it as a change with adventures to be experienced.

Northern Wisconsin is not just a place where our family spends a two-week vacation every year, during this era. It is a place that we live for. We spend most of the year planning ahead for this magic time. We practice fishing techniques, prepare our tackle, mend our swim suits and polish our cameras. You must experience it with us!

* — * — *

Toward the end of July 1929, the Beloit area is in the grip of a relentless heat wave. Della, being three months pregnant with her second child, sits in front of an old, small electric fan. The phone rings and she moves quickly to answer it. She doesn't want it to awaken nineteen month old Jackie, who is napping on the sofa.

She lifts the tube-like ear piece off the hook of the tall tubular phone with her left hand and puts it to her ear. With her right hand she picks up the rest of the phone and speaks into it, "Hello."

"Hi, Honey. How are you feeling?" asks Ella.

"Hi, Ma. Oh, I'm doing okay, but it's so darn hot. Last night it was so hot in our bedroom. My hair was wet. I kept pushing it up and moving, trying to find a cooler spot on the sheet and my pillow. I felt like a dog turning circles in its bed. I can hardly wait 'til tomorrow, so we can head to Long Lake."

"I'm going to run up to Jones Hardware on West Grand Avenue and get a new flashlight for the trip. Your Pa can hardly wait, too. He says it is stifling at Fairbanks. People are passing out right and left. It's 92 degrees here today."

"A few factories have closed in Rockford. Elton, says it's awful hot at Barber Colman, too. He's really excited about the fishing trip."

"Are you all packed?"

"Yeah. I've got everything packed up."

"Well, I'd better run. You take care of yourself. We will pick you up about six in the morning."

"Okay, Ma. You be careful. It's getting rather stormy looking. Bye - Bye."

"I will. Bye, Honey."

Eli pulls into Houghdahl's Camp late Saturday afternoon, July 27th. It has been a long hot ride. Along the way, picnic hampers yielded fried chicken and potato salad packed in ice, fresh raspberries, dark rye bread with butter and oatmeal cookies. The thermoses of cold tea and lemonade helped to refresh them. All are travel weary and happy to get out and stretch.

"Three hundred miles is a long drive, to this north west portion of Wisconsin," exclaims Della.

"Della, we can go into Spooner for groceries in the morning. Elton and Pa can go fishing first thing," says Ella.

"What we need to do now is get our beds made up. Elt, you can bring in that box marked `sheets'," says Della. "Boy, I hope it doesn't storm up here tonight, the way it did at home last night."

"That was a bad storm, alright," says Eli. "I'll help get the running board luggage racks unpacked. You women keep an eye on little Jackie."

Everyone is happy to crawl into bed early for a renewing sleep. Even little Jackie sleeps well through the night. A breakfast of coffee and doughnuts tides them over until supplies are purchased. The men head toward the pier before the women are ready for town.

"You guys better catch some fish for supper," Ella calls after them.

"Don't worry, we'll catch the big ones," yells Elton.

The groceries have been put away, and lunch is on the table. The women hear the happy bantering of the men, as they come to the back door holding a large stringer of fish.

"Wow! You did catch some big ones. What have you got there?" asks Della. She holds Jackie up to see the fish.

"Fishy fishy," says Jackie, as she patty-cakes with her hands. "Daa-dy fishy."

"Hi Sweetie," Elton says, "I caught a northern pike, two crappies and a bass. Pa caught the largest northern pike, three crappies and two perch. They were really biting this morning."

"Put them in this big pail of water, until after lunch," says Eli.

Jackie & Della on steps of cottage at Long Lake.

As they sit at the lunch table visiting Ella says, "I picked up a Sunday paper in town. That storm Friday night did much crop damage over by Darien. There are many acres of grain down, and lightning struck several buildings. At North Manchester there were high winds and heavy rain. The rivers were over their banks and some bridges had to be closed for several hours. There was a lot of crop damage."

"I knew it was a bad storm," says Eli.

Monday the women make another trip to town, and that evening Della says, "Boy, we better be really careful around the water. Twelve people drowned over the weekend. The heat is causing many people to run to the lakes and streams, and people are going in the water that don't know how to swim. Over at Sturgeon Bay three young girls were wading and stepped in a hole. A man tried to save them and all four drowned. Three people drowned at Merrill, and at Watertown one drowned at Silver Lake and one at Twin Lakes. They say a total of twenty-six people have drowned in Wisconsin since the heat wave started a week ago."

"Good grief, that's terrible!" exclaims Elton.

"I was talking to the woman in the next cabin, and she says some Wisconsin lakes have got too many northern pike in them. That's a new complaint," says Ella.

"I was talking to a man that's probably her husband," says Eli. "He says that a couple of guys over near Rhinelander caught a muskellunge in the Chain Lake. It was a real monster, weighing 45 pounds and measuring 53 inches. I'll bet that put up a tremendous fight! They'll probably have that one mounted."

"Yeah, I would surely think so. Earlier this year a 67 year old woman caught a 26-pound muskie in Lake Thompson near

Rhinelander. The lakes over that way must have some great muskie fishing," Elton adds.

Thursday, August first they hear the news that hundreds of people are battling forest fires about a hundred and eighty miles east of them. It is a twenty-five-mile radius around Soperton and the small villages of Tounsend, Lakewood and Carter. The land has recently been cut over for lumber. Waste products cut away from the trees are very dry and acting like fuel. They fear for Pine Falls and Poplar River. They suspect a firebug.

Eli rows the boat, and Elton sits in the back seat. They inhale the fragrance of pine.

"It sure is peaceful out here," Elton says. "I can't understand why anyone would want to destroy such wilderness beauty."

"I can't either. Sometimes you wish you could just stay here forever. There is a weedy patch up here a ways. I think it might be a good spot to try for some big crappies. Who knows what might be down there?" says Eli. "That's a nice rod and reel you have Elt."

"I really like it. It was a good buy. Della got it for me for Father's Day, you know." Elton tosses his baited line into the water. He is looking for something in his tackle box, when suddenly he hears his reel spin and sees motion from the corner of his eye. He jerks his head up, just as his new rod and reel goes flying out of the boat into the water. "Oh, no!" He shouts.

"Somethin' sure hit it. Can you see it, Elt?" Eli asks.

"No, but it's got to be down there somewhere. I'm going in, and see if I can find it." He pulls off his shoes and socks and takes off his outer clothing. Standing on the seat in the back of the boat, he dives into the weedy water.

Eli grabs hold as the boat pitches. He leans forward to see if he can see him. He sees him surface, and then go under again.

"Don't get tangled in those weeds!" Eli calls in alarm.

Finally, Elton comes near the boat. "Here, Pa, I've got it. Can you take it? I've got to get out of here. Something's in this water!"

Eli lays the pole in the bottom of the boat, and reaches out to help pull him in. Elton manages to pull himself up over the edge of the boat, splashing plenty of water in with him. He sits in the back seat, and begins rubbing his skin, vigorously.

"Wow! You look like an alligator. You are covered with bumps. You must be allergic to something in there," says Eli.

"Gosh, I must be. I itch like crazy. We'd better head back, so I can bathe in some soda water," Elton says.

Elton nearly goes wild with itching, as Eli pulls the oars with as much energy as he can muster . . .

87

The days fly by, sightseeing, fishing and letting Jackie splash in the water. They are cooled down, refreshed and filled with happy memories to draw on in the future. Early Saturday morning they start the long trek back to Illisconsin.

* — * — *

Through the years, a variety of family and friends will share the vacation adventures, in northern Wisconsin. It is a valuable part of our life in the place we call Illisconsin. These adventures will always be among the greatest treasures kept in our personal memory chests.

A newspaper clipping in Grandma Wessell's photograph album states: "August 14, 1937 - Mr. and Mrs. Leonard Wessell, Claude Alexander of Winterset, Iowa and Mr. and Mrs. E. E. Singletary left Saturday a.m. for two weeks vacation at Columbus Lake in northern Wisconsin." Mama's brother, Uncle Leonard, Aunt Dorothy and her brother "Bud" vacation with Mama and Daddy while we four "kiddies" stay with Grandma and Grandpa Wessell. Though we love to go up north, any stay with Grandma and Grandpa is an adventure, too.

Tommy, Gene and Jackie prepare to go fishing.   *Aunt Dorothy & Uncle Leonard.*

Early July 1938 we are at Flynn's Resort on Columbus Lake, near the little town of Clearwater Lake on Hwy. 45, five miles south of Eagle River. We have come with Daddy's brother `Uncle Gordon' and Aunt Cora and our cousin's Marilyn and Myrna. Daddy's sister `Aunt Vera' and Uncle Henry Seils and our cousin Freddy have come up on the train. The children range in ages - Jackie 10, Gene 8, Tommy 7, Freddy 6, Marilyn 4; I am 2 and Myrna 1.

Such fun we have climbing in and out of the boats and playing in the water. We build sand castles and fill pails with water and sand. We throw some at one another and fight a bit. The older kids climb around on the pier and jump off into the shallow water. We hang on to the inner tube and Jackie pulls us around.

We are having a lively time, when all of a sudden Jackie looks around and says, "There should be seven of us. Who is missing? Where is Myrna?" she yells, with panic in her voice.

Everyone looks around where we are playing. There is no sign of her, just water everywhere. The water that has been such a wonderful environment of happy play, now becomes a dreaded enemy. Fear invades us! Tommy looks at the live fish box fastened to the pier. He notices something in the water under the box. "Yikes!" he yells. He hurries to the box and pulls Myrna out from under it. She coughs and spits up some water, as everyone comes running. By the grace of God, she was discovered in time and has no ill effects. We all shudder to think what would have happened if Tommy hadn't noticed her when he did. Surely God is watching over us!

Part of our group sightseeing. Tommy, Daddy, Patsy,
Aunt Cora, Myrna, Jackie, Mama and Gene.

A week flies by and we go for a Sunday afternoon ride, sightseeing. All thirteen of us pile into Uncle Gordon's old car. Some of us are on laps and some are on little folding stools. Every time we stop and tumble out, one after another, people stare as though we are doing a magic trick. Thirteen of us descend upon a little restaurant for our evening meal. It takes awhile to order and be served. Outside the sky has grown dark and ominous.

The wind is wildly flapping the green canvas awnings. By the time our food arrives, rain slams against the windows, thunder explodes above us and lightning flashes in brilliant and jagged streaks. We small fry clamor to our mother's laps, and everyone wears an expression of deep concern. We eat because the food is before us, but everyone has lost their appetites.

"We need to get back to the resort," says Uncle Gordon.

"Yes, I think we should get moving," adds Daddy.

The restaurant owner comes to our tables and says, "You folks hadn't ought to leave, yet. Why don't you wait until the worst of the storm is over. A man came in, from several miles south of here, and said a tornado touched down."

"I think it has let up some and we should get back to Flynn's Resort on Columbus Lake," says Uncle Gordon.

Amid much squealing and scurrying in the rain, we squeeze back into the car. The storm is lessening, but there is water everywhere.

"You'd better take it pretty easy, Gord. Some of this water over the road looks deep," says Daddy. "There are some trees down; we'd better watch for power lines."

When we finally reach the resort, the owner meets us at the entrance. "A dam has given way on one of the lakes and we are flooded. You won't be able to drive the car to the cabin."

"Oh no," comes a chorus from the women.

"It has stopped raining; we will have to wade in," says Uncle Henry.

"You boys take off your new leather shoes, and roll up your pant legs. Jackie take your shoes off," Daddy instructs. "Hang on to each other. I'll carry Patsy."

"Cora, you hold on to Marilyn, and I'll carry Myrna," says Uncle Gordon.

"Freddy, you take my hand," says Aunt Vera.

"Mama, it's dark. I don't want to wade in that water," cries Jackie. "Do we have a light?"

"Stay by me, Honey. The men will lead the way with the lights," answers Mama.

"I ain't gonna walk barefoot in that stuff," Gene whispers to Tommy. In the confusion no one notices that the boys take off their pants and leave their new shoes on.

"Oh, Mama. Ohh - eeek -Yikes - Help," Jackie screams and squeals with each step she takes, and Marilyn does, likewise. The water is over the women's knees.

Everyone steps on sticks, pine cones, stones and stumbles on tree roots. Finally we reach the cabin and climb the steps to the door. Someone lights a kerosene lamp and the mucky horde enters the cabin. Such fun cleaning up the mess! "There is a leak

90

in the roof in our bedroom," says Aunt Cora. Uncle Gordon drags the spring and mattress out in the main room and they set it up on four chairs.

In the morning the men wade down to the pier and bring the boats up to the back door. From now on, every time anyone goes anywhere, for the rest of our second week of vacation, it is by boat from the back door.

"Come on, Vera, get in the front of the boat. Jackie and Patsy get in the next seat. Cora, you, Marilyn and Myrna can squeeze into the back seat. I'll row us over near the car, so we can go to town," says Mama.

Later, Mama rows the boat to the clothes line. Aunt Cora and Aunt Vera balance precariously, trying to hang up clothes. "Careful!" Mama yells. She tries to steady the boat that rocks suddenly to one side. "Oops!" cries Aunt Vera, grabbing for the clothes line.

The children swim right by the back door. The men leave from there to go fishing, and take the boat to go after all the water that is used. Their most unpleasant chore is taking the used 'thunder mugs' up the lake a distance, and emptying them in the woods.

A ride out to the tornado area reveals much damage and strange phenomena. We see a frying pan driven half way into a tree. We are thankful God spared us this kind of disaster.

Many vacations will be more convenient, but none will be remembered with more groans or laughter.

* — * — *

Late July 1939, Grandma and Grandpa Wessell accompany us to Chrissy Hensler's on Squaw Lake, near Rhinelander. We are all ready to go swimming. Daddy has on his new, dark blue, wool swimming trunks. Gene has dark brown wool trunks and Tommy rust colored wool trunks.

"In June, The National Clothing store had these wool swim suits with built in support. The men's were ninety-eight cents, so I let the kids get Elt's for Father's Day. The boys needed new suits and they had them for forty-four cents so I bought them," Mama says.

"They look like nice suits," says Grandma.

While we are swimming in the lake, a man from the cabin next to ours comes up and asks, "Are you folks from Beloit?"

Grandpa says, "We are. Our daughter's family is from South Beloit, Illinois. We say we are all from Illisconsin."

"That's a good one," the man chuckles. "I hear they recently dedicated the big new outdoor swimming pool in Beloit. My brother lives down that way, and he worked at building that pool."

"It's a beautiful pool," says Daddy. "They had a big water show on July 16th to dedicate the opening of the pool. Famous swim stars from the Medinak Athletic Club competed against each other. The city manager, A.D. Telfer, and other local officials took part in the dedication ceremonies."

"It was a beautiful water show," says Mama.

July 20, 1940 at Little Star Lake.

Gene, Jackie and Tommy cling to pier.
Patsy and Mryna on pier. Freddie and
Marilyn in the water.

Same group.

Chrissy has her own generator, so the cabins have electricity. She shuts the generator off at nine o'clock. After that time, if we want light we have to use kerosene lamps.

One day Daddy takes us to Rhinelander, to go through the logging museum. After a time of enjoying the museum, we come out to get in our car.

"Where is our car?" cries Mama.

"We left it right here," says Grandpa.

"What the . . . whatever could have happened to it?" asks Daddy.

"Did someone steal it?" inquires Grandma.

We all look around, and see it nowhere. We start walking down the block, which is a slight hill.

"Oh my . . . Will you look at that!" exclaims Daddy.

"I'll be . . . would you believe that?" asks Grandpa.

The car has rolled down the street, crossed the road, headed for the river, and has come to rest, barely caught by the edge of the bridge!

Each resort and vacation offers a special memory. In mid June 1941 we are at Lavender's Resort on Long Lake near Mercer and Hurley. Mama's cousin, Arlene Puttkemery, is with us to help with some of the work, so Mama can enjoy the vacation, too. Arlene is frying pancakes for breakfast. As she turns the pancake she takes the pancake turner and pats it down.

"Don't pat the cakes down, Arlene; you'll make them heavy," cautions Mama.

Next to the back door is a gasoline pin-up lamp, which has a mantle in it. Every time someone goes out the back door and allows the screen door to bang shut, it breaks the mantle in the lamp. This is a constant source of frustration!

We take a drive to an area where there is a narrow gauge railroad. A blueberry bog runs along beside it. Everyone helps to pick the medium size wild blueberries, from the low growing bushes. Gene helps Arlene fill her bucket. Tommy yells as he steps in a wet spot and sinks to his ankle.

"Be careful where you step. There are some wet places," says Daddy.

Thirteen year old Jackie takes my hand. It's difficult walking for a five year old. I help Jackie fill her pail.

Back at the cabin the berries are rinsed and some kept for fresh berries on our cereal. The greatest treat of all, are the fresh blueberry pies that Mama makes in a little oven that sits on top of the stove burners. Um - um - good!

One noon we are having lunch. On the table sits a plate of Gene's favorite cake. Temptation is overpowering him. He has had his piece, but could easily find room for another one. "Look there's a deer," he shouts, pointing to the window. Everyone looks toward the window. Mama and Arlene jump up and run over to the window. Quick as lightning, Gene grabs another piece of cake. Mother says, "Where? Where's the deer? I don't see any."

I see Gene grab the cake. He is wolfing it down as everyone returns to the table. "Gene grabbed more cake," I squeal. Everyone laughs.

"You rascal," Mama exclaims.

* — * — *

In 1942 we vacation at Irv's Log Kabins on South Two Lake near Lake Tomahawk, Wisconsin with Aunt Cora, Uncle Gordon and cousins Marilyn and Myrna. We stay in the cabin called "Sunny Slope."

One morning Daddy says, "Patsy, do you want to go out in the boat fishing with Daddy for a while?"

"Sure, Daddy," I answer.

"Well, come here and I will help you get into your life jacket," he says.

I am not fond of this hot, fat, olive green, uncomfortable thing, but I know it's the only way I am allowed to go out in the

93

boat. Daddy rows to the middle of the lake and sits quietly holding his fishing pole. Grey clouds cluster above us, there is not a breath of air stirring. The lake looks like colorless glass. We are too far from shore to watch the trees, birds or whatever animals might be flitting around. How long have we been sitting here? It seems like hours. Nothing is happening. Daddy seems lost in some far off world. I wonder if he even cares whether he catches a fish or not. I begin to fidget. I'm not sure fishing with Daddy is such fun; he's too patient.

A wind begins to blow us a bit, and I think, "at least we're moving." We hear a rumble and Daddy says, "A storm is coming up. We'd better head for shore."

We are a long way from our cabin area. The wind blows the water into rapid waves. We bob around, and Daddy pulls hard on the oars. "I think we should go up on shore until this storm blows over," he says. Rain comes pelting down.

The boat bounces wildly, and water splashes in. I am frightened. "Daddy, are we going to tip over?" I cry.

"No, just hang on to the seat. We'll be okay," he says.

We finally reach shore, and Daddy pulls the boat up on land and helps me out. We stand under birch trees. He pulls me under his rain coat, and we huddle there with the rain falling around us and dancing on the lake. The sky explodes with thunder and flashes jagged streaks of lightning. I will always carry this picture in my mind. Before long we climb back into a wet boat, where Daddy uses a can to bail water out of the bottom. Sitting in the middle of a quiet lake was boring, but a storm created excitement that will live in the memory box for a lifetime. Daddy rows toward the cabin. Suddenly a fish yanks my line. "Oh! Daddy, I've got something," I yell.

"That a girl. Hang on tight. Reel it now. You've got him. It's a nice bass, Honey," Daddy says. He scoops it into the dip net, then puts it on a stringer and fastens it to the outside of the boat. When we reach the pier, Mama is there waiting, relieved to see us.

Irv is our guide to the "place where the fish really bite." The men go in one boat and the women go in another. Mama rows out into the Rainbow Flowage. Clouds cover the sky and make the water look like endless darkness. This is the strangest looking lake I have ever been on. Tree trunks stand like a forest in the water, some are dead and some still have green needles. The water looks threatening. "I guarantee, you'll catch fish," Irv says.

We get a few bites but we aren't catching any. "I guess we aren't holding our mouths right," says Mama.

"You've gotta set the hook, Della," Irv chides. "Be careful

94

where you are going, there are stumps everywhere. The fish like it up close around these trees." Every few minutes, Irv commands us, "Set the hook."

We begin to realize that he means we need to give a good yank when we feel that tug on our line. Our spooky environment starts to pay off. We are all soon catching fish faster than we can take them off the hooks, and put them on the stringers. Aunt Cora, Jackie, Marilyn and Myrna don't like taking the fish off the hooks. Mama and I can hardly fish; we are so busy baiting hooks and taking fish off for everyone. "We are going to have a wonderful mess of fish for the fish fry," says Mama.

Friday night is the all camp potluck and fish fry. All week the people at the resort pit their fishing skills against one another to catch the most, or the biggest fish to contribute to the event, which will climax the week's vacation. We are among the lucky people who are spending two weeks at the resort.

"Daddy, are they really going to have a wild badger fight?" I ask.

"Well, Irv says he has a friend that will bring one in tonight," he answers.

Some of the resort guests and family displaying (catch) for the fish fry.

As we walk down the sandy path, the fragrance of spruce, pine and hemlock pleases our nostrils, and the fallen needles crunch beneath our feet. How could a Friday night fish fry bring such excitement?

"Mama, will they have the badger fight?" I ask, tugging on her arm.

"Be careful," she cautions, "You'll make me drop the potato salad."

Aunt Dorothy with a muskie and a large stringer
of fish. Aunt Dorothy and Uncle Leonard are
often at Irv's Log Kabins at the same time we are.

As we draw near the lodge we hear the robust banter of the mingling people.

"Boy, smell those fish frying," exclaims Daddy, as we gather around the stone fire grills, where the fish lie bubbling and spattering in the huge iron skillets. The feast is joyfully consumed amid the gaiety of everyone gathered around the picnic tables, as tall tales of the week's fishing adventures are swapped.

As the last crumbs are cleared away, Irv announces, "Everyone clear back and form a circle. We will bring the German shepherd, Rudy, out on a leash and will let the badger out of his cage. Now stay clear. Badgers are ferocious fighters, and we don't want anyone getting hurt. We think the dog can handle the badger, but stay back."

Irv goes into a shed and soon the dog starts barking. The shed door opens as Irv and another man pull a wooden cage through it. Both men wear heavy jackets and leather gloves. Irv's glove is covered with blood. Pandemonium breaks out when they drag the cage forward. The other man has Rudy on the leash and tries to calm him as he scratches and claws at the cage. By now, most of the children and half the women are on top of the picnic tables, and it's a terrible commotion as they screech, scream and squeal! Irv holds a rope that is obviously fastened to the animal in the cage. He yells, "Get back! Get back! He's coming out!" With that, he releases the spring catch on the cage, gives a yank on the rope, and . . .

The whole crowd emits a simultaneous gasp, then explodes

into roars of thunderous laughter as . . . out sails a chamber pot with a roll of toilet paper inside!!! Rudy lurches backward on his haunches and stares at "the beast" with a quizzical look on his face!

Bar and Irv's home at his resort.

As new guests arrive the following week, excitement will build about the badger fight that will take place Friday evening at the all camp fish fry; but no one will reveal the mystery of Rudy and the beast!

It is dark now and the sky twinkles with stars. "Hey, Bill," Mama says to one new camp friend, "Have you ever seen stars through a coat sleeve?"

"Stars through a coat sleeve? No. I can't say that I have," he says. "Do they look closer or brighter?"

Mama says, "Oh, you've got to see for yourself. Take your jacket off. Come over here by the table and I'll show you."

He follows her advice, and she places the armpit area over his face. "It's got to be held up really straight," she cautions. She gets it just right, and says, "Now look straight up through the sleeve." As soon as she says this she pours a glass of water down the sleeve.

The crowd roars with laughter. Bill is a good sport, he sputters and laughs. "Boy, you better be on the lookout, Della. I don't get mad; I get even," he laughs.

Making new friends, teasing and playing tricks on each other, and sharing fish stories of the ones that got away, are all part of the vacation magic that will live with us through the years. Before we leave, we are planning our return.

*　—　*　—　*

In July 1943 we are at Irv's Log Kabins again. Jackie's friend, Ruth Riley, is vacationing with us. The girls are close friends,

97

but they have a fair amount of disputes between them.

"Ruthie, please come help me make our bed," Jackie calls.

Ruthie is looking through a magazine, and doesn't care whether the bed gets made or not. Jackie is getting upset with her. She calls again, with no response. "I am not going to fight with her," Jackie says to herself. She carefully makes up her side of the bed and leaves Ruthie's just the way she crawled out of it.

Jackie and friend Ruthie on pier.

Daddy and the boys are out fishing. Mama decides that we gals can go fishing in the other boat. Jackie is in the front seat, I am in the next, Mama is rowing, and Ruthie is in the back seat. Mama stops near a patch of water lilies. The water is about five feet deep, and crystal clear. We can see the beautiful sunfish, bluegills and perch swimming around below us. If anyone makes a noise in the bottom of the boat, they dart off, but soon come back.

It is a perfect, sunny summer day. The different shades of green trees are complemented with the black and grey trunks. White birches mingle with the evergreens. A Kingfisher swoops between trees and out over the lake.

Jackie says, "I don't like to touch the worms."

"I'll put the worm on your hook," I offer.

"Jackie, you are a sissy," Mama chides, "You are fifteen and Patsy is only seven, and she has to bait your hook?"

"I don't want to touch the worms, either," says Ruthie.

"Oh, you girls are helpless," Mama shrugs. She digs in the can for a worm and puts it on Ruthie's hook.

I take a worm and look at it. "The boys say the fish can't get the worm off so easy, if you poke the hook in one end of the worm and thread it up on the hook," I say. I push the hook up the length of the worm, as it squirms. Inside I feel uncomfortable, like I have just murdered something. I shudder. I throw her line in the water and bait my own hook. We adjust our corks for the depth of the water.

It is fun to watch the fish. If a small fish comes up to investigate the worm, we just pull it closer to a larger fish. Jackie's cork goes under; a fish is running with her worm. The line bends her pole. She gives a yank. "I've got him. I've got him," she yells. She pulls it into the boat. It is a beautiful, large sunfish with greenish - grey sides and a bright golden belly. It is flopping wildly in the bottom of the boat.

"Take it off the hook, and put it on this stringer, which is fastened to the extra oarlock," Mama says.

"I don't want to touch it," Jackie squeals.

"Why'd you come fishin'?" Mama asks.

"I'll do it," I say. I remember how Daddy showed me to slide my hand from head to back to hold down the fin. I get the fish off the hook and it flops wildly, right out of my hand. It flops all over the bottom of our green boat. Jackie tries to pull away from it, while I try to catch it. We all shake with laughter.

Between rumbles of laughter Ruthie says, "Oh, I've wet my pants."

Now we all hold our sides, as she wriggles out of her under panties. "How will I dry them?" she asks. Without waiting for an answer, she puts them on the end of a cane fishing pole and waves them in the air.

People sit in other boats close by. We all laugh so hard, we nearly wet our pants. I still haven't caught the flopping fish, so I put my foot on it. I am finally able to pick it up and get it on the stringer. Now Mama and I both have a fish on our lines. I have laid my pole down during all this commotion and I grab it, just as it starts to roll out of the boat.

When we get back to our cabin, Daddy and the boys are cleaning fish. I take our stringerful out to the screened in cleaning hut, and help them scale and clean the fish. Well, at least, "I" think I'm helping.

Mama and the girls prepare supper. The large, black, iron skillet is hot with melted grease waiting for the fresh fish. Another one has fresh sliced potatoes and onions frying. Ruthie is slicing tomatoes, and Jackie is setting the table.

"Della, be sure to fry the little fish up crisp. That's the way they are good," Daddy says.

"Mother, are we going to have watermelon tonight?" asks Gene. "Do you want me to open these cans of green beans for you?"

"Yes, to both questions, Gene. Tommy, you can go outside and bring the swim suits and towels in off the line," says Mama.

"Okay, Mom. Boy, supper sure smells good," Tommy says.

I like to catch fish much better than I like to eat them. They taste good, but I hate getting bones in my mouth. I'm glad we have lots of other good things to eat.

We take a ride into Rhinelander and go to the Logging Museum. Daddy takes pictures of us kids by the big scoop boat that was used in the rivers during logging procedures, and by a set of huge wagon wheels that were used with the timbers. We climb on the old locomotive for another picture. The railroad car behind the engine says `Thunder Lake Lumber Co.'

Rhinelander Loggine Museum boat. Jackie, Gene, Ruthie and Tommy.

Gene, Ruthie, Jackie, Tommy and Patsy - train.

Our pine scented vacation lingers in our hearts.

* — * — *

Gene and Tommy stand in the green grass of the side yard. They hold their fishing poles up, and with a snap of the wrist send the fake plug on the end of the line flying through the air.

Tommy, Gene, Jackie, Ruthie & Patsy - wheels.

"Oh dang, I got a backlash," exclaims Gene. He picks at the line in his reel, trying to unsnarl it.

"Why, don't you hold your thumb on the line, like Daddy says?" I ask. I walk up to see what his snarl looks like.

"Oh, Perch, why don't you mind your own business?" he scowls.

"You Snot, Poop, Brat. Quit calling me Perch!" I snap.

"Hey, Perch, you're gonna get in trouble if Ma hears you," Tommy warns.

"You quit it, too, Snot, Poop, Brat," I scream.

"Patsy, get in the house. If you can't talk nice, you get yourself in here," Mama calls through the open kitchen window.

"See? I told you," says Tommy. "Dad doesn't call you his black-eyed-spit-fire for nothing. Get in the house, Perch."

"You boys quit teasing her or you'll answer to your father," Mama calls.

It is mid June 1944 - Jackie is 16, Gene is 14, Tommy is 12, and I am 8. The past months have been a terrible adjustment, since Grandpa Wessell's death in October and Grandpa Singletary's last month. This reinforces Mama and Daddy's decision that we need to go for our wonderful vacation therapy, although our nation is at war. The defense transportation director in Washington, D.C., Joseph B. Eastman says, "the only patriotic way is to stay home." Some motorists have been arrested for using illegal gasoline rationing stamps. But the director of recreation for the Conservation Department of Wisconsin says, "A legitimate cache of `A' coupons and a clear conscience are the only passports necessary to a Wisconsin vacation." Grandma is living with us now and we all need the lift that is available in our two-week vacation in the north woods of Wisconsin. The frenzied anticipation of it is drawing to a climax, with only two weeks to wait.

101

Gene and Tom head out to the back yard and watch Daddy roll back a wet piece of burlap from a large sunken galvanized tub.

"Here are the old coffee grounds Mother said you want for the worm box," Gene says. He hands Daddy the small grey, granite pan. "These worms are for fishing, aren't they, Dad?"

"Yes. Someone told me that worms benefit from having coffee grounds mixed in the soil, so I think I'll try it."

"Why do you like to have worms in the garden?" asks Tom.

"Because worms eat their way through the soil, and leave their body waste near the surface which acts like fertilizer. They make little tunnels through the soil and that helps the rain water go down in the earth where it can do lots of good," Daddy answers.

"I've heard that when you chop a worm in half, both halves live and develop new bodies. Is that true, Dad?" asks Gene.

"No, the head half often lives and regenerates new tail segments, but the other end never redevelops internal organs that are needed to live."

"You mean they have a mouth at one end and a butt at the other?" asks Tommy.

"Well, I guess, you could say that. They have a complete digestive tract."

"Dad, why do birds have trouble pulling them up out of the ground? Even I have trouble pulling them out. It's like they have hands hanging on to something," says Tommy.

"Most species have setae."

"Setae? What's that?" both boys say at the same time.

"It's short bristle like hairs on their bodies, which helps them inch along, and cling to the walls of their burrows."

"What makes them feel so slimy?" asks Gene.

"The worm's body has a transparent membrane over the skin. Their glands give off fluids that keep it moist and they breathe through the membrane."

"Do we have enough to take on vacation fishing?", asks Tom.

"We've probably got enough angle worms, but I want to go out to the cemetery tonight and see if we can find some night crawlers."

I come skipping up in time to hear Daddy's reply. "To the cemetery? Why the cemetery?" I ask.

"Because I know a spot where there is a drippy faucet. If we get a good rain, we could go out at night looking for them around here, but we haven't had rain lately."

"Why do they like rain? Do they like to swim?" I ask.

"No. When there are heavy rains the water floods them out of their burrows. We'll go out to the cemetery tonight and look

102

for night crawlers. They are much larger than these worms."

I'm not sure what to think about this idea. Handling worms and fish are no problem to me, but going to the cemetery at night? I had better not let the boys know that I'd rather not go there after dark.

Daddy, Mama, Grandma, the boys and I go in the car to the cemetery. Grandma is waiting in the car while we go in search of the large night crawlers. Daddy and Mama each have a flashlight.

"I don't know if we should even be in here at night," Mama whispers.

"We just need to be quiet and watch where we are going so we don't step on headstones or anything. You've got to grab them fast when you see them or they'll pull back into their holes," whispers Daddy. He shines his light on the ground and adds, "Scatter on either side of this faucet."

The boys each carry little pails, with some dirt in them. They start diving after the night crawlers. I look where the lights shine on the ground. I can see the large, pinkish-brown worms lying on the wet green grass. Some are only part way out of the holes, and I know that these are the ones that can rapidly disappear. Everyone is searching and grabbing.

Well, almost everyone. I look away from the light. It's terribly dark out there. What is that over there? I think I see some dark shapes. There are two that are rather tall and slender. Oh, oh. They are moving around. They are swaying. Are they ghosts? It's not cold out, but goose pimples run up and down my arms. I see them move again. The hair begins to prickle on the back of my neck. It feels as though it is standing up on end. There is a warm breeze blowing. Why do I feel cold? I see those two creatures move again. They are swaying more. Suddenly, there is a loud flapping of wings, `Caw, caw, caw! ' I look up and discover that the lights have moved and I am in a darkened place alone. Someone screams. Is it me? A light shines toward me.

"Patsy, what are you doing? You aren't helping much. What's the matter?" Mama asks.

"Noth - nothing. Mama, what's moving over there?"

"Over where?" I point and Mama shines her light to reveal two small cedar trees slightly swaying in the breeze.

"I think we have enough. We can go now," Daddy states.

In the car I snuggle up close to Grandma. "Are you afraid, Honey?" Grandma asks.

"No, I mean - well, Grandma, there's lots of dead people out there."

"Don't be frightened, Honey. The dead people aren't going to hurt you any. It's living people that can hurt you," she says. She puts her arm around me, and pulls me close.

"Scaredy-cat, scaredy-cat," says Tommy.

"Look who's talking," says Gene. "Remember one night last summer when you were out in the kitchen? The back door was open, and Mrs. Nicolls came up on the back porch. You ran full speed to the living room and took one big leap into Mother's lap."

Everyone in the car bursts out laughing.

The two weeks fly by rapidly. We all go to bed the night before we are to leave, with the idea of getting up early in the morning to start out. Everyone is excited. No one can sleep. As always happens, about midnight Daddy and Mama turn on the lights and say, "Everyone get ready. We are going to leave now."

"Yippey - Yippey!" the cry goes up in each bedroom. In no time we are in the car heading north.

"It really is wonderful that family and friends have given us some of their gasoline coupons so we could make this trip," says Mama. "I just hope we don't run into any trouble with law enforcement."

It's a warm night and cozy with seven of us in the car, so we have some windows down a bit. Daddy drives as the rest of us doze, off and on. Mama has been nervous about traveling with the wartime restrictions. Speed limits have been lowered to 35 miles per hour, and it is almost impossible to buy new tires. She is dozing when suddenly, there is a shrill whistle. She jerks upright, clutching her chest she asks, "What's that? Is it the police?"

"Relax, Della. I think it is a farmer. I don't know why they blew a whistle, but they are harvesting something in the field out there," Daddy responds.

"My gosh, my heart is nearly beating out of my chest!" she says.

We continue through the night, with some sleeping and some talking. It's a long trip to Herman Lamer's resort and mink farm at Heaford Jct., on Muskellunge Lake. We get travel weary. We stop at a gas station in a small town. Tommy is the first one out and runs in to ask the attendant, "Do you have a bathroom?"

The attendant looks at him with a mischievous look, "What do you want to do, take a bath?"

Eventually there are streaks of daylight and the ruby sun peeks over the eastern horizon. Gene has been fidgeting for several miles. "I wish I could turn around and sit on my front," he moans.

As always, we arrive before the stores are open. We get out to stretch and walk around town a bit. Then we all pile back in the car and wait until 8:00 a.m. for the grocery store to open. We eventually all traipse around the grocery store wanting everything we see, but settling for what Mama chooses.

When we get to the resort, we wait again. The cabin will not be available until 11:00 a.m.. Everyone is tired and out of sorts, but our first whiff of the pine scented air lifts our spirits. A stroll down to the lake perks us up, and we beg to go swimming. Of course, we can't do that, either, as our swim suits are not unpacked. We take a short hike and snack on some fresh fruit and sweet rolls.

Swimming, fishing, hiking, eating and using the outhouse. We are having a wonderful time, and have about a half week of vacation left, when Daddy becomes ill.

"Elton, you can't monkey around any longer. You are not getting any better. I am concerned about you. You have to go to a doctor," Mama says.

"I guess you are probably right. We had better drive in to Tomahawk," Daddy replies.

None of us are prepared for the discovery. Daddy must undergo emergency surgery immediately. He has a ruptured appendix.

While Daddy is in the operating room, Mama breaks down. "My God, my God, please help us. Oh, Lord please be with Elton and heal him. What shall I do?" She turns to Grandma. "I don't know what to do. We only have a few days left at the cabin. Elton will certainly be here longer than that."

The doctor comes out to talk to us, "Elton is a very sick man. He came through the surgery all right, but he has peritonitis. His recuperation is going to take awhile. He will be in the recovery room for a couple hours or so. If you have things you need to do, now might be a good time."

"Della, you should take the kids and I back out to the resort. You can check with Lamer's to see what they can suggest for you staying on up here. Maybe Elton's brother, Gordon, could come up and get the kids and me, and take us home," advises Grandma.

"Yes, Ma. I suppose you are right. Let's go. I need to stop at the gas station, too."

Mama pulls into the Mobil Gas Station with the big red flying horses on the sign. Luke and his brothers run the gas station. They are part Indian, and are friendly, helpful men. Mama tells Luke about Daddy's emergency surgery, and our predicament.

"I sure am sorry to hear that. I hope he gets along just fine. Now don't you worry one bit. Since you need to stay, just come in and I'll see that you get whatever rationing coupons you need for gasoline," he says. He pats Mama on the shoulder. He fills the gas tank, checks the water, oil, tires and washes the windows before taking the money. "If there is anything we can do to help you, just let us know," he adds.

Back at the resort Mama tells Mr. and Mrs. Lamer what has happened. "Don't you worry. You can stay right in our home with us, as long as you need to," says Mrs. Lamer. "You may call your brother-in-law from here, right now, if you'd like to."

Uncle Gordon agrees to come after us on Saturday. God is watching over us. He has provided for compassionate people to meet our needs. This has been a wonderful vacation with challenges and a sad twist of fate, but one that will live in our memories a lifetime.

* — * — *

In summer 1945, the Henry Busker family, our neighbors and friends, are with us at Gibbons' Resort on Moen Lake near Rhinelander. This resort is a disappointment. The cabin is old and the roof leaks, but we make the best of it. One afternoon while everyone else is out fishing Grandma and I play "Ice Cream Parlor." The old cook stove, with no fire in it, makes a wonderful freezer full of ice cream pails. I can lift each lid with the handle. It makes a great ice cream scoop, too. Grandma orders and eats endless cones in different flavors.

Dad and the boys have been fishing and now they row toward the resort. They row through a channel between lakes. Coming into the lake, Gene casts out his line and gets a terrible back lash in his reel. He pitches it in the bottom of the boat.

"Here, try mine," Dad says. He hands him his pole.

Gene casts out and S M A C K. Something hits hard and bends the pole sharply. Gene plays the fish, letting him go with the line, and then quickly reeling in the slack. Out it goes again, then the big fish swims toward the boat.

"Reel it in! Quick, take up the slack!," yells Dad.

"Wow, it looks like a big one!" yells Tom.

Gene races to reel in the slack. Again and again the fish repeats his antics, while excitement mounts. Gene finally brings him up along side of the boat.

"I'll get him with the dip net," says Dad. He scoops him up and they lift a thirty two inch, sixteen pound Muskie into the boat. Though he is just a keeper, it was fun catching him, and he is still a lot of fish!

Bathing beauty in a boat on Moen Lake. Jackie - 17 years old - 1945.

Patsy's prize catch from Moen Lake. 9 years old - 1945.

    Back at the cabin Mother announces that we need more ice for the old ice box. "You boys can take this burlap up to the ice shed by Gibbons' house and bring back a block of ice. Be sure you do a good job of wiping the saw dust off it first!" she commands.

The boys hike down the path through the woods. "Hey, Gene, let's stop and get our pack of cigarettes out from under the rock and have a puff before we get the ice," suggests Tommy.

"Yeah, let's," says Gene. They stop along the path and roll back a rock, and remove the cigarettes that they have hidden there. Gene lights one and then helps Tom light one.

"Dang! These mosquitos are terrible," complains Tom, slapping at his arms.

"They'd eat ya alive," agrees Gene, dancing around, swatting himself. "We don't dare stop walking, or they will carry us off!"

"Let's bury the cigarettes and get out of here," Tom says snuffing his out.

"Okay, these beasts are awful!" says Gene, doing a slap dance.

At the ice shed Gene brushes the sawdust off the ice, while Tom swings the burlap bag to ward off the mosquitoes.

"Do you hear that ski plane flying low over the building?" asks Tom.

"Yeah, I hear it," says Gene. "But, it's only a mosquito!"

At the cabin supper is ready. Mother says, "After supper, Iris, Eleanor and Bertha Busker are coming over to our cabin to play cards. The men want to try some night fishing."

While the women and girls share laughter playing cards, the men and boys battle the mosquitos out in the middle of the lake.

Soon pitter patters sound on the roof, as rain comes pelting down. "Oh oh," says Mother. "The guys are going to get wet. I'd better put the coffee pot on. We'll have some coffee and cake when they come in."

"Do you think they'll have a lot of fish?" my friend, Bertha asks. "If they do, they'll have to take time to clean them."

"I hope they don't catch any," I say. I'm still pouting because they wouldn't let Bertha and I go along.

There is a lot of stomping of feet and shaking water from coats as the guys come onto the front porch with their fishing gear. "Well, where are they?" asks Eleanor. "Where's the fish?"

"They are in the lake," answers Mr. Busker.

"Did you have fisherman's luck?" asks Grandma.

"Yep," says Dad, "A wet butt, and a hungry gut!"

"The only bites we got were mosquito bites. If it hadn't been for our mosquito repellant, we'd have gotten eaten alive," states Mr. Busker.

"I can smell it. It stinks!" says Jackie.

"Coffee's ready," announces Mother.

The women chatter over who got beat playing cards, while

108

the men talk about the gigantic fish they know they'll catch.

* — * — *

In 1946 we are heading to Harper's Lake Resort, near the town of Rib Lake. Once again, the Henry Busker family accompanies us. About fifty miles into the trip Mr. Busker's car begins to wobble. "Oh oh, I think we have a flat tire," he announces. One look at the back tire confirms it.

Daddy stops our car and offers help. They partially unload the trunk to get to the spare tire and car jack. When the tire is changed, and everything and everyone loaded back into the cars, we go on. We stop at the nearest town to have the tire patched at a gas station.

Twenty miles down the road Dad says, "Looks like Hank is pulling off. I wonder if he's got tire trouble again?" We stop and sure enough. Mr. Busker is unloading the car again.

"By gosh, Elt. I got another one," he grins.

Getting back into our car, Daddy says, "He is pretty good natured about it. We'll stop in the next town for another repair job."

With the repair made, we travel on toward our destination. Within thirty miles we see Mr. Busker along side of the road looking at another tire. He is scratching his head and flashing his broad grin, "I guess, we've got another one." Again the unloading, reloading and stopping in the next town for a patch.

When we stop for the fourth flat tire, Dad says, "Hey, Hank, is it flat on the top or the bottom?" Everyone laughs and the men change the tire.

"I can't believe anyone can experience that many flat tires without getting upset," Dad comments.

After six flat tires on Buskers' car, we arrive at the resort and Mr. Busker is still smiling and ready to have a great time fishing. "Anyone with such a patient and jovial personality should make a fine vacation companion," says Dad.

One evening we are gathered in the Buskers' cabin. The adults are playing cards. Bertha and I are playing with paper dolls.

Suddenly someone is trying to pull the screen door open. There are two men talking loudly. One says, "Is this the bar? Which way is the bar?"

It is obvious they don't need a bar. They are already drunk. Mr. Busker says, "Just go straight down that way," and he points toward the lake.

They stumble down the steps, stagger down to the lake and walk right off the end of the pier. There is a loud splash and then a chain of cuss words. "What the ——? The lake came up to meet me!"

109

The afternoon is just right for fun at the lake. We have waited an hour for our lunch to settle and now we are in our swim suits. Once we get used to the shock of the cold water on our warm bodies, the water is wonderful. We are in the water an hour or so when I look at my feet. I climb up on the pier.

"Eek—what are these?" I scream. My feet have several dark things that look like chunks of worm-like jelly stuck tight to my skin. "Get these off me!" I scream. "What are they?"

"They won't hurt you," says Gene. "They are just blood - suckers."

"They're what?" I scream. "Get them off me!"

"They are leeches," says Tom. "They have a sucker at one end of their body. That's how they attach themselves to people. They make an incision in the skin and gorge themselves on blood. They'll drop off. Don't get panicky. They won't hurt you."

It's too late to avoid getting panicky! I'm petrified. "Get them off!" I scream. In a bit, they begin to drop off, and I begin to calm down. I'm in no hurry to go back in the water.

It is the Fourth of July and the boys are shooting off fire-crackers. Tom is now 14 and Gene 16. "Watch this," says Gene. He lights a firecracker and places a tin can over it. "See how high this can is gonna blow." Nothing happens.

"What's going on here? Why isn't it going off?" He waits a minute and then picks up the can. Nothing happens, so he picks up the firecracker and blows on it. KA - POW!!! It explodes right in his face. We all scream. The adults come running from the cabins.

There is no blood, and there are no burns, but Gene is stag-gering around in a daze. Mama screams, "Gene, are you all right? What did you do?"

"I can't see very well. I'm dizzy," Gene says.

Mama and Daddy help him into our cabin, where he lies down. Mr. Busker comes over with a small glass with something dark in it. "Give him a few sips of this," he says.

Gene takes a few sips, "What is this?" he asks.

"It's blackberry brandy," he answers. "It will help you."

In a while Gene is feeling better.

"Do you realize how dangerous those firecrackers can be?" asks Dad. "You might have blown off some fingers or disfigured your face. You were extremely lucky."

"I won't try that again," Gene agrees.

In the evening we are sitting near a group of people near Rib Lake watching fireworks. A fellow in front of us says, "I heard you mention Beloit. Did you folks hear about that policeman in Beloit that caught a musky last August? The Beloit Daily News reported that he was fishing near Rhinelander when he caught a 21 3/4 pound muskellunge. When he took it to a taxidermist for mounting, he was startled to find that the fish contained a full capped bottle of beer."

"That's a heck of a way to drink beer - bottle and all," laughs Mr. Busker.

"When he showed it to a brewer in Rhinelander, they gave him two cases of beer," continues the fellow. "The guy says the fish battled for 35 minutes and gave `spirited resistance' although the cap was firmly intact on the bottle. He was planning to have the fish and beer bottle mounted on the same plaque."

KA-BOOM - BANG - BANG - with a tremendous burst of color in the sky, the grand finale unfolds.

* — * — *

In 1949 when I am thirteen, we vacation at Indian Lake Resort near Eagle River. Spotlight, our dark brown cottage with white trim, sits above the lake, on a green lawn scattered with birch and evergreen trees. The resort is operated by a jovial Swedish couple, Rudy and Molly Helstrom. They had previously owned a bakery, so Molly continues to make bread and rolls to sell to the guests. The aroma of fresh baked bread keeps us on a continual hunger quest, even when our stomachs are full.

Gene drives, Tom and I, five miles to Sugar Camp Lake. It is a beautiful golden sand beach with clear water sparkling in the sunshine. I'm not a good swimmer, but I dive from the pier. The water is shallow and I am inexperienced. My head goes swiftly through the water and slams into the bottom of the lake, with a spine wrenching jolt. I am dazed and frightened. I have wrenched my neck, but the Lord is watching over me, I might have broken my neck and become a paraplegic. He has other plans for me.

Arriving back at the resort, we are greeted by cousin Fred Seils. He is vacationing close by at Uncle Gordon's cabin, on Kathan Lake. The sun lights up his plump, ruddy, freckled face and beautiful red hair.

"Hey, I've heard that black bears have been coming down to feed at the dump in Lake Tomahawk. Do you guys want to go with me, to see if we can see any, tonight?" he asks.

"Sure!" we all say at once.

Just past six thirty, Fred turns into the road leading into the dump. It is rutted and full of pot holes. He hits a pot hole rather hard. I fly up from the back seat hitting my head hard on the framework of the car.

"Ouch!" I yell. This is almost more than my poor head and

111

neck can take in one day. Now I have a goose egg on my head.

He slows to a stop. We sit a few minutes. Two other cars pull in, slowly, and stop.

"There! Look over at the edge of the dump. It's a big one," Tom says. He points to a black bear working his way through the piles of garbage and debris.

"There's another one over there," I say. "It's not quite as big. Look at that dumb woman; she's getting out of the car."

"She better get back in. They say a woman got mauled pretty bad, here, last year," says Fred.

She snaps a couple of pictures, and starts to walk closer to the bear. Just then someone in her car opens the door and yells, "Get back in here!"

The bear lifts its head and starts toward the woman. She turns, rapidly, and in a flash, she's in the car.

Grandma stays on at Aunt Dorothy and Uncle Leonard's cabin near Lake Tomahawk. Shortly after we get home from vacation, we are notified that Grandma has fallen and broken her leg. She has a cast from her foot nearly up to her hip. She will have to stay longer. We are all concerned, and disappointed that she won't be home soon.

Cousin Fred Seils with his beautiful red hair.

Jackie & Grandma with her broken leg in a cast.

"That's his plane landing now," says Tom. Mother, Dad, my guest - Myra Newnham and I follow Tom toward the plane.

112

Tom's friend, Melvin Anderson, is arriving at the airport in Rhinelander, Wisconsin, this cool July day in 1950. After greetings, we get in Dad's car for the ride through forested country to Uncle Gordon's cabin near Eagle River.

Melvin Andersen descending from the plane

Evening finds us in a hot game of ping-pong at the extended, round dining room table. The little white ball often goes astray, ricocheting off rafters, creating a merry ruckus.

"Myra, breathe deep. The fragrance of the Spruce and Pine woods is beautiful," I say. I carry a pair of oars as we head toward the lake.

Friend Myra Newnham in boat on Kathan Lake at Uncle Gordon's cabin.

113

Climbing into the green boat, Myra says, "The lake is like glass. Look at the reflections. The sun has warmed these wood seats."

"It's untied, I'll push us out, the water is clear and shallow here. We'll go out farther," I say jumping into the boat.

"It's really quiet out here. Listen to the birds singing in the woods. Look! A little black and white bird swooped down over that group of yellow water lilies," Myra exclaims.

We are out in the middle of the lake when Myra shrieks, "Pat, look at those spiders."

I nearly jump out of the boat screaming, "Where?"

"Under your seat!"

The boat rocks violently as I scramble to another seat.

"Whoops! Be careful," Myra exclaims. "I have never in my life seen such big, black, fuzzy looking spiders. They are bigger than silver dollars!"

"Shall we jump in the lake and let them row back?" I ask.

"I can't swim!"

"Neither can I!" The spiders move toward the front of the boat and I jump back to the rowing seat. With oars flying, I row to the pier. If it were a race, we'd surely win. We both jump out and tie up the boat.

Uncle Henry & Aunt Vera Seils, Mother,
Dad & Uncle Gordon at his cabin.

In the evening, Mother takes Myra and me to a dance over at Lake Tomahawk. Aunt Dorothy is chaperoning a group of the town's teenagers. The recorded music encourages even the shy kids to seek a partner. A few boys ask us to dance. After refreshments, Mother drives us back through the night woods to Uncle Gordon's.

Myra and I are atwitter about the cute boys, and the fun we had. Aunt Dorothy has asked me to spend an additional week at their cabin, across from the Wisconsin River, on County trunk D, near Lake Tomahawk. Mother and Dad take me to Aunt Dorothy's, where I bid my friend, Myra, and the family, "Good-bye."

Aunt Dorothy invites area kids to the cabin. She takes us to Big Carr Lake swimming; even a moonlight swim. We push furniture back in the cabin, wind up the old Victrola and dance.

Uncle Leonard, Mother and Aunt Dorothy Wessell in their cabin.

Before the week is up, I am involved with my first case of puppy love. For several months, correspondence, of the sweetest nature, and little gifts, will fly between Lake Tomahawk and South Beloit. And then as swiftly as its arrival, it vanishes.

115

Chapter 8
Sometimes We Hurt
(1930-1950)

Life in Illisconsin is difficult in the twenties, thirties and early forties. When sickness strikes, people don't always go immediately to the doctor or call him to the house. Home remedies are sometimes tried first. Pain is sometimes inflicted in trying to correct a health problem.

Three year old Jackie is sick and Della finds it necessary to flush the bowel. A few days later her Grandpa Singletary is visiting. Jackie climbs up on his lap and chats. He plays with her and encourages her to talk. "Grandpa, have you ever had one of those squirt things used on you?" she asks.

Trying to keep from laughing, Grandpa says, "Well, now, I'm not sure."

Jackie says, "Grandpa, the other day I was sick. Mama used one of those squirt things on me and - pow - she nearly blew my brains out!"

* — * — *

It is summer, 1938. Jackie and Ruthie Riley are ten years old. They are playing house on our large, white, front veranda. They have Jackie's doll cupboard and table. The table has a green cloth and is set with Jackie's toy china dishes. The cream color dishes have a blue band around them with a tan circle in the center encircled with a fine black ring. At one edge is a small clump of orange and blue flowers. Jackie's doll, dressed in pink, sits in her tan, wicker doll buggy. Ruthie's doll, dressed in yellow, sits in the small, green wicker rocker. The girls sip tea, and feed their children.

Seven year old Gene and six year old Tommy are running around the yard playing cowboys and Indians. They have suckers on wood sticks. Gene says, "Come on, Tommy Hawk, let's attack the girls' house." With a war whoop they come charging up the stairs and climb up on the porch railings.

"Help," yells Ruthie, "They are going to attack us."

"Oh! Protect our children," screams Jackie.

They dance around, threatening the girls. Gene has his left hand full of wooden clothes pins and the sucker in his right hand. Just as he is about to do his wild attack, he loses his balance and falls to the sidewalk about five feet below.

His scream brings Mama running from the house. "What's happening?" she cries. One look at Gene confirms her fears. The blood is running from his mouth and head. The wood sucker

116

stick has gone through his lip and the wood clothes pins have gouged his forehead to the bone.

Aunt Kay, who is Daddy's brother Ivan's wife, is visiting us. When old Doc Thayer arrives, Gene is still moaning and crying. Gene gets one look at the doctor's needle and cries, "No! No! Don't do that to me! Get away!"

Daddy says, "It's alright, Gene. He is going to help you to get better. Those gouges must be stitched or they will never quit bleeding."

"No! Daddy, no!" Gene wails.

"You don't want them to leave big ugly scars, do you?" asks Aunt Kay.

"Hold still now, Gene," Daddy says. He takes his arms and holds him firm on the couch, while Aunt Kay sits on his feet.

At two, I am frightened and crying as hard as Gene. Mama picks me up and leaves the living room. In the kitchen, she tries to comfort me, but it is difficult to do when she is crying, too.

The life of cowboys and Indians is hazardous, and sometimes they get wounded.

* — * — *

In the crisp days of autumn, Mama has the pantry shelves filled with colorful jars of home canned fruits and vegetables. She is happy to have a bountiful supply set aside for the onslaught of winter, like the red squirrels that have been burying nuts and berries in the ground.

With the colder days, other little animals are trying to prepare for winter also. That is why Mama is preparing the mouse traps, by tying tiny pieces of bacon on them. She has a newspaper on the kitchen table, where she is working. "Patsy, do not touch these. They are dirty, and they bite hard. Don't touch!"

She has one set, and steps to the kitchen window to see who is in the side yard. My four year old mind is curious. I think, "those are sure funny looking things. I wonder how they work? Will that bacon come off?" I reach my index finger out and touch the bacon. SNAP! "Ow! Ow!" I scream. I hold my hand up with my tiny finger clamped in the vice-like grip of that dreadful trap.

"Oh, no!" Mama yells, as she leaps to my side. Her hands shake, as she pries the metal clasp open. "Oh, Honey," she cries. She picks me up and rocks me back and forth. Carrying me to the sink, she runs cold water on my finger. It is red and swollen.

"Oh, Patsy, Patsy. Why didn't you mind Mama? Now you are going to have a very sore finger for a while." I cry, as I snuggle against her. I am sorry, and her love is such a comfort to me.

* — * — *

It is mid winter with snow covering the ground and cold

117

winds whistling at the windows. Colds and flu have been circulating in the shops, schools and in our home. Ten year old Gene is ill. Daddy has come down with a bad cold and is feeling rotten. A remedy of the day is camphorated oil rubbed on the upper torso.

"Della, where is the camphorated oil?" Daddy asks. He is rummaging around in the medicine cabinet over the kitchen sink.

"Mother is upstairs, taking care of Gene," Jackie answers from the dining room.

He continues to look, but doesn't see it in the cabinet. He glances up and there it is, sitting on top of the refrigerator. "Well, what's it doing up there?" he mutters. He is in the process of rubbing it up the front of his neck and all over his chest, when Mama comes into the kitchen. She takes one look at him and becomes hysterical. She is laughing so hard she can hardly talk. "Elt, that's —- not —- camphorated —- oil," she manages, between spasms of laughter.

He sniffs it, and gets a funny look on his face. "Well, WHAT is it?" he asks.

Still laughing so hard she can barely talk, she says, "It—is—Gene's—urine sample—that I—have ready—to—take to the—doctor."

* — * — *

One evening Daddy has pressed a pair of his pants. He sets the hot iron on the kitchen table to cool before he puts it back in the cupboard. I am at the table with a paint book. I have a dish of water and a brush. As I paint the designs, color comes up off the page like magic. Mama is going to run next door to Mrs. Nicolls house for something. She stops to caution me. "Now don't touch that iron! It is very hot and it would burn you!" The boys come out to the kitchen and are fretting over some project.

In a few moments I look at the upright iron, it peaks my curiosity. I wonder if it is still hot. I reach out with my right hand, extending five little fingers. Without any thought of the previous caution, I press five fingers onto the bottom of the iron. My scream brings Daddy and Jackie running. Almost immediately I have five large blisters. Daddy grabs a can of Cloverine Salve, from the medicine cabinet over the kitchen sink. Jackie wraps her arms around me and kisses and hugs me. Soon Mama is home and she soothes me too. "Do you remember what Mama said to you, Patsy?" she asks.

"I'm sorry," I cry.

"I'm sorry, too, Patsy, because now you have the pain of not obeying what Mama asks of you," she says. But she hugs me close and kisses me.

A few days later, my step grandmother - Rachael Singletary, takes care of me one morning so Mama can run some errands. "Patsy, would you like to play squirrel?" she asks.

"How can I do that?" I ask.

"Grandma Rachael has hidden some peanuts, with shells on, around the house. You can be a squirrel and look for them."

For an hour or so I search in every nook and cranny, squealing with delight at each discovery.

When Mama arrives, Grandma Rachael says, "We should run a needle through those blisters and let the water out."

I'm not sure I like that idea, but Grandma Rachael holds a needle in the fire of a match awhile, and then slips it in one side of the blister and out the other. It doesn't hurt, and she does all five of them. It isn't long until they heal up.

I like Grandma Rachael and am puzzled when she and Grandpa are divorced. Mama says some of the family interfered.

* — * — *

It is wash day in our old limestone cellar. At five years old, I am fascinated with that old, grey metal, electric, Maytag washing machine that stands on legs. It has a hose, with a hook on the top, which fastens on the top side of the machine. When Mama is finished washing, she will unhook the hose and lower it into a piece of galvanized downspout, which has an elbow. She will fasten it on a wire loop. This will carry the wash water to the floor drain. The water in the two large rinse tubs, which sit on a long table, will be hand dipped into the machine to drain out.

Mother removes the lid on the machine. I smell the warm fragrant soap suds, and the bleach in the one rinse tub. Something in the center is rotating back and forth, making a swish - swish sound. She moves a gear shift on the side of the machine, and the motion stops. "Oh my, Mama, why are you pulling up clothes and feeding them into the rolling lips on the machine?" I ask. "That looks like fun." The clothes come out flattened together, and land with a plop into the funny smelling water. I help push them down.

"These are wringers. They squeeze the water out, so I don't have to wring them by hand," Mama answers.

Our quiet is broken with the shrill sound of the telephone ringing. "DON'T TOUCH ANYTHING!" Mama commands. She climbs the stairs to answer the phone.

I look at the machine. Surely, it won't hurt to push a few hankies into those rollers. "Ow-w-c-ch!!!" I shriek, in pain.

Mama flies down the stairs two at a time, as one of her shoes sails through the air. As she wrenches the monster off my wounded thumb, she is shaking and crying, and I am whooping it up. "Patsy, Patsy, when will you obey Mama?" she cries. "You

119

could have been crippled or even killed!" She cradles me in her arms; I feel her love and forgiveness. I didn't mean to be naughty, I just have a great curiosity. My scare and sore thumb are punishment enough.

* — * — *

During Tommy's adolescence, he is plagued with allergies and a variety of minor, but painful medical conditions. He is in the kitchen bathing his eye with hot compresses. He has an inflammation of one of the sebaceous glands of the eyelid. Our neighbor friend, Erla Nicolls, has stopped in to visit with Mama. "What's the matter with your eye, Tommy?" she asks.

"I have a sty on it," he answers.

"Oh, Tommy. You know how you get those don't you?" she asks.

"No. How?"

With a mischievous look on her face she says, "They say you get those from peeing in the middle of the road."

Tommy blushes, as we all laugh.

Several days later he has a bout with hives. He is in misery with itching as those terrible welts cover his body. We have just finished lunch in the kitchen. Tommy gets out of his chair and faints, falling to the floor. Greatly alarmed, Mother runs to him, kneeling at his side. "Someone get me some water, quick!"

Gene grabs an empty water pitcher and hands it to her. Only later, will we see the humor in it. Right now, this is a frightening thing. Jackie gives her a glass of water, and she splashes a little on his face. He awakens, and Mama bathes him in baking soda water. The itching relents and gradually the hives disappear.

As if the sties and hives aren't enough, Tommy endures a time of painful boils. Presently Grandpa Wessell's sister, Mama's Aunt Sue Ramboldt, is visiting us from Colorado. Tommy has an extremely painful boil on his forearm, near the elbow. The circumscribed inflammation has formed under the skin, generating a pus buildup. It has a pointed pustular tumor and a central core. It is deep red, and has the appearance and feel of a volcano building pressure. Tommy moans in agony with it. Aunt Sue says, "Tommy, I know a way to pop that core out of there and relieve the pressure and pain."

Tommy looks up, as he continues to apply the hot epsom salt compress. "How, Aunt Sue? It hurts so bad."

"Della, get me a small, clean, white cloth and a pair of shears, please," Aunt Sue says.

Mama finds the cloth and gives it to Aunt Sue with the shears. She cuts a small hole in the cloth, less than a half inch.

"Here, Della, put this hole over the boil and take hold of both sides of the cloth and pull down firmly. It will hurt a lot at

120

first, but it will be worth it, Tommy," Aunt Sue says.

Mama looks at Tommy, as though she would rather not do this, but she follows Aunt Sue's advice. Tommy flinches and cries out.

Almost immediately, the skin breaks and the volcano erupts. All of the crud and the core flow out onto the cloth, which is disposed of. Relief and gratitude register on Tommy's face.

* — * — *

When my next door neighbor friend, Jimmy Nicolls and I are six years old we have measles at the same time. A policeman comes to our homes, and tacks a big red placard on the houses near the front doors, to warn people that we are in quarantine. This is done for all childhood diseases that are considered contagious.

After the first couple of days, when we are feeling a bit better, Jimmy and I are allowed to play together. We must either be in a darkened room or wear sun glasses. We think this is rather neat. We get a holiday from school, receive gifts for being ill, and can play together!

* — * — *

When the loose teeth come, I wiggle them back and forth, impatient for them to come out. The boys convince me to let them tie one end of a string around a tooth, and the other end around the door handle. They open the door and then slam it shut. It works! My tooth is hanging from the string on the door handle!

* — * — *

I hear yelps and moans coming from the kitchen. "What is happening?" I wonder. I peek my head around the corner, and hear another outburst.

"That's got to come out of there, or it is never going to feel any better," Daddy says.

Tommy is perched on the edge of his chair, looking rather peaked. He has his shoe and sock off, and Daddy is sitting in front of him with a pocket knife.

"These ingrown toenails have got to be kept dug out at the corners, or they are going to be so sore you won't be able to wear your shoes," Daddy says. He inserts the knife in the corner again and cuts out another chunk of nail. Tommy shrieks again, and Daddy dabs his toes with mercurochrome, leaving a red stain all over them . . . No pain, no gain!

* — * — *

It is early August 1943. Having suffered a stroke, Grandpa Wessell is confined to bed at his home on Riverside Drive in Beloit. Eleven year old Tommy, and thirteen year old Gene, are at the old pump house down by the river.

"I brought some wrenches down to see if we can get that

leaky pipe off," says Gene.

"That's good. I know Grandpa would want us to get this fixed, so we can pump water from the river to water the lawn," answers Tommy.

"Grandpa has a piece of pipe here that we can replace it with," says Gene. The boys work together, and remove the section of pipe, but they can't get an elbow off that needs to come apart.

"I'll take it up to the garage, and put it in Grandpa's vice. Then I probably can get it apart," says Tommy.

He trudges up to the garage and unscrews the huge vice to open its mouth. He places the pipe between its teeth and winds it tight onto the pipe. Taking a wrench, he pulls hard, trying to unscrew the elbow from the pipe. It is corroded and doesn't budge. Leaning into it and using his weight to force the wrench, he tugs with all his might. The huge vice is not bolted to the work bench. Suddenly it slides to the edge of the bench and starts to fall. Instead of jumping back out of its way, Tommy tries to catch it. The heavy vice smashes to the floor, taking with it part of Tommy's left index finger. He shrieks in pain and terror, as he races through the back door of the house.

"Oh, dear Lord. What happened?" Mama cries.

Tommy is as white as a ghost, and the blood is streaming down his hand. Grandma comes out of Grandpa's room. "Oh, no!" She grabs a towel and wraps it around his hand. "Hold it up, Tommy. Let's take him to the front porch and set him in a chair. So it won't upset Pa so much," Grandma says.

"I'll call the doctor," says Mama. Then she looks at Tommy's finger. "Oh, God help us. Part of it is missing!" She runs out to the garage and picks up the chunk of flesh and fingernail that lies on the garage floor. When she comes in, she is nearly as white as Tommy.

"You'd better sit down," says Grandma.

I stand back in a corner, terrified.

It seems less than five minutes, when Dr. Gunderson pulls into the driveway.

"Well, Tommy, let's have a look. The bone is exposed, and there is nothing left to stitch. About all I can do, is clean it up and dress it." As he begins to cleanse and work on the finger, Tommy almost passes out. "We'll just have to keep changing the dressing often. It will heal eventually, but it will probably always be sensitive," he concludes. When he finishes dressing it, he adds a guard.

It is painful for weeks. Tommy goes to have the finger redressed. There is no soaking to remove the dried blood bandage that adheres to the wound. The doctor pulls it off, as white-knuckled Tommy soars through the roof. This is repeated often throughout the convalescent period.

An ounce of prevention is worth a pound of cure!

* — * — *

I come out of my miniature bedroom, off Grandma and Jackie's bedroom, on a Sunday morning in early July 1944. The house seems strangely empty. Daddy is in the hospital in Tomahawk, Wisconsin, where he just had emergency surgery for a burst appendix, while we were vacationing. Mama is staying up there with Lamers, the people who own the resort where we were. Daddy's brother, Uncle Gordon, came after the rest of us and brought us home yesterday. Gene and Tommy are still asleep in their room across the hall. As I come into the room, Grandma is swinging her legs out of bed.

"Grandma!" I gasp with wide eyes. "What is the matter with the back of your leg?"

Jackie is awakened, and rolls over to look. "Oh, Grandma. What is it?" she asks with alarm.

"I don't know. What's the matter?" she asks. She tries to twist herself around to look at the back of her leg.

Behind her right knee is a place, larger than a grapefruit, which is purple-black with a large, dark brown knot, the size of a kidney bean, in the center.

"Grandma, we'd better call the doctor," says sixteen year old Jackie.

We get dressed and go downstairs. When Dr. Gunderson arrives, he looks at Grandma's leg and says, "My gosh, Ella, it is a gigantic woodtick! Where did you get that?"

"Well, I probably got it when we stopped at that park yesterday on the way home from up north. We ate our lunch at a picnic table, in a wooded area."

"This woodtick has been gorging itself on blood all these hours, and it is as big as a large kidney bean. I'm going to take it out with these tweezers and put some antiseptic on it," he says. "You keep an eye on it. You can put iodine or mercurochrome on it a couple of times a day. With your diabetes, we don't want this to get infected. Where are Della and Elton?"

Grandma tells him the story of our interrupted vacation.

"That's too bad. Keep me posted how you and Elton are doing. I'll be going now."

* — * — *

The year 1945 brings an epidemic of polio, and parents worry for their children. When I run around playing outdoors, Mother calls, "Patsy. I want you to quit that racing and tearing around. You should not get overheated. There is a polio epidemic and that is a terrible disease. Look at you. Your face is all red. Now I want you to quit it. You settle down, or you are going to have to come in the house!"

In June, my eight year old neighbor friend, Barbara Kissling, becomes quite ill. The illness continues for weeks. She is puzzled because her friends don't come to see her or to play. Mother calls to see how she is doing, but there is no diagnosis, yet. Parents are panicky, and they are not taking any chances.

Barbara becomes very ill. She burns with high fever, and members of the family take turns sitting with her through the long nights. "Mother, see the beautiful girl in the lovely white dress. Oh, Mother she is so beautiful."

"Where, Barbara? Where is she?" asks her mother.

"Mother, don't you see her? She has such a beautiful white dress. Oh, Mother, will you buy me a beautiful dress like that?"

The diagnosis comes. Barbara has polio.

By August twentieth, seventeen people, in Rockford, Illinois have died with polio. Citizens are so fear stricken, they agree to allow the government to experiment, and to spray half of Rockford with the powerful wartime insecticide DDT. It is a mercy mission for the powerful plane, brought here from the canal zone especially for the experiment. The great olive-drab B-25 plane, one of two equipped with spraying devices, roars low over the roof tops of Rockford from Truax Field, Madison, Wisconsin, spraying the city with 1,650 gallons of the miracle insecticide. The experimental nature of the test is emphasized by Dr. John R. Paul, Yale University poliomyelitis authority, here to supervise the test, according to the Beloit Daily News.

Barbara continues to see the beautiful girl in the lovely white dress. She beckons to Barbara. One day Barbara's fever subsides. The beautiful girl in the lovely dress smiles at Barbara and walks away. She doesn't return. Barbara starts improving day by day. By the end of September she can go back to school. Her mother continues to give her wonderful care.

"Barbara, use that foot. Don't you drag it. Walk on it!" her mother calls. As Barbara goes off to school, and out to play her mother continues to call to her, "Barbara, don't limp. Don't favor that foot. Use it!" At home she says, "Barbara, would you like to play at Mother's sewing machine?"

"Oh, yes, Mother. That will be fun." She spends long periods of time working the treadle with her lame foot.

It will be many years before Barbara understands why her friends stayed away when she was ill, or why her mother allowed her to play with her treadle sewing machine so much, and especially why the beautiful angel in the white dress watched over her . . .

* — * — *

On a cold, Saturday afternoon, mid-winter of my twelfth year, I knock on the Kisslings' front door. I am dressed in my sister's old, green snowsuit, and I carry a pair of old, black shoe ice-skates. Mrs. Kissling is going to take a group of the neighborhood girls ice-skating out to the lagoon on Riverside Drive, in Beloit.

Mrs. Kissling comes to the door. I wonder what is wrong. It looks as though she has been sunburned or something.

"Come on in, Pat," she says. "I've just had a terrible disaster."

"What's the matter?" I ask in concern.

"I'm all burned," she says. She points to her face and neck, which is so red. "I got scalded with steam. I just did a stupid thing. I tried to open the pressure cooker without releasing the steam. I've never used one before."

"That's sure too bad. Do you have some Cloverine Salve or something to put on it?" I ask.

"Yes, I was just rubbing some on it. Come look at my kitchen!" she says.

I walk into the kitchen, and I don't know whether to laugh or cry. A cooked beef roast and potatoes are scattered around on top of the stove. Beef broth, onions and bits of potatoes are decorating the ceiling and walls. I guess, we all decide that it won't do any good to cry, and we burst out laughing.

"Mrs. Kissling, it makes me think of the saying, 'When all else fails, follow directions'," I say.

Barbara has let the other girls in the house. Mrs. Kissling, in her usual upbeat attitude, says, "Come on girls, I'll take you to the lagoon. I'll come back here and wash my kitchen, then I'll be back to pick you up."

The other girls have pretty white shoe skates, with colorful tassels on the toes. They go right out to the ice and skate well. I want to blame my second hand black skates, with the deep shanks to the blades, for not being able to stand up. It really is my weak ankles and fallen arches. While the other girls skate around, I wobble from one side of my ankles to the other. I am cold, and thoroughly exhausted by the time Mrs. Kissling returns. I can't make my feet or ankles work another step. While the girls laugh mercilessly, I crawl to the car, over the crusted snow, on my hands and knees!

* — * — *

It is 1950; Grandma sits down in a living room chair. As she bends her leg, a sharp steel pin pops through her knee, protruding an inch. Grandma broke her leg last year and had to have pins put in her knee. Now we are all frightened. Is she going to need surgery again? A call to the doctor dispels our fears. On his advice, Grandma pulls the pin straight out with her fingers. It is over three inches long. She puts mercurochrome on her knee, leaving the red stain.

Somehow, we continue to survive the accidents, pains and home remedies!

Chapter 9
Holiday Celebrations
(1941-1948)

November 15, 1941. "Hello," says Mama, as she picks up the telephone receiver.

"Hi, Honey," Grandma responds. "Did you notice McNeany's ad in the Beloit Daily News last night?"

"Yeah, I did, Ma. I'd like to do some Christmas shopping there."

"They have fifty Christmas cards for $1.00. The ad says there are many designs to choose from. That seems a little high, but I like the idea of having our name imprinted. It would eliminate a lot of writing."

"I'd like to send Elton to look at the fur trimmed coats; they have advertised, on the second floor. They have Persian, Silvered Fox and Sable dyed Squirrel. But, I suppose I can get by with my old coat another year."

"If you want to go, I'll pick you up, after lunch."

"The kids go back to school about 12:45. I'll be ready then."

When they arrive at the store, Mama, says "I brought their ad out of the paper. I want to find these head scarves on the main floor. They are 27 inch wool squares in luscious patterns, florals and plaids. It says, create distinctive blouses, table covers, skirts and even dresses of them. Claims they are gay and exciting at 69 cents. They would be nice for the girls. Maybe they'd make good gifts for the teachers, too."

"While you're looking down here, I'm going to take the elevator upstairs," says Grandma.

Grandma says, "Hello," to the lady running the elevator.

"Good afternoon," she replies, cheerfully.

The lady starts the elevator and it doesn't line up with the floor level when it reaches second, so she pushes buttons and the elevator jerks as it stops again. She pulls a long lever to open the door.

A sales lady comes up to Grandma. "Hello. May I help you?"

"Yes, please. I saw your ad for the better dresses that were originally priced up to $8.98, on sale for $3.88," says Grandma.

The sales lady leads her to a special rack. Grandma looks through the dresses. She chooses one for herself, and two for Mama's Christmas gift. Then going to the blouses, she selects a white one and a pink one at $3.00 each.

Mama chooses the scarves, and then looks at the ad and sees the turbans advertised in jewel tone fabrics, at $2.98. "Hum,

127

Hats for the mood - elegant! Sparkling colors and plenty of black and brown, sizes 21 1/2 - 23," she says, to herself. "I'll get this black one for Ma."

When they meet again, both have their arms full.

"I don't have much Christmas shopping left to do," says Grandma.

"Neither do I," responds Mama.

On the way home Grandma says, "Thanksgiving is coming up fast. I'm glad your family and Dorothy and Leonard are coming."

Thanksgiving 1941. We are at Grandma and Grandpa Wessell's home. The aroma of chickens roasting, mingles with that of Hubbard squash, potatoes and cranberries. My taste buds work overtime. How much longer 'til dinner?

Fourteen year old Jackie is helping Grandma, Mama and Aunt Dorothy in the kitchen. The boys and Blackie went outdoors, and Grandpa, Daddy and Uncle Leonard are in the living room listening to the radio. At six years, I am happy to entertain myself in Grandma's bedroom.

I open the closet door. Wow! There, on a small table, sit three pumpkin pies. Grandma's closet is cold. The pies look so good! I bend over, with my nose close, and smell them. Umm, they smell spicy and delicious! They are dark, golden bronze, and so glossy. I wonder what makes them so shiny? Reaching out my right hand with five little fingers extended, I gently touch the center of a pie. Oh, oh! When I lift my fingers, there are five little fingerprints in the middle of the pie. I lick my fingers, and hurry out of the closet.

The last plump, juicy, chicken leg has been eaten, and everyone is stuffed with dressing, and whipped cream fruit salad. Mama and Jackie stack plates, and Aunt Dorothy carries serving dishes of leftovers from the dining room table to the kitchen, while Grandma goes for the pies.

"I think a little mouse has gotten into one of my pies," says Grandma. I don't know why everyone is looking at me! I am getting nervous, then Uncle Leonard and Grandpa burst out laughing, and I know I'm safe this time. I don't mean to be naughty; I just have curious little fingers!

* — * — *

It is an evening, close to Christmas. Mama and Daddy have gone somewhere for a short time. I am lying on the living room floor, in front of the tall Christmas tree. The colorful lights make me feel cozy. Tinker toys lay on the floor, and I am busy sticking dowels into round disks, making animals, and all sorts of things.

Jackie is busy in her bedroom upstairs. Gene and Tommy have been in the kitchen and now they come into the living

128

room. They look at the few wrapped packages under the tree.

"I wonder what's in these?" says Tommy.

Gene picks one up and shakes it. It rattles, and that increases his curiosity. He picks up another one and reads the label, "To Patsy, from Grandma Rachael. Don't you wonder what's in this package, Patsy?" he asks.

I pick it up and shake it gently. "I don't know what's in it," I answer.

"Wouldn't you like to know?" asks Tommy.

"Maybe we could each open one enough to peek, and then wrap them back up," Gene suggests.

My eyes light up, "Could we?" I ask.

"We'd better hurry. Mama and Daddy said they wouldn't be gone long," says Tommy.

The boys open one end of each package, carefully. I look as they slide mine out far enough for me to see a box containing three circus animals, brown, pink and yellow, made out of bath soap. Quickly they put them back together, carefully trying to lick the Christmas stickers to reseal them.

I will always remember these cute, small, soap animals. Not because they are a spectacular gift, but when it is time to open them Christmas eve, there is no surprise! The fun of opening the package is gone. I have learned my lesson, and don't want to sneak a peek again!

* — * — *

A few days before Christmas, we visit our friend Walter Anthony, at his small home on Vernon Avenue. Tony is always kind to us kids. He opens a large, flat, white box and tells us to take a cookie. My eyes pop, when I see the cookies inside. They are the largest Gingerbread men I have ever seen, about ten inches long! They have raisins for eyes, nose, mouth and buttons down the front. Mama, Jackie and I know what will be in the wrapped gifts to us. It will be Tony's traditional gift of Evening in Paris cologne in various shaped, cobalt blue bottles.

He surprises me one year, with a set of Blue Willow china doll dishes, and brings me Uncle Wiggly books, which I love.

Through the years Grandpa Wessell creates a variety of wonderful, wood toys and furniture for us. When the boys are small, he makes them a locomotive with wheels and tie-rods and a semi truck. Both are large enough that they can sit on them and scoot along. Later he makes each of them buck saws and cross bucks painted red, and also makes jointed, wood dancing dolls on strings.

For Jackie he makes a large blackboard on legs, a large desk, a white doll cupboard about three feet tall and a white doll swing. He makes me a narrow, rosy - pink dresser with mirror attached, and matching hinged lid seat; a red, doll cupboard, about two foot high and a red swing. Though made from orange or apple crate materials, these creations will be treasured even when we are of an age to have our own grandchildren.

Christmas at Grandma and Grandpa Wessell's home is an experience of love and joy. This year, of 1941, Jackie and I will each receive a small, stuffed black and white panda bear. A special taste treat is the soft, fat sugar cookies in the shape of Santas, stars, reindeer and snowmen. Grandma fills them with love and sprinkles them with colored sugar or tiny beads of candy.

The joy of Christmas abides in our hearts as we continue to gather with friends and loved ones. New Year's eve is fast approaching. Early in the morning of December 30, 1941, Mama answers the telephone. We hear her saying, "Oh my word! Oh no! How bad are they hurt? When are you leaving? Well, you be careful, Dad." She hangs up the phone and says to Daddy and the rest of us, "That was your Dad. He had a call from the Mark Greer hospital in Vandalia. Jen and Floyd had a terrible car accident. He is driving down there this afternoon."

(Aunt Jeanette is Daddy's youngest sister. She is eighteen years younger than Daddy, about twenty four years old at this time. Her husband Floyd is a lieutenant in the 128th Infantry of the 32nd Division, as commander of the headquarters detachment, on duty at Ft. Livingston, Louisiana.)

Tommy, Jackie, Gene, Patsy and the Christmas pandas.

Uncle Floyd & Aunt Jeanette Monroe.

"Oh no!" cries Daddy. "His leave was short and they were hurrying home to see the family. They probably drove all night. Are they badly hurt?"

"Floyd has a broken ankle, Jen has two or three broken ribs, and both have facial cuts and severe bruises. It happened about ten miles north of Vandalia, Illinois. They are painfully, but not seriously injured."

"How did it happen?" Daddy asks.

"Floyd had driven all night, and must have dozed. The car struck a concrete culvert abutment."

"I suppose they really messed the car up, too," says Elton.

"They are lucky to be alive! It rolled over and ended up with its wheels in the air. In spite of Floyd's broken ankle, they say, he miraculously freed Jen from the tangled wreckage and dragged her to safety, just before the car burst into flames. They couldn't save any of their clothes or possessions, and it killed their little dog," Mama says, in tears.

"They are lucky to be alive." Daddy says, with big tears welling up in his eyes. "Did Dad know how long they will have to be in the hospital?"

"They think they will be out in a couple of days," Mama replies.

"What a rotten way to start the new year!" Daddy exclaims.

"It all depends on how you look at it. It may be a blessed way to start the new year. They have a lot to be thankful for. They have their lives, and each other," Mama replies.

* — * — *

It is 1943, our first Christmas season without Grandpa Wessell. He has been gone only two months, and we are all dealing with our grief. Mama does what she can to cheer us up. Friday evening December third she says, "Look at the ad for this movie at the Majestic theater. You kids can all go see it tomorrow."

Jackie starts reading the ad in the Beloit Daily News, "'Wintertime' with Sonja Henie, Jack Oakie, Cesar Romero, Carole Landis and Woodie Herman and his orchestra. It says, happy songs and hilarity in the happy playground of the North. Melody - romance - sensational Sonja - glitter - glamour with stars all around her, and the splendor of snow crested Canada, at her twinkling feet. Sat. 'til 6:00 - 27 cents, evening 36 cents, children 10 cents (plus Fed. war tax)."

"Wow. That sounds good. She's a great skater," says Gene.

"Is there a cartoon?" asks Tommy.

"Yes. A color cartoon - 'Corny Concerto' and some other short features," Jackie says. "It should be good. Thank you, Mother."

I clap my hands in excited anticipation.

* — * — *

As I come up the sidewalk around the end of our back porch, I can smell something cooking. Coming home from school this

131

winter, Wednesday afternoon, I stop before the back porch. I stomp snow from my feet, and negotiate the three slippery steps. As I enter the back shed, Mother calls, "Take your boots off, I've just finished the floors." I smell something cooking that invites me to hurry in.

"Umm, it smells so good. What is it?"

"Homemade soup," Grandma answers.

"Homemade soup for supper? Oh goodie! Are you going to make dumplings, Grandma?"

"Yes, I'm going to make dumplings, Dumplin," Grandma smiles.

"Oh boy, you're getting the Christmas decorations out," I exclaim to Mother.

Red chenille wreaths, with red light bulbs, hang in the windows. As I enter the dining room, I see the royal blue, two foot tall tree in the center of the table. Its branches which fold up, have been pulled down. The lights, with the narrow pointed bulbs, plug into a five point, ornate, bronze light fixture above it. Small red cranberries decorate the branches. The tree's white, square, wood base sits on Mother's Quaker Lace tablecloth. A tiny white berry ends each blue bough. On either side of the tree is a triple, crystal candle holder containing spiraled, red candles.

A couple of nights ago when we were at the tree lot ———

"The sign says, `Fresh Trees,' but I'm sure most of them are cut before Thanksgiving. They top out tall trees in the north woods and start bringing them down during hunting season," Gene informs us.

"Well, I want a double needle Balsam. They hold their needles best," says Mama.

It's cold and the wind blows across our foreheads like an arctic blast. I stomp my feet, wiggling my toes inside my shoes and boots. They feel tingly. I pull my thumbs back and curl my fingers up inside my gloves, trying to warm my fingers.

"This tree looks pretty good," says Mama. Gene turns the tree this way and that. "But I guess, we'd better look them over. We might see one we like better."

Continuing through the lot, Gene and Tom turn the trees this way and that. Here a branch missing, there a crooked trunk, here a bare branch, there a trunk too fat . . .

We all shiver and shake; we have walked full circle. Gene lifts the first tree we looked at, and Mama says, "I think this one will be the perfect size for the corner of the living room. It has a nice shape and the trunk should fit the stand." Mama pays the man $1.50 and we leave. "Merry Christmas," he says.

We all sing out, "Merry Christmas." ......

132

I say to Mama, "May we put the tree up before Jackie's birthday?"

"Yes, Jackie's sixteenth birthday is this Friday, December tenth. We will put the tree up after supper tonight," Mama replies.

Gene and Jackie come stomping up the back steps, just getting home from high school. Mama calls the same caution to them about the clean floors. Tommy comes down from upstairs.

"Gene, you and Tom can get the tree fit into the stand, out on the back porch. Then bring it in to the corner of the living room. You have time to do it before your Dad gets home for supper, if you get moving," Mama says.

When Daddy arrives, the tree is sitting in the living room ready to be decorated.

Grandma lifts the pot roast from the large, blue enameled, roaster pan of vegetable soup. She slides it onto a platter, then drops dough from a tablespoon, into the gently simmering soup. Onions, celery, potatoes and golden carrots, simmer in the clear broth. "Don't anyone lift the lid for ten minutes," Grandma cautions. "If you do, the dumplings won't be tender and fluffy in the center." Time is up. Mama lifts them out, onto a platter. They are the size of large biscuits.

"What do you put in the dumplings, Grandma?" Jackie asks.

"It is Betty Cheney's recipe for `Never Fail Dumplings' (Betty Cheney is Aunt Dorothy Wessell's best friend.) It takes 2 cups flour, 1/2 teaspoon salt, 2 teaspoons Baking Powder, 2 Tablespoons butter, (cut into dry ingredients with a pie blender), add 1 egg, and 3/4 cup milk and blend. Drop dough, the size of an egg into simmering liquid. Cover pan with lid; Cook ten minutes without removing lid."

"I'm going to make these some day when I'm grown up, Grandma," I say. "I love them."

After supper and clean up, we decorate the tree. The narrow, pointed light bulbs in different colors are a real challenge. When one light bulb burns out, the whole string goes out. Considerable time is spent changing bulbs, trying to discover which one is the culprit. Mama has some bulbs that are fancy shapes of houses, santas and elves. The large, colored, shiny balls with colored stripes around them, were Grandma's. On the tree top is a shiny, ball-like ornament with a spire. Red cranberries hang over the branches. Quarter inch wide twists of aluminum, about five inches long, silver on one side and red, green or blue on the other, hang on threads and twirl with air currents.

Gene and Tom play "Tiddly Winks," "Pick Up Sticks" and "Chinese Checkers" on the floor in front of the tree. I sit close by with my wind-up train on its three foot circular track. Placing

133

small match boxes under the track to create hills, I watch the train climb. A composition santa rides on the caboose. A large eared mouse sticks out of the pack on his back. The family enjoys the tree's warm glow.

"I remember when Jackie, Gene and Tommy were small, I used to read Christmas poems to them, and substitute different words in places. They would get so excited, and say, `No, Daddy!' Then they would say the word that should be there," chuckles Daddy.

"Remember, when we'd go for a ride in the fall and gather nuts, when Jackie was little?" asks Mama. "She'd say, `Let's crack some nuts an aud ob us eatim,'" laughs Mama.

"Elton, do you remember how you used to buff the waxed floors?" asks Grandma.

"How?" I ask.

"I used to set the boys on a gunny bag and pull them around the floor, with them laughing and squealing," smiles Daddy.

"Christmas is for remembering," says Mama.

* — * — *

Saturday afternoon, December 9, 1944. Jackie, now a senior in high school, celebrates her birthday a day early. Her friends, Corrine Strand, Corinne Griffiths and Ruth Riley are joining her for a movie; I am invited. "What is the movie, Jackie?" I ask.

"`And The Angels Sing.' This is what the ad says, Starring Dorothy Lamour, Fred MacMurray, Betty Hutton, Diana Lynn and Mimi Chandler. It is Paramount's greatest comedy with music! The entertainment is Heavenly and so are the bodies. There is the Dangerous Angel, the Reckless Angel, the Sassy Angel and the Falling Angel. Fred tries to make love to a singing sister act—all four of them! A Simply Super Show, With a Super Duper Cast of Super Troupers!"

At nine years, I am thrilled to be included. Mama gives Jackie money for popcorn and drives us to the Majestic theater. The girls have to pay 35 cents for tickets, but mine costs only 12 cents.

Such a joyous outing, but the world news shown on the screen is sobering. When we get home, Daddy is sharing highlights from the front page, of the Beloit Daily News, with Mama. The headlines: "China has successfully weathered one of the gravest military crises of the war, a high government spokesman declared today in announcing the rout of a strong Japanese invasion force that had penetrated within 65 miles of the big American air base at Kweiyang."

"American infantry knocked out 12 bitterly-defended pillboxes with flame-throwers, grenades and cannon, and plunged deeper into the maze of Siegfried line defenses northwest of

134

Saarlautern today after smashing the strongest German counter-attack yet uncorked east of the Saar river.

"Some 600 counter-attacking Germans with 11 tanks stabbed back into American-held Dillingen, two and a half miles north west of Saalautern and six miles inside the Saar basin, at 6:20 a.m. yesterday. The battle swayed back and forth through the streets and houses of the town for more than 10 hours, but the battered enemy finally withdrew at 5:00 p.m."

"Diplomatic observers believed today that the United States and Great Britain were far from agreement on allied policy toward liberated European governments despite British Ambassador Lord Halifax' assertion that `substantial understanding existed between the two Allies.'

"British Prime Minister Winston Churchill's fighting speech and his vote of confidence from the House of Commons yesterday strengthened belief among American authorities that the policy breach would remain until the next Roosevelt-Churchill-Stalin meeting."

"The Japanese acknowledged for the first time today the severity of the earthquake that ripped across' central Japan Thursday afternoon, and revealed that war plants and residential areas were damaged in Osaka, the empire's second city."

"Good grief!", exclaims Mama, "I think, this horrible fighting is going to go on forever. I'm so sick of it."

"Well, if you think you are sick of it, imagine what it must be like for those who have immediate family fighting in it," responds Daddy.

"I'm sure it's horrible for them. I have cousins in the service. I pray for peace every night," Mama concludes.

Monday night, December 11, the Daily News carries a report to the American people on the coming battle of Japan. It is an official U.S. Treasury advertisement prepared under the auspice of the Treasury Department and War Advertising Council.

"With the war in Europe not yet won by a long shot—and the war in the Pacific hardly begun—America is in no position to settle down for a "long winter's nap."

"The plain truth of the matter is, we have not yet begun to wage full-sized war in the East. And neither has the Jap.

"The Allied Military Command has estimated that it will take years, not months, to lick Japan.

"One and a half to two years after the defeat of Germany is regarded as the absolute minimum.

"Sometimes, Americans are apt to forget that the Jap is bred, fed, and trained for one thing - to expend himself fighting us.

"No Jap even considers defeat, for that is something the Empire of the Rising Sun has never experienced. His faith in the

135

`Divine' Emperor is supreme, unquestioning, final. What happens to him, his body, his family are all incidental in the present pilgrimage for divine supremacy.

"Japan's present army numbers about 4,000,000 with 2,000,000 more men available and fit for military service who haven't been called up to date. Another 1,500,000, between the ages of 17 and 20, are not subject to the draft.

"In addition to millions of native workers, Japan has a potential slave force of 400,000,000 conquered people..."

In spite of the war, Christmas eve arrives in our little town. Mama prepares the traditional oyster stew. We kids think the only thing good about this is the quick clean up of dishes. We drink the broth, but hate the oysters. Tommy bravely decides to eat one. We all watch him as he swallows, it returns, he swallows again, it returns. At the third return, Mama says, "Tommy, get rid of it. I don't think you are ready to enjoy oysters."

The suspense is too great; we want to open the presents. "Let's remove the soup bowls," says Jackie. We devour the Christmas cake, and quickly do the dishes.

We go to the living room, where the Christmas tree glows in colorful warmth. The boys play Santa, giving out the gifts. We appreciate useful clothing, and love the books, games and toys.

I open a long, narrow package and remove a metal bowling alley about twenty inches long and five inches wide. At one end, stands a little metal man with a spring action arm. Setting it on the floor, I put ten wooden bowling pins, about an inch and a half tall, on the round spots at the far end. I pull back the man's hand, place a marble in the indentation, and let the arm spring forward. "Oh, I knocked three pins down," I exclaim.

"Good for you, Honey. I'll play it with you sometime," says Grandma. At times during the evening, Grandma wipes her eyes. We take turns wiping our eyes. It isn't the same without Grandpa.

"We need to move along, if we are going to the midnight service at Second Congregational church, in Beloit," says Daddy.

It is hard to set aside our new treasures. I grab up my new scarf and matching mittens. "I can wear these to church," I exclaim. We stack our gifts, don our coats and head to church.

Inside, the church glows with soft lights. Its sanctuary is large. The north window is a huge, beautiful, bright colored, stained glass scene of three figures on a path. It intrigues me, but it will be many years before I know that it is Jesus with Cleopas, and another follower, on the road to Emmaus, after Jesus' crucifixion and resurrection. This wonderful story in Luke 24, is the reason Jesus was born the Christ Child in Bethlehem. I am awed by the magnificent church, the choir in black robes with white collars, the flickering candles on the altar, the powerful voice of Rev. Studebaker, the glorious music of the majestic pipe organ, the choir's anthem and the congregation's joyous singing of carols. I don't realize, I feel the powerful presence of God.

Oh happy Christmas in our home! Aunt Vera, Uncle Henry and Freddy have come on the train, from Madison. Aunt Cora, Uncle Gordon, Marilyn and Myrna come from 1150 Vine St. in Beloit. Everyone chatters happily about their Christmas gifts, some wearing new apparel.

Aunt Vera opens a large, round tin of rosettes she has brought. My eyes pop to see such large, thin, crisp cookies in fancy, dimensional shapes. "I make them by dipping a special iron into a thin batter, and then dipping that into hot grease," she says.

Cousins Myrna & Marilyn Singletary.

Mama and Grandma have prepared a feast. A rosy pink ham, mashed potatoes with milk gravy, green beans with bacon and onion, cranberry-orange salad, wheat buns and pickles await the hungry crowd. Mother's spectacular mince and pumpkin pies top off the noon meal.

Marilyn aiming a snowball at Myrna

The adults spend the afternoon visiting. Marilyn, Myrna and I go upstairs to my miniature, hide-a-way bedroom, and play with our dolls. Tiring of that we go outdoors for a breath of fresh air, snap a few pictures and throw a snowball or two.

At supper time, we all come back to the table and overeat for a second time this day. Our day has been one of joy and family festivities. But in many parts of the world, men and boys sacrifice much, suffering and dying in the sickening war that goes on.

Monday evening's paper reveals the war skirmishes of Christmas day. "'Christmas Day Landings End Leyte Battle' American forces set their sights for other Philippine islands today after completing the capture of Leyte, where Gen. Douglas MacArthur said the Japanese lost 113,221 men in their worst military defeat in history.

"'Ninth Air Arm Knocks Out Record Bag Christmas Day' Airmen of the Ninth tactical air force were credited today with one of their greatest bags of the war in Christmas Day strikes at the German spearhead in Belgium, knocking out more than 1,100 vehicles and 35 planes."

* — * — *

Dressed in our best clothes, Daddy drives our family to Aunt Vera's house, on East Mifflin St. in Madison, Wisconsin. Uncle Gordon's family comes from Beloit, and Uncle Ivan's family from Elroy for Thanksgiving 1946. Aunt Vera's home is small, but she sets a table in the basement for the young folks, and thus feeds twenty-two.

Aunt Vera, Uncle Henry and cousin Fred greet us, and

immediately we savor the aroma of the feast. Mama, Grandma, Jackie and the aunts work in the kitchen, and the men visit in the living room. Uncle Henry takes a Bromo-seltzer to fight off one of his many headaches. We kids go to the nicely finished attic room to play.

Fred opens a closet, at the top of the stairs. A black and white cardboard skeleton swings full length, its green eyes looking at us. I wonder if this is what Grandma means, when she says every family has a skeleton in their closet. Fred says it is left from a Halloween party. Occasionally an adult comes upstairs to request we lower the noise.

The pilgrims couldn't have had a greater feast. Golden brown turkey with dressing, mashed potatoes with gravy, apricot-pineapple-jello salad with mayo sauce, relish tray, Aunt Vera's marvelous refrigerator rolls with the yeasty smell, cranberry sauce, Hubbard squash and green peas. We are miserably stuffed. Aunt Vera wants us to clean up the bit left in a serving dish. We can't possibly eat another bite! Of course, we have room for pie.

It is fun seeing Uncle Ivan's family from Elroy that we seldom see. One darling little dark haired girl, and five handsome boys! Uncle Gordon takes a car full of kids to the movie theater, down on the square, near the state capitol. Afterward, we return to Aunt Vera's and gorge ourselves, again, before heading home.

A week before Christmas 1946, Aunt Dorothy and Uncle Leonard drive up from Chicago. Mama opens the large box that Aunt Dorothy brought. It contains pink wintergreen Divinity, Pale green peppermint Divinity, and white vanilla Divinity with nuts in it. There is rich chocolate fudge with nuts, and Uncle Leonard's famous Peanut Butter fudge with nuts. Such Christmas Sugarplums!

Christmas 1948, our family spends the day at Aunt Cora and Uncle Gordon's home. Uncle Gordon prepares a goose in the electric roaster. In the scrumptious feast, Aunt Cora includes her large, tender, Baking Powder Biscuits and home canned pickled peaches. Eating excellence!

Biscuits = 2 cups flour, 4 teaspoons Baking Powder, pinch salt, 3 rounding tablespoons Crisco, 1 cup milk. Cut shortening into dry ingredients, mix in milk. Drop large, egg size, spoon of dough into sauce dish of flour to coat and mold lightly with hands. Place on baking sheet, flatten slightly. Bake at 375.

Pickled Peaches = 1 cup cider vinegar, 1/2 teaspoon cloves, 1 1/2 cups water, 1 teaspoon cinnamon, 2 cups sugar. Bring to boil. Place peaches in syrup and bring to boil. Heat one minute. Put peaches in cans. Pour syrup over peaches. Seal. (As you run out of syrup, make more and add to old.) Can use this on store bought canned peaches. Just drain off their syrup - put this syrup on instead.

Their tree shines bright with colored lights and balls, and is totally covered in fine spun glass Angle Hair. I look at the colorful light shimmering in circles, and wonder what a real angel's hair would be like. Marilyn and Myrna each play Christmas music on the piano for us. Marilyn shows us the figurines she has painted in dainty detail. I wonder where my talent is.

Through the years, we continue to celebrate Thanksgiving and Christmas with family gatherings, festive decorations, delicious food and Christmas eve church service. We miss loved ones that go on to Heaven and rejoice in the family gained through marriage. Savoring traditions, we celebrate!

Chapter 10

Experiencing Beloit and Area Businesses
(1940-1948)

Mama fastens the rhinestone pin at the neckline of her elegant black dress. She picks up the matching earrings, and places one on an ear, screws it down snug, then does the other one. Picking up a pretty pink atomizer bottle from her dresser, she aims it toward her, and squeezes the bulb two or three times. I see the fine mist float through the air and settle upon her. At once, a delightful fragrance teases my nose.

"Mama, you are beautiful," I say. "I love you."

"Thank you, little Patsy; I love you, too," Mama responds. "This hair is a problem though, I need a permanent."

"It looks pretty, Mama, I wish I had curly hair. Where are you going tonight?"

"We are going next door, to the Nicolls' house, for our card club. Dorothy Rosenthal is coming to stay with you, Jackie, Gene and Tommy." Mama slips a rhinestone bracelet around her wrist and fumbles around with the clasp, until finally, it catches. "Okay, Honey, let's go down stairs," she says.

I follow her downstairs. She sits in the living room chair, near a lamp, and thumbs through the evening paper.

"The Arlette Beauty Shop, at 425½ East Grand Avenue in Beloit, has a special on a steam oil permanent wave for $2.00. The ad says, 'we are permanent wave specialists. Our permanents look better and last longer. Every permanent wave guaranteed for six months'," she says.

"Why do they call them permanent if they only last six months?" Daddy interrupts. "They ought to call them impermanents!"

"Oh, Elton, you're goofy," Mama laughs.

"I'm going to jot the Arlette Beauty Shop's phone number down - 318. Patsy, you are nearly five. Would you like a permanent for your birthday?"

That's how I happen to be upstairs, looking through a large window down onto East Grand Avenue. There are people and cars moving about. It is 1940, just a few days before my birthday.

"Come on Patsy, It's your turn," says the beautician.

Mama is in a chair, under a machine. She looks like something from outer space, with an electric cord coming down to each curl. Suddenly, another lady under the same kind of machine yells, "Help, help, this is getting too hot!"

The beautician leaves me and runs to tend the woman. She hurries back, sets a booster seat in the beauty chair, lifts me up, puts a large, green, plasticized apron around me, and pulls me backward. My neck lies in the groove of her beauty parlor sink. I've never laid backward to have my head washed before.

Each strand of hair is pulled through a thick felt pad, before the metal curlers are rolled down. She leads me toward the machine. I have heard of electric chairs. I wonder if this is it? I thought they were for bad people. I haven't been bad. Well, not terribly bad. It gets too hot and I cry out, too. The beautician runs over to adjust it.

"What stinks?" I ask.

"It's the chemicals in the permanent solutions," laughs the beautician. "That's what makes your hair curl. It smells like ammonia."

I think there must be a way that would smell better.

Mama's hair is all combed out now. She looks pretty. Soon my hair is combed. I look in the mirror. "Oh my, is that me?" Now I know why women endure the torture chamber. "Mirror, mirror on the wall, Who is fairest of them all?"

* — * — *

"Are we going to lots of stores, Mama?" I ask. Grandma has one hand and Mama has the other as we walk east on West Grand Avenue, in downtown Beloit.

"I have to stop at Second National Bank a minute," says Grandma. She pulls me toward the door.

Finished with her banking, we continue toward McNeany's on the corner of West Grand Avenue and State Street. A policeman, in a dark blue uniform and cap with a silver badge, strolls his beat. He nods and smiles at us. "Good morning. It's a nice mild day for November," he says.

"Good morning," chorus Mama and Grandma. "I hope it stays this way," adds Mama.

McNeany's showcases

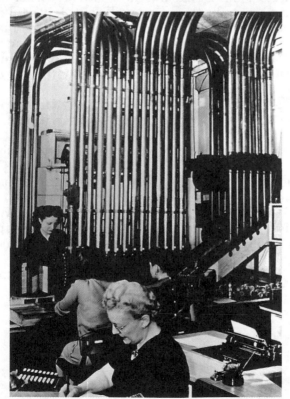

McNeany's tubular vacuum money exchange, second floor office.

From the collection of the Beloit Historical Society.

We turn at the entrance to McNeany's department store. The show cases are filled with beautiful displays of winter clothing. Manikins wear elegant party dresses, and winter skirts and sweaters, for women and girls. Wool shirts decorate the windows with red, blue and green plaid for men and boys. Leather gloves and belts accent the display. "Come in" they say.

These walkways, between the store and the showcases, are often an invitation for youngsters to ride their bicycles in and out, around and around. Sometimes the policemen get after them. One has to be careful not to get hit by a bicycle. As we enter the store, the revolving door frightens me, and I hurry along, close to Mama.

Mama goes to the cosmetic counter. I stare at the woman behind the counter. She has black hair, ruby red lips and long fingernails that match her lips. Impeccably groomed in a black suit with a white blouse, she emits a sweet fragrance. Smiling at me she says, "Where did you get those pretty curls and those dark brown eyes?"

"I had a permanent," I smile back.

Mama selects a Revlon lipstick, and the sales lady writes up a receipt. When Mama gives her the money, she puts it in a tubular container. Twisting it shut, she holds it to a large tube that sucks it up, like a vacuum cleaner sucks up a sock. Soon it comes flying back down with a thud. The lady opens it and gives Mama her change and the receipt. I watch with eyes of wonder.

Grandma suggests that we go around the corner to Murkland's Shoe Store. She sits down and the clerk asks if he can help her.

"I am looking for some house slippers for my husband," she says.

"I have just the thing for you," says the young clerk. "These slippers have a flexible sole for extra comfort. See how they bend?" He bends the slipper backward toe to heel. CRACK! We all jump at the noise. The red faced clerk looks down at the slipper that is broken in half. Grandma can't hold a straight face. She bursts out laughing, and we all laugh.

"I think you better show me something else," Grandma laughs.

Grandpa J.C.F. Singletary in his office.

Climbing on the x-ray machine, I stick my feet in the opening.

"Do you want to see where your toes are, in your shoes?" another clerk asks.

I smile, and he turns the machine on. Looking through the viewer, I see the bones in my feet. They look like a green skeleton. Mama looks, and says, "You are going to need some new shoes soon."

Grandma chooses a pair of slippers for Grandpa. "Let's go over to Ford Hopkins and have some lunch," she says.

We walk back, past McNeany's, and cross to the northwest corner. Entering Ford Hopkins we walk through a long narrow aisle, past drug store supplies, and find a booth. It is a dark atmosphere. The waitress brings water and menus. Grandma and Mama order soup and sandwiches for us. Grandma is visiting with the waitress, who is an acquaintance of hers.

The waitress is talking about the large containers, which the food comes in for the restaurant. "One day I opened a large can of spinach, and right on top were four horse apples."

Mama and Grandma gasp. "My word!" says Grandma. "Someone must have done that deliberately."

"Well, I opened a can of beets once, and when I dumped them in a pan I heard a klunk. I searched through them and discovered a rock!" says Mama.

Grandma pays the bill, and Mama says, "I should stop up to Dad Singletary's office for a minute." We cross the street to the east, enter the Goodwin Building, and take the elevator to the second floor. Grandpa welcomes us to his office. I observe the large old ledgers on the shelf, and Grandpa's big desk.

As we leave, Mama says, "Come for supper tonight, Dad."

Grandma says, "Let's walk up the street a couple of doors to McLellan's dime store." Entering the store, I notice how the extremely narrow floor boards dip and rise, as we walk across them. They creak, too! As we go by the candy counter I ask, "Can I have some candy?"

"May I have some candy?" Mama corrects.

"Me, too!" I squeal. Grandma buys a small, clear, glass train filled with balls of candy. They are the size of BBs, in bright colors. "Thank you, Grandma. Thank you."

"I think we'd better go home, Della. I'm getting pretty tired," Grandma says.

"Yes, I'm tired, too," says Mama.

Well, I'm sure not! I hope they aren't thinking about a nap!

* — * — *

Mama takes the four of us kids and Grandma to Rockford, for a special outing, in the summer of 1941. "Let's go through the

146

Kress Store," says Grandma.

"What's the Kress Store?" asks Tommy.

"It's a dime store," says Mama. "Yes, we will go there."

As we enter the store, I am surprised at its size. It is a huge store. The endless counters are dark wood, about three and a half feet high. Like McLellan's in Beloit, it has extremely narrow, dark boards for flooring, and it creaks when we walk on it. Some counters that I find interesting have bright colored scarves, hairbows, barrettes, jewelry, toys, coloring books and paper dolls. When we come to the candy counter, I smell the chocolate, and see the big, colorful gum drops, orange slices, jelly beans, flat yellow butterscotch discs the size of a quarter, Boston baked beans and malted milk balls inside the glass cages.

One counter is filled with embroidery projects. I see pillow cases, dresser scarves and tea towels that are all stamped with blue line designs for embroidering. Embroidery floss in every color imaginable is neatly lined up in rows. There are envelopes of designs on sheets of paper that can be ironed on your own material, for embroidering. Various size needles and embroidery hoops are here, too. Grandma buys a few pieces, and Mama buys a ball of white crochet thread for crocheting around the edges.

The boys enjoy looking at some model airplanes, wind up cars, military trucks and tanks. There is even a Charlie McCarthy car that races around, tilts up on one end, turns around and goes back again. It is like one the boys have at home.

Everyone has fun looking at the wonderful things available. We decide to go to Bishop's cafeteria on Main Street for lunch. Such a delight to see the beautiful display of colorful and delicious food. But, oh my, what to choose! Mama and Grandma guide us, and waitresses help carry the trays to a round table. A waitress brings me a red balloon man with cardboard feet. A cute bus boy with dark curly hair winks at me, and teases me. I may have to add him to my list of boyfriends, most of whom are married men.

* — * — *

Late spring 1947, Myra Newnham and I settle into a booth in the cafe at Strong's Drug Store, across from the Northwestern depot in Beloit. We chat about our sixth grade class, having been in a new room created in the school basement this year. Myra asks how much school I missed, when I had my appendix out on March tenth. We like the man teacher, but we are glad that school will soon be out for the summer. Our burgers and coke arrive, we chow down and leave.

Having walked across town, and across the bridge, we enter Kresge's 5 and 10 cent store. We wander up one aisle and down the other. I find a small, fat, black book.

147

"Look, Myra; this is a Holy Bible. I don't know much about it, but I want one," I say. I give fifty cents to the girl behind the three and a half foot high, counter. In another aisle, I see some light, aqua blue, hobnail tiny dishes. "These would make good ashtrays," I say. "I'm going to buy them for Mother's Day." I give the girl fifty cents for two of them.

We wander into the other side of the store. I am wearing my Girl Scout uniform, because there is a special function late this afternoon.

"Oh look, there's a booth for taking pictures. Let's have our pictures taken," says Myra.

When I get home with the pictures, Daddy is pleased with them. He sends Mother and me to town, later, to have enlargements and colored ones made.

* — * — *

In March 1948, Grandma, Mother and I go shopping in Beloit. Grandma is going to buy me a new dress for Easter. We go into Three Sisters dress shop. I pause in the entrance to look at the pink marble like entry. It has a large, gray circle about four feet across, and in the center, in black is the silhouette profile of three women. I think this is quite classy! Unfortunately, after looking at many pretty dresses, we haven't found the right combination of material, color, print, size and price.

We aren't ready to give up, yet, and we enter J. C. Penney's. As we look around the main floor at various things, Grandma remembers she wants a piece of material for a pillow cover. The material is at the back of the store. Browsing through the various bolts of material, she finds a pretty gold color, and has the sales clerk measure and cut it. She chooses thread to match, and gives the clerk her money. The clerk closes the bill and money into a tiny metal cage and fastens it to a wire.

I watch as the miniature, car like, container travels over the wire, rounds a bend and goes upstairs. All over the store they travel along on different wires. Like a gigantic, mechanical game in action, these little cars do business all day. Soon the tiny metal cage makes its way back down the wire to the counter, and the clerk removes Grandma's receipt and change.

Mother decides to look for some work socks for Dad, so we all head down the creaky basement stairs. Reaching the bottom, we can't believe our eyes. A clerk, in rubber boots, says, "If you tell me what you want, I'll try to find it for you." She stands in six inches or more of water. High water from the river behind the store seeps into the basement. The clerks wade around with rubber boots on. They walk through the water creating waves like a lake. Mama purchases the socks from the stair steps, where we stand above the water.

We climb the stairs away from the water, then go up another flight of creaky, stairs to the dress department. The clerks are friendly and we chat with them, but we don't find a dress. I see a red felt hat with a brim and black band. I try it on, admiring myself in a mirror. Grandma says, "The hat looks cute on you. I'll get the hat, and maybe we can find a dress in the catalog."

Mother wants to go to McNeany's, so we cross the street. Inside, we take the elevator to the second floor to women's lingerie. Corsets and brassieres fill the counters. They take things serious in this foundation department. Specialists sponsor showings for women on certain evenings. One should be correctly fitted for foundation garments. The garments have metal stays and some have lacings. I think of Aunt Dorothy, who is a large woman, but she never looks sloppy. She says, "proper ladies wear proper foundation garments under their good dresses."

Mother purchases what she came for and our shopping excursion is over for today. Grandma is right. We find a dress in the Montgomery Ward catalog. It is grey with red flowers to go with the hat.

* — * — *

In August 1948, a group of ladies in our friend and family circle goes to the world famous Wagon Wheel Lodge in Rockton, Illinois for a lunch celebration. This is a rustic lodge filled with antique displays, and massive fireplaces. We like the Trophy Room, with the huge, live tree growing up through the roof. The red and white check table cloths accent the rustic setting. Many people enjoy the Garden and the Martha Washington rooms. Various movie stars and celebrities often visit here.

Our group includes Dad's sister - Aunt Vera Seils from Madison, Grandma, Jackie and myself, plus the August birthday celebrants. Those with August birthdays are Mother, her cousin

Madeline Ennis, Aunt Dorothy Wessell and neighbor friend - Erla Nicolls.

The waitresses wear long, heavily starched colonial dresses in soft pink, green, yellow or blue. Most of us order the chicken salad for which the Wheel is famous. Delicious, little, hot cinnamon rolls are included. We choose different desserts, but several of us order Schaum Torte. It's a delightful baked meringue with strawberries and whip cream. If the meringue isn't made just right, and weather can affect it, they get tough and become difficult to eat.

The minute Aunt Vera touches the torte with her fork it jumps off her plate, into her lap. "Oh my!" she exclaims. With a red face, she tries putting it back on her plate. Everyone laughs. Luckily it landed in the cloth napkin. For years she will talk about the time she plopped the torte into her lap!

Chapter 11
Maintaining Our Home
(1940-1948)

Daddy gives specific chores to Gene and Tommy. The reel type hand mower is kept sharpened, and they mow our 2 1/2 city lots. On Saturdays they push the big, old, iron wheelbarrow, full of tin cans and trash, down the road two blocks to Zemples. They live high above the Rock River, and have a place they are trying to fill. Sometimes I go along. The boys don't always like a nearly five-year-old sister tagging along, but occasionally they are charitable. The iron rim of the wheel makes a loud noise as we hurry along. When they give me a ride home, it bumps and jiggles my insides, but it is fun.

When the days turn crisp and the elms and maples scatter their yellow, green and brown leaves over our yard, it is time to rake. Gene gets out some ropes and the boys turn their work into playtime. They rake long rows of leaves. Gene hitches Tommy to the wheelbarrow as a horse. The boys spend the day toting leaves to the pile, out in the back yard, where they burn them. "Giddy-up. Let's go'" says Gene as they trudge along with their load of leaves.

"Whoa - whoa!" Tommy whinnies, kicks up his heels, and off they go again. By supper time the horse and farmer are glad to trot into the house where Mama's delicious supper is waiting.

Mama is upset with Daddy because he has a habit of going into the living room and sitting in the dark. "Elton, for Pete's sake turn on some lights," she scolds. I think this is Daddy's way of relaxing while the kitchen work is being done. Soon the hustle and bustle of the family joins him.

On cleaning day I crawl around underneath the dining room table and dust the ornate legs and cross bars for Mama. She polishes and vacuums. Today she tugs at the living room furniture and pushes it into new places. "It looks pretty, Mama," I say. I look at her tall glass lamp filled with colored sand. It sits on a table that is now where the big overstuffed chair used to be. I hear thirteen year old Jackie out in the hall, working her way down the stairway, with a dustmop. Many hands make light work, and soon we're done.

In the kitchen, Jackie, Gene and Tommy fight their way through the dishes. I am coloring in a book at the dining room table. Mama comes in the back door from having taken some garbage out. Suddenly, there is a terrible crash with the sound of breaking glass, followed by a string of loud cuss words. Like

151

popcorn bursting out of a kettle, we all dash to the living room. The room is dark. Mama turns on a light and there sits Daddy on the floor with the table knocked over, and Mama's sand lamp broken all over the floor. He is sitting where his chair used to be! We kids are a bit frightened, but Mama bursts into laughter, and then we all feel safe to laugh. Daddy is not very happy as he tries to clean up the mess. Mama helps. This ends Daddy's sitting down in the living room in the dark.

* — * — *

In 1940, Jackie - 12, Gene - 10 and Tommy - 8, are responsible for doing the dishes, and cleaning up the kitchen. They do not work well together. When supper is finished, Tommy has a habit of running to the bathroom. "He's doing his disappearing act again," laments Gene. "We'll get him when he comes down. It's my turn to wash the dishes tonight."

"I don't think so. You don't do a very good job of washing. You better let me wash and you dry," commands Jackie.

"No! It's my turn to wash!" wails Gene.

The dishes are all scraped and stacked up before Tommy gets back to the kitchen. Gene gives him a shove toward the corner of the kitchen. "Where have you been? You always disappear when its time to do the dishes!"

"Let me out. I had to go to the bathroom," cries Tommy.

Gene grabs the meat fork and brandishes it toward Tommy. Jackie reinforces the ranks to hold the scared little rabbit in the corner.

"Are you going to be here when it's time to do the dishes next time?" asks Jackie.

"I had to go to the bathroom," whimpers Tommy.

"You heard her. Are you going to be here when it's time to do the dishes next time?" demands Gene. He gives Tommy a little poke with the meat fork.

At age 4, this scene frightens me as I watch from the doorway. "I am going to tell Mama," I cry.

"You'd better not," yells Gene. "Are you gonna be here next time, Tommy?"

"Yes. Yes, I'll be here," squirms Tommy.

Jackie and Gene let Tommy out of the corner. I hug him around the waist.

The next day is Saturday, and Jackie, Gene and Tommy are again fussing about the routine of doing dishes. Mama and Daddy are outside.

"Gene, you washed dishes last night. It is my turn to wash them this noon," Jackie exclaims.

"You have washed them more than once in a row. I'm going to wash them now," Gene states.

152

"Then get them clean!" Jackie yells.

Tommy is there with a dish towel waiting for a dish. "I've got to go to the bathroom," he says. He darts out of the kitchen, through the dining room and up the stairs.

"You brat. Get back here!" yells Gene. He goes to the doorway, then he sees Jackie heading toward the dish water and runs back to the sink. "I'm washing," he states. Giving her a shove out of the way, he washes a few plates and puts them in the drainer.

Jackie looks at them and yells, "You stupid dope. You aren't getting them clean and you haven't even wiped a place off, on the table, where I can set the dishes." She grabs at the dish cloth in his hand. He tugs at it and they wrestle around. Finally Jackie gets the dish cloth and wads it up in a knot. With all her might, she throws it at him. He ducks. CRASH! There is the sound of breaking glass as the dish rag sails through the kitchen window.

Within a minute Daddy is standing in the kitchen. "What do you think you're doing? Why can't you work together to accomplish your responsibilities? Can't we ever depend on you? Now you can both work to pay for the window. And don't ever let this happen again or you will get the tar knocked out of you!"

* — * — *

I look to make sure no one is around upstairs or down; then I lie over the varnished stair rail and slide to the bottom. I open the hallway door and gasp. The dining room is empty except for the large table and buffet. Someone has covered them with an old white sheet.

Mama calls from the kitchen, "Come on, Patsy. Your breakfast is ready."

"Mama, what happened to the dining room?" I ask.

"Well, Honey, we are going to take the wallpaper off the dining room, and put some pretty new paper on."

Mama carries pails of warm water to the dining room. Daddy brings stepladders in from the back shed. They start soaking the old wallpaper by dipping rags in the water and rubbing them on the walls. They keep doing this for a long time.

After breakfast, I wander around in the dining room. For years the old ladders have been spattered with different colors of paint and now I am curious to see if I can climb one.

"Patsy, get away from that ladder," scolds Daddy.

Mama and Daddy scrape the walls with spatula-like tools. Wall paper crinkles up in rippled ribbon like strips as the tools scrape through to the bare wall. The room feels warm and steamy. I try pulling some paper off, and it is fun to see how long a strip I can get before it breaks. It begins to smell funny, like musty paste. As I walk around, bits of paper stick to my shoes. The room sounds hollow and our voices seem to bounce off the walls.

153

As the paper comes off and exposes the bare walls, I can hardly believe my eyes. The room looks like a blackboard jungle.

Mama stands back and looks about the room. "I can't believe anyone could be stupid enough to put such a color paint on the walls. Every room in this house was painted with this junk when we bought the place," says Mama, in disgust. The dining room walls are such a dark gray; they look black.

Eventually Mama and Daddy clean up the mess and scrub the walls. Then Daddy lays a narrow board down on one edge of the table and on top of that, he rolls out a lead cutting strip. After a great deal of measuring and marking, he takes the handle of a tool with a sharp, round disk on the end. He presses it firmly, rolling it across the paper to cut it.

It is fun to watch him dip a wide brush into a bowl of something that looks like white gravy. He calls it wallpaper paste. Slopping it on the back of the paper, he brushes it every which way. When it is well coated with paste, he laps it over with two pasted sides together.

With it ready to hang, he climbs the ladder and starts pressing it on the wall up near the wood molding. Mama helps him maneuver it, and after a bit it sticks to the wall. He takes a brush nearly a foot long and brushes it this way and that. The pale salmon paper has pretty white and pale blue designs.

Sometimes things don't go well and Daddy gets pretty upset. He says some funny words I don't understand.

"Patsy, it's a beautiful day. I think you might like to play outdoors awhile. Jimmy is playing in his sandbox next door. You can play with him until lunch time," says Mama.

It is fun watching the wall papering project, but Mama has that, `I mean now' tone in her voice.

I go out to play with Jimmy.

A few days after the wall papering is done, Mama decides to wash the sheer curtains for the dining room. She gets out some funny looking strips of wood that are full of pins.

"What are those, Mama?" I ask.

"It is the curtain stretchers," she answers.

She measures the curtains, then adjusts the strips of wood to the right measurements marked on them. She tightens the sticks in place with a wing nut, and leans the stretchers against the back porch railing.

She has washed the curtains by hand, and now carries them out in a metal dishpan. Looping part of the length of curtain over her arm, she starts putting a corner of the curtain on a corner of the stretcher. She works carefully pushing the curtain onto the sharp pins.

Occasionally she cries, "Ouch!" as she pricks her fingers on

154

the pins. If she gets blood on her clean curtain, she says some strange words. I think maybe it's a foreign language!

When the curtains are dry, she pulls them off the stretchers. In the house, she threads them back on the curtain rods. Climbing up on a dining room chair, she puts the rods up, and the curtains look white, and crisp. The dining room looks fresh and pretty.

Mama and Daddy wall paper the living room, too. They carry the carpet outdoors and drape it over two clothes lines. With a long handled, flat, wire carpet beater they whack the dirt out of it, while they try to stay out of the cloud of dust.

* — * — *

Along with the war effort Daddy saves and collects scrap iron. When he has a wheelbarrow full he wheels it about two miles to Lerner's junk yard, across the river, at the east end of South Beloit. The boys often go with him.

In summer 1945, Jackie has just graduated from high school, and is working for Dr. Gunderson. Gene and Tom are teenagers and I am nine. With seven of us in the house, wash day means hard work. The old wringer washer is swishing back and forth, back and forth. I smell the La Franz bluing and the Oxydol soap powder in the blue, sudsy water. The two, large rinse tubs sit on the table in back of the machine. I smell the bleach in one tub. Before we came down stairs, Mama broke off a couple chunks of Argo starch and cooked it in a sauce pan of water. Now she pours it in a metal dishpan with warm water. When aprons, house dresses and Daddy's shirts have been rinsed she dips them in the starch and wrings them out by hand. She is careful to dip only Daddy's shirt collars, because he doesn't like stiff shirts.

Mama carries many baskets full of heavy, wet, clothes up the cellar stairs, out the side door, and around the house to the south yard. She goes to the back shed and brings out coils of rope and a bag of clothespins. Putting a rope loop over a hook by the kitchen window, she goes to the large maple tree, several feet away, and winds the rope around the tree. Stretching as high as she can reach on her tip toes, she pulls the rope tight. She continues to go from hooks on the house, to trees and posts in the yard, until the entire side yard is like a huge spider web of clothesline. With the weight of the clothes, the lines begin to sag. Then she gets the wooden props out of the garage and hikes the lines up in the middle.

"It's hot," Mama says, mopping her brow.

I am not too warm, but I know that Mama is working hard. The batch of overalls is especially heavy, and throw rugs worse yet.

Mama calls her neighbor friend, Delores Milner. "Are you

155

using all of your lines, today, Delores?"

"No. Help yourself, Della," she answers.

So Mama carries a basketful across the back yard and fills the rest of Delores's lines. When the last item is hung, she goes to the cellar again and empties the washing machine and rinse tubs, and sweeps the last of the water down the floor drain. Throughout the day she checks the clothes, as they dry she folds them and carries the baskets back in the house.

"Dang those stupid birds!" Mama exclaims. "Look at this nice clean sheet."

I look at the long purple streak on the white sheet. "Poor Mama, those birds are naughty," I say.

Mama spreads the huge mound of clothes, which needs ironing, out on the kitchen table. Using a ketchup bottle, with sprinkler top, she sprinkles the clothes and rolls them up tight. She heaps a basket full. Grandma helps with the endless ironing, and she prepares much of our supper on washday. Mama works so hard!

Remnant of washday. Tommy, Jackie, Gene & Patsy.

* — * — *

"Are you making your soft, fat sugar cookies?" I ask.

"Yes, Honey. I think this cold fall day is a good time to light the oven and bake some treats," Grandma answers.

"You put lots of margarine in them don't you, Grandma? Do you remember when you had to mix the little packet of orange powder into the margarine to color it?"

"I surely do! What a nuisance that was! Then margarine came in a plastic bag with an orange color capsule in it. We had to pinch the capsule to break it, then knead the oleo until it was colored," Grandma responds. "The oleo and buttermilk makes the cookies so good. Your Dad works hard, and he likes these cookies because they aren't so sweet, so I'll make some for him."

"Why can't they buy margarine in Wisconsin?" I ask.

"Because it is a dairy state and the farmers want people to buy butter," says Grandma. "The people of Wisconsin come to Illinois to buy oleo. This really helps the neighborhood grocery stores to do a great business."

* — * — *

It is a mid winter night, when I am thirteen. It has been snowing all afternoon. Dad and I are all bundled up in warm clothing, ready to shovel sidewalks. Dad has made a pusher with a three foot long two by four, mounted on an old shovel handle. He starts pushing snow out of the driveway.

I go to the east end of our sidewalk on Illinois Street and shovel toward Eighth Street. A corner property makes a lot of sidewalks to shovel. I work my way several feet down the walk throwing great mounds of snow onto the terrace and lawn.

Stopping for a rest, I am struck by the beauty of the night. Looking toward the street light on the corner, I see large, fluffy, white flakes floating toward the ground. The snow has transformed everything into rounded mounds, with a mantle of white. Smoke rises in wispy clouds from chimneys of homes around the neighborhood. Warm, inviting lights glow through most of the windows. Toward Beloit's business district the sky glows red from the lights. It is so quiet I can almost hear it snowing. It isn't cold; I am even steamy inside my warm coat. Oh little town of South Beloit, how still you are tonight. The quiet is broken by an occasional scrape of metal shovel on cement, as neighbors begin to shovel here and there.

I continue to shovel. The terrace now has a high bank of snow. In the morning school children will try to walk on the high banks, as I did when I was younger. They will knock mounds of snow onto the clean sidewalks, and Dad will get upset, as he has for years. Dad has finished the drive and starts the little walk around the house, as I head around the corner on South Eighth Street.

Finally, we finish the walks, the paths to the garbage can and burner, and we are tired, yet happy to be a part of God's winter

157

creation. We clean off our shovels and stomp the snow from our boots. We brush the snow off our clothes. It has stopped snowing. Just as we head up the steps to the back porch, we hear a familiar sound. "Oh no!" moans Dad. The snow plow sails by, leaving mounds of heavy snow in the end of the driveway and throwing some back on the side walks!

* — * — *

Before bedtime, Dad goes to the basement, as he has every winter night for years. He shovels big chunks of coal into the furnace, and banks it for the night. Beside the big furnace, sits what looks like a baby furnace. It is a coal furnace that heats the water. He takes a small hand shovel and feeds the mouth of that furnace with coal small enough to go through the opening.

In the morning, he will come down and do the same thing before he goes to work. Mother will feed it during the day. I have come to the basement after something, and follow Dad up the stairs.

"You make me think of Gene when he was a little tyke," Dad says. "He used to follow me down in the cellar. I would get up the stairs before he did, and I'd turn the light off. I'd say, `Where are you, Gene?' and he'd answer, `I'm down sutty in da gark.'"

"He used to say lots of funny things when he was small," I say. "Mother tells about the time she got after him for something outdoors. She sent him in the house. When she came through the kitchen doorway into the dining room, Gene was standing there with his fists up like a boxer. He said, `Do you want to make something of it?'"

Dad laughs, "Yeah, and your mother couldn't keep from laughing. He used to be afraid of dogs, too. We went on a picnic at Stores Lake once. There was a St. Bernard there, and we couldn't get Gene out of the car."

"Are you two telling stories?" asks Mother, as we come upstairs laughing. She is in the kitchen packing Dad's lunch.

Man works from sun to sun; woman's work is never done!

Chapter 12
Play Daze
(1940-1950)

Spring 1938 - Patsy with neighbor friend Jimmy Nicolls

Patsy - "umm, the flowers smell nice"

Our quiet neighborhood rambles into blocks of two story homes with a sprinkling of bungalows. Huge sprawling American elms and maple trees shade the manicured lawns. Spring 1940 is bursting out all over; the scent of lilacs teases our noses. Daddy's tulips make splashes of red and yellow, near the orange Oriental poppies in his long, narrow flower beds. Twelve year old Jackie takes my hand and guides me across the green side lawn. She carries her doll in the other arm. We are going to visit Jackie's girlfriend, Geraldine Wanninger, who lives two blocks southwest of us. We will play in her neat playhouse at the back of their garage.

"I hear horses coming," I say. We look up the sidewalk and see Gene and Tommy clomping toward us. They each have tall, tin cans strapped to their feet, like stilts. Clippity clop, clippity clop, they trot by us, enjoying the spring day.

* __ * __ *

On a glorious sunny summer day 1942, Margie and I kneel, breathless at the edge of the magnificent swimming pool. Sap-

159

phire blue water laps the shores of the circular basin. A variety of leafy green foliage, in various shades, grows around the edge and an outcropping of jagged rocks form the eastern slope. One area is a manicured lawn. Here lovely maidens stroll about. Their long flowing gowns of rosy pink, fuchsia and white are exquisite.

"Where is he? Is he ready?" I ask.

"He'll appear soon," Margie answers.

We catch our breath, when suddenly the sleek athlete appears on the high diving board, in his iridescent green and brown diving suit. He pauses momentarily in unique form, then with a superb jump he goes up - up - up. As though by magic, he spreads filigree wings as he soars beyond the pool.

We are in awe of Mr. Grasshopper and the Hollyhock maidens. Margie's mother's La Franz laundry blueing creates the lovely sapphire blue water in the white enameled wash basin.

We must hurry to catch more performers for our water show. Grasshoppers do swim, don't they?

* — * — *

The robins have left for the south lands. What was the spectacular dress of fall, now lies on the ground, like clothes carelessly dropped on the floor after a dance. The trees stand bare bracing themselves for the onslaught of winter, waiting to be dressed in fluffy white coats.

Neighbor friends - Patsy, Jimmy Nicolls and Margie Milner

But this day is a reprieve from the torment of winter that is a threat around the corner. Today the sun plays hide and seek with fluffy clouds that float overhead in a subdued blue grey sky. The air is crisp, like a bite into a rosy red apple newly harvested. A perfect playday for the neighborhood children gathered in our side yard.

It doesn't take Margie, Jimmy and I long to gather mounds of

160

leaves with our rakes. We run and jump into the mounds, flop around and send leaf children dancing into the air. We laugh and shout with the exuberance and freedom of children. The leaves provide manna for our activities.

"I know what let's do," I announce. "Let's make a big house of leaves and then we can play house."

"Good idea," says Jimmy. "Let's build it in your big, side yard between your house and mine."

"Okay. You can be the father, I'll be the mother and Margie can be our little girl," I agree.

"Yeah," adds Jimmy.

"Why do I always have to be the child?" asks Margie.

"Because you are the littlest," I say, with a note of finality. "We need to make long lines of leaves into squares and rectangles so we can make the kitchen, living room, dining room and bedrooms."

"We can make the living room bigger," says Margie.

"Yes, and don't forget to leave openings for the doorways," I add.

We work busily with our rakes to create a leafhouse, not unlike a modern floor plan which none of us has ever seen.

Mama has taken a package to the garbage can, and walks over to our leaf house. "Hi, Margie. How's your gizzard?" Margie giggles and answers, "Okay." She knows Mama will always tease her with that question. "Have fun kids," she adds, heading for the house.

Like little beavers we prepare our home and play house while the air grows cooler. The hours slip away like the birds going south. The sun is lowering toward the western sky. We hear the first call coming from the brick Dutch colonial home that sets in back of Jimmy's back yard.

"Margie, time to come in now," Mrs. Milner calls.

Hardly before she is done calling, Mrs. Nicolls steps out the back door on the south side of the house Jimmy calls home.

"Come on, Son. Time to get ready for supper," she calls.

I hurry to put the rakes in our garage and enter our back door to the warmth and good smells of Mama's cooking.

* — * — *

Early one sunny summer day in 1943, I finish my breakfast and hear someone calling for me.

"Patsy, Pat-t-t-sy," calls Jimmy. He stands at the foot of our back steps with his wagon.

I open the door and say, "Hi, Jimmy, I'm glad you brought your wagon. Let's pretend it's a boat and the sidewalks are rivers."

"Okay, let's find some heavy sticks to use for oars," he says.

He pulls the wagon down to the public sidewalk and climbs in. Going to Daddy's small pile of branches beside the garage, I find two sturdy sticks, about our height, for oars. I pick out two that are longer and skinnier for our fishing poles, take them to our "boat" and climb in.

Such a lovely day for a trip down the river. It's warm and difficult navigating our boat on such a long river. The turbulent water makes it difficult to keep from getting tipped over. We can't go too close to shore because we can see bears prowling around, and we don't have our guns with us. Coming to a calmer area, we decide to throw out our anchor and fish. The fish are biting, and we soon have a stringer full. When a big one hits on Jimmy's pole, we nearly tip over trying to land it.

"Jimmy, sit still. You are going to tip the boat over," I cry. "And watch what you are doing with your fishing pole. You nearly poked my eye out."

"Let's pull up the anchor and move down the river," Jimmy suggests.

In a short distance we encounter a rapids. The boat starts rocking violently and we are nearly pitched into the water. "Paddle hard," I scream.

"We aren't going to make it," yells Jimmy.

But we do, and we finally come to a beautiful spot where we can go up on the bank and cook our dinner. We just get our boat unloaded when we hear Jimmy's mom ringing the hand bell, calling him to lunch.

After lunch I stand calling at his back door. He comes out and we head to the sandbox in back of his house. "Let's make some sand pies," I suggest.

"I'll get some water from the bucket by the faucet," he says.

We mix water with the sand and pack it in little tins. Dumping them on the board at the edge of the sandbox, I sprinkle the tops with dry sand, like sugar. "We have some very good-looking cakes, Jimmy. Do you want to eat my cakes?" I ask.

With a mischievous look, all his own, Jimmy picks up one of my little sand cakes, takes a bite, and starts chewing. Then he coughs, spits and runs in the house for a drink. I hear some loud words and know he's in trouble with his mom. I guess it's time to go home awhile.

* — * — *

At fifteen, Jackie often goes to call on her girlfriends. Though I am only seven, she takes me along. Jackie never considers me a tag-a-long, but enjoys a motherly role with me. I especially like to go to her friend, Corrine Strand's home, a block away, on Shirland Avenue. Her mother speaks with a strong Norwegian accent. She welcomes us with her pleasing smile. In the same area we visit Ruthie Riley and Elsie Blotter.

Returning home we find Gene sitting on a high stool on the back porch with a cloth draped around him. With a comb Daddy lifts his hair up and goes snip, snip, snip with the scissors. He takes the hand clippers and squeezes them repeatedly as he glides them up the back of his neck. As he finishes, he takes a soft bristled baby hairbrush and whisks the loose hair away from his ears and neck. Then he removes the cloth wrap.

"Come on, Tommy. It's your turn for a haircut. It's too hot in the house, so we'll have our Barber Shop on the back porch," calls Daddy.

I remember how I hated to have Daddy cut my hair straight around. I'm glad Mama lets me have permanents now.

Because my siblings are four, six, and eight years older than I am, they are often off playing with their own friends. Some days I play in the house alone. I never have trouble entertaining myself, and have a few unique pastimes.

I enjoy playing marbles, and sometimes play in the living room. Making a large circle on the floor with a piece of string, I scatter marbles in the center. With my large shooter, tucked between my thumb and index finger, I snap the marble out trying to knock a marble out of the ring. Marble games are a popular sport through our grade school days. Two Turman brothers win national marble championships in different years. They bring honor to Riverview School, and we are all proud of them.

We learn to be gamblers at a tender age, by playing "Pot," which is a marble game played for keeps. Fights often arise when the kids disagree on who really wins the pot of marbles. A fight among our friends is seldom just verbal, so we usually end up in trouble with our parents, also.

I have a cloth bag of deep blue, clay marbles that had been my father's about 1908. They are smaller than our glass marbles, and are irregular in shape. They are not only unique in character, but also in the imaginative way I play with them. I line the marbles up on the floor in the order of a classroom full of desks. Each marble becomes a student with its own name. You would be amazed at all the things I teach these students! Some get an airplane ride in a glass ashtray.

Eventually the marbles will be lost, along with all of the empty hours that can be filled with such contented fantasy.

* — * — *

The Old West is a cultivated part of our heritage in 1943, and is portrayed on radio programs and at the movie houses. Who wouldn't want a splendid horse like that of Roy Rogers or Gene Autry? Actually, I am quite privileged. I have only to hike about a block to ride the most magnificent steed. There is a matched

163

pair of steeds owned by our Swedish neighbors. I am fortunate enough to be a friend of their youngest daughter, Alice.

It is no easy chore to mount either of these massive creatures. Just to get them bridled and saddled up is a feat nearly impossible for us. Sometimes we fall, trying to get mounted, but it is all so exciting that we endure the abrasions for the thrill of the ride!

Once mounted, it is hang on for dear life! These beasts can go like the wind and we have to cling low to stay in the saddle. It is the most exhilarating experience a youngster can hope to encounter. Over the plains and up the slopes we race until the horses are heaving and snorting. We often have to bring them home more slowly, for we know we must not abuse them.

Each time we take them out we encounter new adventures. Sometimes bandits chase us, but we are too fast for them. We see lots of wild animals, and sometimes we stop to talk to other range hands. Often we strap on our guns, because we never know what kind of situation we might encounter. At the end of the day we are tired, but happy. When we climb down from the huge cement porch stair rails, we feel bow legged and just as wobbly as though we had ridden a real horse.

Patsy & neighbor friend Alice Anderson (six years old)

For diversion, we go to their back yard and hitch two saw horses up to their big old farm wagon. We spend hours riding the range. "Giddy yap," I say. When it's my turn to drive the team, I sit in the wagon seat and snap the reins. I make the horses move out at a good clip. "Whoa whoa," I call out. We have to stop for supplies, and sometimes we give people a ride to the next town.

* _ * _ *

I curiously look toward 110 South Eighth Street as men carry furniture in from the moving van, in late summer of 1944. Soon I discover that a couple in their thirties, Monte and Hilda Kissling, are the new owners. Their darling, seven year old, blond daughter, Barbara, is one year and eight months younger

164

than I am. Barbara and I will eventually develop a friendship bonding us like sisters. Across the street to the west and three houses north, new neighbors will bring new adventures to my life.

One of our first adventures happens behind Barbara's house. Neither of us has ever climbed a tree before. My beloved maple tree, at home, is much too large for me to climb, but there are some fruit trees in Barbara's back yard that beckon to us. My maple tree is too large, here is one apple tree that is too small, but this cherry tree is just right. The limbs are low enough that we can pull ourselves up, use the limbs as steps and work our way out along one of the largest, sturdiest limbs. We both perch on the limb, and discover that it makes an excellent spring ride. The limb swings and sways, as the leaves dance with adventure around us.

"Patsy, this is fun!" Barbie squeals.

"It's like riding the red Mobil horse that has wings," I agree. We bounce and fly up and down, back and forth, giggling and laughing in excited delight.

Suddenly, there is a loud crack, like a rifle being fired, and Barbie and I fly through the air. Abruptly we have been bucked off our flying horse. The great, rock-ribbed horse lies dead at our feet, its flailing limbs subdued. We look at each other in shock, the scope of what we have done begins to register. A car rolls into the driveway and Barbie's Dad gets out. Such timing! Immediately, we know he is not happy.

"What have you been doing in that tree? Now, look what you have done! You have broken half the tree down. That would have produced a lot of good cherries. You stay out of those trees!" The tone of his voice reflects his anger at us.

We look at each other, wondering how such happy fun could end in such a catastrophe. I am afraid I may never be welcome to come back. We brush ourselves off, and rub our bruises. Well, all adventures have an element of risk.

Forgiveness is such a beautiful gift! I am welcomed back, with no grudges held against me. Barbie's house is a gathering place for the neighborhood girls. The back shed-like porch provides us a great playroom. Mrs. Kissling donates several nice dresses and high heel shoes. We dress to the nines, and attend lavish affairs. We dine in elegance and dance in the moonlight. On an ordinary day we do our housework, send our children out to play, and scold them when they are naughty. Sometimes we expand our play area to the two car garage.

Mrs. Kissling buys a hammock and hangs it between two of the fruit trees. We have a fabulous time swinging together in the hammock. It is a challenge to get in and out of it, without getting in the squashed apples that lie on the ground underneath it.

Sometimes there are a few little doggie doodles, besides the apples to avoid. Barbie has a small, short haired, tan and white dog, called Tiny. Often Tiny plays with us, dancing around and nipping at our heels. One day the little dog comes racing out the back door. Excited to see all the kids, it runs some wide circles and races out front, right into the road. To our horror, a car is coming, and we watch as Tiny is killed. "Oh! No! No! No!" Barbie cries. We all cry, as Mrs. Kissling gathers Tiny up in a cloth. We will all miss the little dog.

School days call the neighbor kids to walk together the four or five blocks to school. We hurry home at four o'clock, and play for a short time before supper. Sometimes we spread out on South Eighth Street for a ball game called "Peggy Move Up." If we don't move out of the street fast enough, when a car comes along, we receive a tongue lashing.

We are playing Jacks on the front sidewalk, in front of Barbie's house, when Mildred comes toward us. Barbie jumps up and says, "Come on, Patsy. Run! Hurry!"

"Don't be frightened, Barbie," I say.

Mildred is very old, probably in her thirties. Her brown hair is cut short, and is straight, like many little girls of this era. She wears cotton house dresses, and a sweater, if it's cooler. When we encounter her, it is because she is on her way to one of the neighborhood stores. Either Patrick's on South Eighth Street or Field's on Shirland Ave. Mildred is mentally ill. Mama says, it is a sad thing, but tells us to just leave her alone and avoid her.

She often goes to the store for a large cardboard box. We never know what she does with them, but that is what she goes after. If we should smile, or say, "Hi, Mildred," she gets upset. She turns around, bends over, and flips her dress up, and sticks her bloomered bottom out at us. Sometimes she fingers her nose at us, and tries to chase us. I am not afraid of her, but I heed Barbie's command, and we go to the back yard.

* — * — *

The summer of 1945 holds major fears for parents. The polio epidemic is rampant. Mama tries to keep us from becoming overheated. From July first to August twentieth, 153 cases of infantile paralysis are admitted to the county hospital in Rockford. It is believed that the polio virus is carried by the common house fly. Our dear friend, Barbie, has been ill since June, because of fears of the unknown, all of the neighborhood children abandon her.

* — * — *

I am ten years old when I run across the street and stand on the sidewalk in front of the house, calling, "Bertha, Berr tha."

Bertha Busker is a year older than I am, and taller. She is slender with brown hair, about the same color as mine, blue eyes, and has a cheery disposition. She opens the front door. "Hi, Pat. Come on in," she calls out. "Oh, good, you brought your paper dolls. Let's play here on the stairway," she says, indicating the stairway, leading to the second floor, which is just inside the front door.

She selects the top half of the stairs with the landing and I begin setting up house on the lower section. The stairs work fine; we can use a different step for each room. The bedrooms have lovely, full color bedroom suites recently cut from Sears or Montgomery Ward catalogs. Each room has the latest 1946 furnishings.

Each member of the paper doll family has the latest fashion wardrobe and each child has an assortment of toys. Most of the morning our doll families interact with one another going to school, parties, dancing, work and maintaining their homes. Of course, they find the need to change clothes often and romance flourishes. Occasionally, Mrs. Busker has a need to go upstairs and she picks her way gingerly up the stairs, being careful not to disturb our setup.

All of a sudden Bertha announces, "I'm tired of playing this. Let's go up to my bedroom."

"Okay," I answer.

We carefully stack the dolls and accessories into organized piles and place them into our boxes.

I follow Bertha up the stairs to her room. She rummages through a stack of magazines and school papers. She spies a flat box and says, "Oh, Pat. I've got to show you what I found in the attic the other day when I was searching for a book."

"You mean the attic behind that little door?" I ask, pointing to a white door of wanes coating, about two feet wide and three feet high.

"Yes. That's where I found this neat paper doll. I don't even remember her. She's really different. I didn't even know I had her. I don't know where she came from. I just love her," Bertha says. She opens the box and takes out a larger than usual paper doll of a young girl. The doll is of sturdy stock over an eighth inch thick, about ten inches tall with pretty life-like colors and coated with a glossy finish. She has a variety of fashionable paper clothes.

My mouth opens with a gasp. I can't believe what is happening. This is my doll! Grandma Wessell bought her for me when we went to Chicago together early last summer. I have been looking for her for weeks. I couldn't figure out what I had done with her. Bertha and I play together at each other's house often. I must have left her here and didn't miss her right away. Eventually she got carried to the attic with other things during a tidy-up time. I stare in disbelief.

"She's . . . pretty," I stammer.

I want to claim her. She's a special treasure from Grandma. This isn't right. I feel like crying. Bertha is so thrilled with the doll; I just can't tell her she is mine.

"We'll play with her sometime," Bertha says.

I bite my lip and swallow.

"Sure," I manage to say, "I'd better go home for lunch now."

It will be fifty years before I reveal the truth.

* — * — *

Mother agrees to let me walk down to Alice Anderson's house, in the middle of the block on Illinois Street. "It will be dark when you come home, Patsy. You telephone, and I will turn the back porch light on, and stand on the porch until you get home," Mother instructs.

Now ten, Alice and I like to lie on her bed and look through the big wish books. She has both, Montgomery Ward and Sears, Roebuck & Co. catalogs. We talk about taking a bus to visit her sister, Ruth, in Milwaukee. We will never do this, but we spend hours planning the new clothes we will order, and discuss all the great places we will visit, when we get there. When it is time to go home, I call to tell Mother I am on my way. Mrs. Anderson turns the porch light on and stands on her porch, also.

Between the two houses it is pitch black. I know I am on the sidewalk, but I can't see much except the shapes of some neighbor's bushes along the way. As I walk along, I hear some noises behind me. I look back, and see two dark forms emerge from behind the bushes. Then I hear loud snorting and growling. I start to run, and two creatures chase me. I run faster, my heart is pounding, and I'm out of breath. "Mother!" I try to scream. I reach the driveway and they chase me right up to the porch.

"You, dang Brats!" Mother yells. "I sent you to walk home with Pat. Not to scare her to death!"

My two teenage brothers come howling and laughing up the back steps.

"You - Snot - Poop - Brats!" I cry.

Dad comes into the kitchen. "Patsy, you are my black eyed spit-fire! You've got to quit saying those words. You boys ought to be ashamed of yourselves."

The boys continue to rock with laughter, at my expense.

* — * — *

In the warmth of summer, 1947, I walk a block north to visit my friend, Joyce Field. Her home sits behind Field's Grocery store, on Shirland Ave. A darling miniature house sits between

168

the store and her home. Joyce greets me saying, "How do you like my new playhouse?"

"It is fantastic, Joyce. It looks like a real house!" I say.

"Come in and I'll show it to you," she says, opening the door. It has screened windows that open. Inside, her toy furniture is neatly arranged to fit the space. She has lovely things to play with. I am impressed by a large, baby doll with brown, lamb's wool looking hair. Everything is so luxurious. She generously shares her toys, and is a gracious hostess in her tiny home. It echoes the phrase, "A place for everything and everything in its place."

At home, I say, "Mother, you should see Joyce's playhouse. It has everything."

* — * — *

In the Fall of 1947 our dear friends, Erla and Floyd Nicolls, get a new baby. Jimmy now has a little brother. They give so much love to their sons. The Nicolls will live in three different homes in the neighborhood. It is interesting that at least seven families live in different homes in our neighborhood through the years, some moving three times.

It is October 1947, Eleanor and Clyde Sudds are hosting a masquerade party. Eleanor is Bertha Busker's older sister, and lives in the house south of Barbara's. Neighborhood playmates are invited. A gigantic, orange harvest moon shines upon the neighborhood. Bats swoop overhead, black cats walk atop the porch rails, and I think I saw something sail by on a broomstick! Scarecrows, hobos, fairies, cartoon and nursery rhyme characters appear from every direction.

We enter the front door, and crawl through a tunnel. Cobwebs brush our faces, a fake bonfire glows in the corner, and snakes follow us along the route. When we reach the end, a ghost stands waiting to shake hands with us. His rubber hand is wet and ice cold.

We sit in a circle and are told that a cat has had surgery and we are to examine the parts that come around. A ball of fur, a bone, slimy - wet - large - macaroni is an intestine, a peeled grape is an eyeball, and soft - stringy spaghetti is brains. When we are done examining all the parts, the cat is said to have been put back together and healing well. Games, prizes and refreshments conclude an exciting evening of fantasy.

* — * — *

The neighborhood and community are deeply saddened on Nov. 3, 1947, by the tragic death of Barbara Kissling's father, Monte. A fiery crash claims his life near Elgin, Illinois. Monte had been the operator of the Blue Diamond tavern.

Grief hangs over their household. Grandparents stay in their

169

home for a few weeks. Eventually, life takes on some normalcy, and Barbie's mom continues to operate the tavern. I begin to spend more time at Barbie's home, and stay overnight often.

Mrs. Kissling meets a lady from Canada. Emily has some problems, and is invited to room at Kissling's for awhile. At one point, her adult sister, Rosy, comes to stay for a time.

I am a pre-teen, with Barbara trailing, in age, by nearly two years. We have spent the night at her home, and we wake up before anyone else in the morning. Snores are coming from the room where Rosy is sleeping; the door is partially open. We decide to play some tricks. Still in our pajamas, we crawl on our hands and knees, to her room. Her feet are uncovered. Trying to stifle our giggles, we quietly take a piece of string and tie it to the bedpost and then tie it on her big toe. We crawl under the bed and begin plinking the springs. No response. We plink a little harder. Still snores. We get bolder, so we push the springs up and down.

Suddenly the snoring stops. "What the —?" We hear a foot moving quickly, then—"Ow!" as Rosy discovers she is tied up. By this time we are giggling and Rosy is getting a ride as we push the springs up, from under the bed. "You rascals!" she exclaims, in a sleepy voice.

Having accomplished our mission, we crawl back to Barbie's room.

* — * — *

Mother manages to provide me with funds for the Saturday matinee and lunch at a soda fountain or restaurant. We look at the newspaper ads for the movies.

"Which one is in technicolor?" I ask. We choose musicals whenever possible. Barbara's mother drops us off at the Lakeland Cafe. We will walk over to the theater, and home afterwards. Surely, I am twelve going on eighteen, as Barbie and I eat hamburgers and fries, and drink our Cokes at the restaurant.

We love the movie, but the fun really starts when we get back to Barbara's house. We create our own theater, acting out the various scenes from the movie we have just seen. Because I am the oldest, and the tallest, I always play the man's part. Like Fred Astair and Ginger Rogers, we dance on the furniture. Barbara's mother is more lenient with us than other parents. I would be in big trouble if I tried that at home! We play records and perform the evening away.

I have been asked to spend the night with Barb. Emily is about to have her baby and Mrs. Kissling must take her to the hospital. Consent granted, Barb and I decide to entertain ourselves by cooking. We often try different recipes in her mom's cookbook, but we are rarely successful with them. We have

170

made taffy that won't pull, popcorn balls that won't stick together, (we ended with a metal dishpan full of syrupy popcorn), and fudge that was runny and grainy. What can we try tonight?

"Do you like macaroni salad?" I ask.

"Sure. Shall we try to make some?" asks Barb.

We cook the macaroni, rinse it in cold water, spread some mayonnaise on it and taste it. There seems to be a few things missing, so we add salt and pepper. It's a strange macaroni salad, but we eat it.

We go upstairs and get ready for bed. I am about to turn the light out when we hear some noise, apparently coming from the basement. We head downstairs.

"What if someone is in the basement?" I ask. "We should each take a frying pan to protect ourselves."

"Oh, Pat, I'm scared," Barbie answers.

We each grab up a frying pan, and open the basement door. Someone is whining.

"It's Inky," says Barb.

We go down the steps and see their black cocker spaniel in her box. She has just given birth to a litter of puppies!

Barb's mom arrives home and announces that Emily has a baby girl. A new baby girl and puppies in the same night!!!

* — * — *

November 1948, several girlfriends have come to help me celebrate my birthday. We go to the old cellar (it took some real talking to convince my father we could have fun in that old basement). Marge Milner brought her accordion, and she plays some music while we dance.

Grandma has prepared sandwiches with spread made from ground bologna, pickle, onion and mayonnaise. A real hit! We have potato chips cake and pop. Afterward we go to the livingroom. Barbara and I go into the little room, which I used for a playroom when I was small, and pull on some colorful Spanish looking attire, including fancy straw hats. We sing and dance the Spanish "Cuánto Le Gusto." With coquettish gestures, we sing of caballeros with dark and flashing eyes. In Cuban motion we emphasize, "If we stay, we won't come back!" The girls hold their sides in laughter, as we gyrate and sing "We haven't got a dime, But we're goin, and we're gonna have a happy time!" All this gaiety celebrates a grand occasion, I am now a teenager.

* — * — *

Barbara's mom lets us do most anything; but to try smoking is out! Barbara and I want to try smoking so I coax Mother. She has a problem saying "no" to my requests. After considerable badgering I say, "You may as well give me some cigarettes because I am going to get some and try it somewhere."

Mother takes us for a little ride in the car and gives me a pack of cigarettes. "You'd better not let your Dad find out or he'll kill us both!" she exclaims.

In spite of my experimenting at various times, I never enjoy smoking. This will not be one of my bad habits.

* — * — *

Memorial Day - May 30, 1950. The family is not celebrating this holiday because Jackie is at the hospital delivering her first child. I can't be part of that, so Alice Anderson and I go to a carnival, at the lower end of Shirland Avenue. We ride the loop-o-plane so many times, the man operating it gives us free rides. The house of mirrors distorts us into long skinny figures, short fat ones, and disjointed ones. Our eyes pop when we visit the tent of the fat lady. An afternoon of strange phenomenon!

Chapter 13
School Daze
(1940-1949)

Green, red and yellow leaves decorate the trees, on this warm, autumn day in 1940. Mama and I chatter with her cousin, Madeline Ennis. It's always fun to visit Madeline's home. She makes us laugh with her special sense of humor, when she shares stories of her family.

"I have more freedom, now that the kids are back in school," says Mama.

"Yeah, I know what you mean, Mary and Danny are in school too," says Madeline. "Well, you're the lucky one, Patsy. You can still join us for cake and coffee, but next year you will be in school. There go a couple kids on bicycles. I'll bet they are skipping school."

"I'll bet they are, too. What the - -? Those little devils! That is Gene and Jackie. They probably think they can ride over here in Beloit, and no one will know where they are. Are they ever going to be in trouble! They went back to school after lunch, or at least, they pretended to," says Mama.

"They are going to wonder how in the world you found out what they were doing!" laughs Madeline.

"Daddy better not find out," I say.

"Maybe this better be our secret for a while, Patsy," says Mama. "Once doesn't make a habit. Let's not make a mountain out of a mole hill."

* — * — *

With the bloom of spring, 1941, sister Jackie graduates from Riverview Grade School. Grandma and Grandpa Wessell, Aunt Dorothy and Uncle Leonard attend the ceremony. Aunt Dorothy's handsome, twenty six year old brother, Bud Alexander, is visiting them. He attends the graduation in his white dress suit, creating a great impression on thirteen year old Jackie and her girlfriends.

Labor Day Weekend claims 515 lives across the nation as people celebrate summer's last holiday. A fourteen inch rainfall causes extensive damage in northern Wisconsin, forcing 2000 people from their homes in the Ashland area. The White, Bad, Mississippi, Wisconsin and Chippewa Rivers are on the rampage, causing principle damage in Ashland, Wausaw and Hayward.

Classrooms open Tuesday, September 2, 1941 in Beloit and South Beloit schools. Upper classmen initiate Jackie, and her classmates, into the freshman class at South Beloit High School.

"Mother, this is awful. I don't want anyone to see me wearing tattered cut-off pants and looking so sloppy. I don't want to go to school looking like a hobo," Jackie wails.

"Don't let it upset you, Honey. All of your classmates have been asked to do the same thing. Just have fun with it. In years to come you will look back and laugh about it," Mother answers.

Gene is going into seventh grade, Tommy into fifth grade, and in two months I will be six years old. Mother has just delivered me to my classroom at Riverview School. There is no kindergarten, so I am beginning Miss Quinlan's first grade. Miss Quinlan is a middle age lady, with a white gauze patch over her left eye. I have never seen this before, and it frightens me. I'm not sure I like it here. There are children I don't know. Neither Mama nor Grandma is here. I put my head down on my desk and cry. Miss Quinlan calls Mama to come and get me.

I remember Mama telling, many times, she didn't want to go to school, and she would turn around and run home. Eventually, Grandma used a little switch on her all the way to school, until she got the idea that she had to stay there. Perhaps a seed has been planted in my mind that I won't like it at school.

Daddy says, "Patsy, you must get used to being away from Mama or Grandma during the day. School is a wonderful place. You will learn to read and write. You will count, draw pictures, and make new friends."

I'm not alone at school. Jimmy Nicolls and Alice Anderson are here, and I soon find that the other kids are fun to play with. Miss Quinlan is kind, but I have a little problem with this idea of being quiet and not talking to the children who sit near me. Who ever heard of having to raise your hand when you want to talk? And going to the toilet not only means raising your hand to get permission, but having to show with one or two fingers, what you intend to do. Now, really! Whose business is that? We have to go to the grey basement and use one of three stalls. One stall is for teachers only, how odd. Who thought up these strange ideas?

My little friend, Marjorie Milner feels sad and left out, because she is not old enough to go to school with Jimmy and me. Maybe we could trade places? She will be in the class with most of our neighborhood friends, Joyce Field, LuAnn Johnson, Carol Kniprath and others. She shouldn't feel so bad, because she has a new little brother about three months old. We don't know it, but in two years she will have twin baby sisters.

We learn our ABC's, are called to the front of the class in little groups, and sit in little red chairs. Eventually we learn to sound out words by using flash cards, and learn to work with numbers the same way. Sometimes we make terrific music in a band. The teacher passes out sticks, small bells on a cloth band, triangular metal tubes with a metal rod and cymbals. I never get anything more exciting than the sticks or bells.

Miss Quinlan says, "Everyone stand, look at our flag and put your right hand over your heart. You are going to learn the pledge of allegiance to our flag. Say these words after me —- I pledge allegiance to the flag, of the United States of America, and to the republic, for which it stands, one nation under God, indivisible, with liberty and justice for all." —- Every morning we start school the same way. We stand and repeat the words. Before long we all know them by heart.

One day Miss Quinlan stops by our home, and gives me two old books to help me learn to read. One is "Ben and Alice." I love the stories about them, their family and pets. It even has a story about a rabbit named Jumpity-hoppity and his trip to New Town. I spend many hours playing school with these precious books.

Jimmy, Alice and I walk to school, with the older kids. It is three or four blocks, depending which way we go. We usually take the sand path that has been created, by neighborhood kids taking a short cut, across an open field. There are several routes we can choose, with different classmates living along the routes.

After school I go to Jimmy's house to play. I am invited in, but Mrs. Nicolls says, "Jimmy can't play. He is being punished for chewing on his shirt collar at school. Jimmy has been told not to chew on his collar, but seeing how he likes to chew on it so much; he can just sit here in the kitchen and chew on it."

I look at my little friend feeling sorry for him. His mother is obviously not happy to have him ruining his shirt collars. She is cooking their supper at the stove. Mrs. Nicolls turns to him with the salt shaker in her hand and says, "Here, see if this makes it taste better." She shakes some salt on his collar. He is embarrassed and so am I. I decide it is better if I go home.

The weeks fly, and on December seventh the Japanese bomb our country's naval force in Pearl Harbor, Hawaii. The long feared and dreaded truth is upon us —- we are at war. Adults talk anxiously about the horrors of the war and the sacrifices we will all be called to make.

A bright spot shines at school. A new girl has joined our class. Marie Troxel has moved from northern Wisconsin, to a home out west of our school. Eventually Marie will become one of my best friends. She is a lively, pretty girl, with brown eyes and dark brown wavy hair that bounces when she walks.

* — * — *

The students are excited. This day the Ladies' Circle group

175

is holding the Bazaar. We have brought pennies and nickels to play games and purchase treats. In turn, each class files down to the Ladies' Circle room in the basement. Finally, we enter the large room. Tables are spread with homemade candy. I see big chunks of chocolate fudge with nuts in it. Our noses savor the aroma of fresh popped corn. The lunch counter has hot dogs. In one corner a fishing booth attracts my attention, I pay my pennies and take the fishing pole. When I swing the line over the partition, a lady behind it fastens a wrapped package on the end of my line. I pull in a trinket. The children have fun and the Ladies' Circle takes in money for special school equipment.

One day we file down to the basement and stand in line for a different purpose. A few children are crying. Some are frightened, anticipating what is ahead. I'm not sure I want to be in this line. When I get close enough, I watch a nurse rub a child's arm with alcohol saturated cotton, and see a doctor poke him with a long needle. This immunization program is free and important. I decide to be tough, and don't let out a peep.

The shots to prevent diphtheria, scarlet fever and whooping cough aren't so terrible to receive, but often leave swollen, sore arms. The doctor starts to administer the vaccination for smallpox, and I'm sure he is purposely torturing me with all these needle punctures. He makes the arms all sore and itchy, and then has the nerve to say, "Don't scratch it!" To add insult to injury, a few days later he looks at mine and says, "It didn't take. We'd better do it again." I have a tremendous urge to poke the doctor a good one, but I know this would be wrong, and I'd end up with more than a sore arm! The vaccination never does take on me. Some kids end up with large scars, the size of a dime or nickel, which they will wear on the upper arm forever.

In September 1942, the Big Shoe Store advertises boys and girls economy grade oxfords, with twenty styles to choose from. They have rubber cork soles, come in sizes 8 1/2 to 3, in browns, blacks, and patents for $1.39. Mama buys me a pair of brown shoes for school. I'm not thrilled with the style or color, but I feel better when I discover that many kids are wearing the same kind and color. It is war time and Mama makes a practical choice.

Jimmy Nicolls has some new brown shoes, too. Unfortunately, when we walk home from school after a rain, he isn't thinking about that. There are puddles along the gutter, and they are so inviting. How can a little boy resist wading in puddles? I am to stay at Jimmy's for a while after school today, and look forward to playing with him. When Mrs. Nicolls discovers the new shoes all soaking wet, she is not happy. Jimmy isn't happy, either, when she sends him upstairs to get ready for a spanking with the fly swatter. I'm not happy anymore, either.

* — * — *

Times are hard for many folks, having just come out of the effects of depression years, only to enter war time. Some families can't or don't provide well for their children, and are not concerned for cleanliness. One teacher, Mrs. Warren, has great compassion for these children. She invites them into the school early, takes them to a room upstairs, bathes them, and provides them with clean clothing. She wants them to have the same advantage that other children have. Because of the father's attitude and temper, she has the children change into their old, soiled clothing before returning home in the afternoon.

At recess we play on swings, teeter-totters and the merry-go-round. Sometimes this equipment proves to be dangerous. The swings have wood seats, attached to chains with metal brackets. Sometimes the older kids like to see how high they can make them go. One day a little girl walks too close in front of the swing. "Watch out, watch out," kids scream. Too late! She gets hit. The blood runs down her face. We see that her eyelid, nearly severed, hangs only by a thread at each end.

The merry-go-round is a stand up style. We push it by vertical bars and then jump on. One little girl, from the south, always climbs to the upper horizontal bars, wraps her legs around them, and hangs upside down, with her underwear exposed. Can you imagine that?

Teeter-totters are even more hazardous. Kids coax someone to get on the end, even help her by lowering it. When she is not expecting it, the scheming rascal slips off the end and lets her down with a crash!

The boys' playground is on the south side of the school and the girls' is on the north side. To the east, across the road from the school, is a ball diamond shared by boys and girls. A teacher always supervises the playgrounds during recess, but she has to walk around all sides, and usually misses what she might be looking for.

Myra Newnham and I play with our dolls under some trees, and sometimes other girls join us. Eventually the dolls give way to jump rope, hopscotch, jacks, softball and tag. When we want to sit and chat, the teacher comes along and tells us to get up and move around.

One day while I am still quite small, a fire truck comes roaring up to the school during recess. I don't know what possesses me, but I run across the street in front of it.

"Patsy Singletary, why did you do that? That is a dangerous thing you just did. What would your mother say? You could have been hit by that fire truck. I ought to make you stay after

177

school. Don't you EVER do that again!" snaps the teacher on duty.

I am terribly embarrassed. It was a stupid thing to do, and I don't know why I did it. Was I showing off, or just being careless? I hang my head without a reply.

In class the teacher uses my actions as a bad example, and I want to crawl under my desk with shame.

* — * — *

Today I run through the sand path with my classmates. Kids of all grade school ages are using the path. Some big boys are riding their bicycles, and we have to jump out of their way. The weeds in the field, on either side of the path, are taller than I am. "Oh, look," says Alice. "Someone has written some bad words in the sand." Someone has taken a stick and scratched some four letter words in the firmer surface at the edge of the path.

"What do they mean?" I ask.

"I'm not gonna tell," says Alice. "I wonder who wrote them?"

Just then Mary runs past and pulls Alice's hair bow off. Alice swings at her, and the fight is on. I try to help Alice and then I'm in it, too. We grab each other by the shoulders and arms and throw each other down. No one really gets hurt. This is only one of many skirmishes on the path, which our parents seldom find out about. Our closest neighborhood friends help defend one another. When our parents find out about it, we are likely to get a severe tongue lashing, and sometimes a good whack.

At times the battles on the path, with neighborhood kids, leave some resentments. One spring morning Daddy looks out at his beautiful flower beds, which are always the pride of the neighborhood, and gasps. About two hundred tulip blossoms have been snapped off at the top, and they lie on the ground. It will be a few weeks before we discover who did it. It is a path foe!

* — * — *

As I come into the back shed, I smell the wonderful aroma of baking apples and cinnamon. I burst through the kitchen door. "Is it apple dumplings, Grandma?" I ask.

"Yes, Honey," Grandma says. With a pancake turner, she begins removing huge apple dumplings from a large baking pan. She sets one gently into a large shallow soup bowl, and it fills the bowl.

I can hardly wait to dig into that wonderful, tender, fluffy, biscuit dough with the spicy apples baked inside, and the spicy syrup sauce on top. There couldn't be a more delicious homemade treat for our noon lunch. Mother sets a pitcher of milk on the table, for the dumplings. "Come on Gene and Tom," she calls, "Lunch is ready."

It takes only a few minutes for our large bowls to be empty, and our tummies bulging. Renewed in mind and body, we run out the door and head toward the school house.

In the future I will think about how privileged we were to have a Mama and Grandma that baked such wholesome goodness for our nutrition and enjoyment. Love went into every dumpling.

* — * — *

The years of lower grades roll by with studies, a variety of teachers and experiences with different friends.

People respect my fifth grade teacher, and most students appreciate her. She is a good teacher, but her sternness intimidates me. I recall her laughing just once, during the year she is my teacher. One morning she says, "Mary, did you bring your report card back?"

"Yes, it's in my lunch sack," Mary answers.

"Well, you'd better get it out, before you eat it," says the teacher. Laughing quite heartily, she appreciates her own joke.

She must be in a particularly bad mood one day. When we file into the classroom after recess, she stands in the doorway, a sentinel with hawk like eye. The teacher has no trace of smile or friendly greeting. She observes every move, as children continue to come in and settle into their seats.

I scribble a quick note to my friend, Marie Troxel, sign it, and hand it to Alice Anderson, as she passes my desk. "Please, give this to Marie," I say. She takes it to her seat and reads it, then she calls to Marie, and throws it to her. Fatal action!

The statue moves swiftly, going directly to Alice's desk. She grabs Alice by the shoulders, shakes her violently up and down, back and forth, as though she is releasing pent up fury, then slams her into her seat. As though an afterthought, she lifts her face and rapidly slaps it back and forth with the palm of her hand.

I turn around quickly and get my books out of my desk. My heart freezes, I expect to be the next victim. She passes my desk, without saying one word to me. She knows my mother. Can it be that she knows the way my mother protects her children, or does she figure I will eventually catch it when she uses her plan? The teacher goes to her desk at the head of the room, and carries on as though nothing has happened.

A few weeks later when our report cards come out, I have a D in deportment.

"What is the meaning of this?" Mother asks.

I play dumb! However, that doesn't fly with my father, and I receive one of his famous lectures. Although I'm not fond of being captive to the lecture, I prefer it to Alice's thrashing!

Many years into the future, I will see the breakdown of discipline in the schools and homes, and the tragic results. Then I will realize the benefit of the strict teachers. ...To err is human, to forgive divine . . .

* — * — *

I will never be a winter person, the cold effects me adversely. It is sub-zero weather, and four blocks to school seems like four miles. Even bundled up, I feel like I have no clothing on. With a scarf wrapped around my face and forehead, I still think I will freeze. Turning and walking backwards with my hand held up over my forehead, I try to keep the cold breeze off my face. I want to cry, but I'd have icicles.

On milder winter days, we have to contend with the boys. They attack us, and throw snowballs at my girlfriend and me. The boys try to wash our faces in the snow. On a white winter morning, this makes me see red! We hate having our faces washed with snow, and I'm ready to fight. When we get hit with an ice-ball, we squeal to the teacher. The teacher calls the boys out to the hall, one at a time. We hear her using her ruler. Each boy comes in with the palms of his hands bright red. But they continue to peg snowballs at us, more than ever.

One day we decide we have had enough. Myra, Alice, Marilyn and I hurry and get a block ahead of the boys. We hide behind some fencing and make a pile of snowballs. When Jimmy, Page, Faye and Willie come along, we are ready for them.

"Ow! Ouch! Wow! Get 'em," they yell. They are no match for us, with our stock pile of snowballs. Our surprise attack sends them running!

* — * — *

Our school always has masquerade parties on or near Halloween. If the weather doesn't allow an outdoor parade, the classes take turns parading through each other's rooms. In sixth grade I am a hobo, with oversize, old, dilapidated shoes. I wear a tattered shirt, and baggy pants with a pillow in the seat.

This year I have my first male teacher. Marie Troxel and I know we won't like having a man for a teacher, but we discover him to be a favorite. I go up to him in my hobo costume. "How do you like my elephant pin?" I ask.

"That's cute," he says.

"Look close at his eye," I urge. When he bends close to look at it, I squeeze a little bulb in my shirt pocket, and it squirts him in the face with water! The kids nearby roar with laughter and so does he. I continue playing my little trick on any unsuspecting classmates I can find.

* — * — *

At graduation and Christmas we always have special plays. Some students play piano solos or duets, a few play accordions or other instruments. Students with special voices sing solos. It is always a challenge to memorize parts for the plays. I am delighted to receive a major part in a few of the plays.

One year the entire school does a major production of a minstrel show. I receive the part of a pastor in a mock wedding.

I am called Mr. Interlockalator. When I ask the bride if she takes the groom for better or worse, she replies, "If he gets any worse, I fix em!" The groom produces a jar ring for the wedding ring. Whereupon, the bride says, "Dat ain't no ring. You gotta hab a ring what am a ring, You ain't weddin no cow!" The entire show is a comedy, with much singing and music. We all have to cork our faces black.

I am sensitive to the feelings of the Negro students. They have parts in the play also, but I'm concerned for fear of hurting anyone's feelings, however, everyone appears to be having a good time. It won't bother me, if they paint their faces white for a comedy about "those po white folks."

* — * — *

I miss school during a variety of childhood diseases, and an appendectomy during grade school. Though a few things catch my interest, mostly plays and reading, no teacher can inspire me until I reach Mrs. Warren's class in seventh grade. Mrs. Warren creates an interest in travel, places and events in geography. She entices me with creative writing, reading for pleasure and knowledge, also in learning grammar basics. She helps me understand the value of math and history. For the first time, I feel truly encouraged to work to the capacity of my ability.

In eighth grade, we are in the same room, but now with only eighth grade students instead of seventh and eighth. I really try to excel now. One day Mrs. Warren calls me aside, "Patricia, you will be awarded the American Legion Award at graduation." I can't believe my ears. I have always expected my good friend, Marie, to receive this honor.

"Thank you, Mrs. Warren," I manage to stammer.

My brother Tom had received this honor when he graduated from eighth grade, also.

Patsy, Jimmy Nicolls - 1943

*LuAnn Johnson, Joyce Field,
Carol Kniprath - 1948*

*1948 - 7th grade - James Nicolls, Myra Newnham, Marie Troxel -
8th grade - Bertha Busker*

The bronze medal I receive has a young woman lowering the American flag, with words "FOR GOD AND COUNTRY" in relief on the front. The back has an eagle, American Legion emblem, and the words American Legion School Award, COURAGE - CHARACTER - SERVICE - COMPANIONSHIP - and SCHOLARSHIP. I am never sure I deserve it, but I treasure it.

High school is so different. I have never been in a class before where bedlam reigns. The coaches teach Math, Biology and Science classes and have no control. Math class at one o'clock is in the room used for lunch. One day a female student screams, "I just got hit in the eye with a meat sandwich!"

Senior boys, as large as the coach, heckle him. He tries to

remove them by the nape of the neck and seat of the pants. Red faced, he struggles with them, without success. There is no order, no respect, and I learn very little! I divide the blame equally between myself, the teacher and the student body. In spite of this, I have a hopeless crush on him. In my annual, one coach writes, "To Pat, come to school more often, I miss that smiling face." And the other one writes, "Good luck to a good girl! But not too quiet a one - You passed."

I do well in the English classes where respect and order are required.

We hear her coming to the door, and the entire freshman English class, of South Beloit High School, stands. Mrs. Gruhlke walks to her desk, holding her tall frame erect. She wears a camel tan suit with tan, green and red print blouse, accented with gold jewelry. Her slightly greying, dark hair is loosely fashioned into a chignon. Determined, curious, but kind eyes set below dark, unruly eyebrows. Her thin lips spread into a wide grin.

Her comments the day before, concerning a class that honored a teacher by standing when she came into the room, have prompted this display of respect. She does not faint, but thanks the class. It is a one time event, but once is better than never.

"I'm sorry, Bill, you know I don't tolerate gum chewing in my class. You will wear it on the end of your nose for the rest of this hour. There is nothing more disgusting than having someone, in a business position, wait on you, while he is smacking and cracking his gum," she says.

Mrs. Gruhlke never fears taking a stand for what she believes in, even if it collides with school administration. She allows us to have debate teams on school policy, and encourages us to stand for what we believe in.

During discussion on essays one day, she says, "I don't mind having a big mouth. I read where it is a sign of strong character." She is disturbed over the way sports interferes with curriculum, and the privileges granted students involved in them. Her encouragement in self expression has a great influence on me.

She encourages us to write essays and poetry, and requires us to memorize picturesque portions of poetry and prose. I shall always be able to recite the portion of poetry required, from "The Lady of the Lake" by Sir Walter Scott. The vivid hunting scene sets lasting images in my mind. Mrs. Gruhlke's influence and encouragement create a desire to express myself with words that create colorful pictures.

* __ * __ *

Social life is different in high school. I join Y-Teens. This group is affiliated with the YWCA, and Mrs. Gruhlke is the sponsor.

All freshman must endure initiation into the group. The program is held in the old gym with the audience seated in front of the four foot high stage. So many new faces and intimidating upper classman make my stomach feel filled with bumble bees. My face burns when they call my name to come to the stage.

On the stage sit three, large, cardboard boxes. A girl blindfolds me and turns me around three times. She instructs me to run and try to jump over each box when she yells, "jump." What I don't know, is that they will remove the boxes before I start to run. The surprise comes to everyone! With the last turn they yell, "run!" I run fast - I feel my body soar through the air as I leave the four foot high stage. I hear a roar of screams - Mrs. Gruhlke's the loudest - I can almost feel the breeze from the gasps - though I am blindfolded I can see them clasping their hands over their mouths.

I land flat on my back on the floor below. Immediately a crowd surrounds me. Someone removes the blindfold. I knew this initiation would embarrass me, but this is ridiculous! I toy with the idea of playing dead.

Mrs. Gruhlke is about to have a heart attack. I can't let that happen to her, so I reveal that only my pride is hurt.

In later years, when I experience back and neck problems, I wonder if more than my pride was hurt. I know for sure, I will never approve of initiations.

Chapter 14
Special Bonding
(1946-1950)

*Pat by cosmos back of Grandma
and Grandpa Kissling's cottage
Lake Kegonsa, Stoughton, Wi.*

*Barbara at end of the pier.
Pictures about 1950*

Summer, 1946, is in full bloom with fully leafed out trees, as red geraniums stand in the shadow of the brightly colored zinnias of Dad's flower beds. The boys argue over whose turn it is to push the reel type mower over our spacious lawn.

They say the days are supposed to be long, lazy and hazy. But there is nothing lazy about my long summer days. I make the most of the freedom from the restrictions of school. A time to run, ride bikes, explore, to see if I can stand up on my playmate's roller skates, a time for picnics and special vacations. I stretch my legs and my imagination.

My bags packed, I hug Grandma and Mother goodbye. Gram tucks a five-dollar bill in my hand as she says, "Be a good girl.

185

Be careful, and have fun."

"It surely is good of Kisslings to invite you for a week of vacation at their summer home on Lake Kegonsa near Stoughton," Mother says. "You must be careful near that Lake. Here come Hilda and Barbara now."

As the car pulls into our driveway, I pick up my bags. Barbs' mom gets out and opens the trunk. She shifts the wooden crate that holds twenty-four bottles of soda pop in a mixture of flavors, and makes room for my bags.

"Hi, Mrs. Singletary. The kids are going to have a great time at the lake. I've got a case of pop and bags of potato chips for them," Mrs. Kissling says.

My eyes widen as I see all that soda pop!

"They'll have a great time swimming," adds Mrs. Kissling.

"Oh, Pat doesn't have a swimming suit with her," Mother says.

"Yes I do, Mother," I confess.

"Don't worry," Mrs. Kissling assures Mother, "Grandpa will keep an eye on them."

Mother hugs me again, "Be careful. I love you."

I know she is fearful of me going, but she is setting me free to find my own wings. I squeeze her tight, "I'll be careful. I love you Mother."

We roll along the highway singing popular songs with the radio. "I'm looking over a four-leaf clover," we sing. Mrs. Kissling lightly taps the car's accelerator and the car jerks in time to the music. We go into gales of laughter.

It is no time until we cover fifty miles, and arrive at Grandma and Grandpa Kissling's summer cottage. They welcome us with open arms and happy faces. I will become the favorite of all Barbara's friends in Grandma Kissling's eyes. I will share many vacations here with them. The Kisslings will become extended family to me. How precious are dear friends! Barb's mom has lunch with us and bids us goodby promising to pick us up in a week.

We tote our bags upstairs to the large attic room that is divided into a front and back bedroom by partition with curtained doorway. Grandpa has our bed made up in the back bedroom. Because of Grandma's large size and leg problems, she doesn't come up the stairs. Besides the beds there are old dressers, trunks and chests holding antique bowl and pitcher chamber sets. We drop our bags and hurry; we can hardly wait to get outside to play.

The afternoon disappears while we explore the woods across the entrance road behind the cottage.

"Let's build a hut," suggests Barbara.

186

"That would be fun. Shall we look for some long skinny limbs?" I ask.

"Sure. Maybe we could weave them together." Barbara says.

Searching the woods, we find several limbs of various lengths. We brace the limbs against a tree, and support some of them with the tree's lower branches crudely weaving them together until we have the frame done. Gathering small leafy branches, we cover the frame enclosing the hut. The blue jays scold us for invading their territory, while the squirrels jump from limb to limb and drop acorns on us. Grandpa comes to the edge of the road. "Barbara, it's time for you girls to wash up and set the table for Grandma."

"Its supper time already?" I ask.

"Guess so. We can play out after supper, 'til it starts to get dark," Barbie says.

We hurry into the kitchen of enticing aromas.

"I didn't know I was hungry until I smelled these hamburgers frying," I say.

Grandma flashes her broad grin and hitches herself across the kitchen. "It always increases your appetite to play in the fresh, lake air," she declares.

With dishes done and put away, we go out and head to the long flights of stairs that take us down the hill to the lake.

"Wow, that's a lot of stairs," I exclaim.

"Just wait 'til we have to go back up!" Barbie smiles.
The door to the white frame boathouse is locked. We walk out onto the pier and look at the lake. "This is a big lake," I say. "Can you swim?" I ask.

"Not very well," she answers.

"I can hardly stay afloat, and I can't swim at all, but maybe I'll learn while I'm here. I love the water," I say.

Our play is strongly influenced by movies we have seen. We sing and dance. The cement foundation projecting about three feet in front of the boathouse makes an excellent stage. The overhanging trees and shrubs at the edge of the lake, on the left side, give us a little privacy. In a strong voice I sing, "Now Is The Hour." The sound carries out across the lake. We have a natural amplification system. Together we sing "Harbor Lights," giving it all we've got. Twilight drops a curtain on our stage and we start our climb back to the cottage.

Grandma sits in her big chair wearing the cotton cap that matches her dress. Her needle goes in and out as she embroiders a tea towel. Grandpa sits in his corner chair reading. Barbie and I wander out to the large, windowed in porch that runs across the front of the cottage. On a square, tiered antique table, sits a huge vase of fresh cosmos, from Grandpa's small flower bed in the back yard. They create such a pretty picture in various pink to deep rose shades, with their dainty, green, fern like foliage. We sit on the floor for a game of Uncle Wiggley. Before we know it, Grandma is saying, "Girls, it's time to get washed up and ready for bed."

We go to the tiny bathroom, off the kitchen near the back door. It contains a small sink and toilet. With giggles, getting teeth brushed and washing up we are finally ready to climb the stairs.

"Now girls, once you go up those stairs. No giggling. You are to go to bed and get to sleep," Grandma commands.

Barbie kisses Gram and Gramps goodnight, and I say goodnight. We start up the stairs pulling the door shut behind us. No sooner is the door shut, before we are convulsed in laughter. Covering our mouths with our hands, we hustle up the stairs and pounce into bed. When the lights are turned off, a bit of light filters in from an outdoor light. We start a pillow fight . . .

There is a loud voice from downstairs, "Girls, go to sleep!" We dart under the covers, head and all, and giggle.

The day's activities catch up with us and we drift off to sleep, in spite of ourselves. But soon I hear bong, bong, bong, and it keeps on bonging. I sit up in bed.   "What's   that?" Barbie sits up, too, and we resume laughing.

"It's just the grandfather clock downstairs," she laughs.

At some strange hour we finally sleep, and in the morning we awaken to a bang on the roof. I roll over and look at Barbie. Something rolls across the roof and then we hear something running up there.

"Are their ghosts up here?" I ask.

"It's just small limbs dropping out of the trees, and squirrels running on the roof," she assures me. She is accustomed to these sounds on the attic roof, but I must get used to them.

By mid-morning we make our way down the flights of stairs to the boathouse. Barbie unlocks the padlocked door and we go inside to put our swim suits on. It is cool in here. A white boat sits to the far side, and along the back wall a shelf holds odds and ends of cans and tools. On the dark cement floor, rainbows of colors shine in an oily spot, and we smell a faint odor of gasoline. This becomes a setting of endless happy times shared. For the rest of my life, when I smell gasoline, I am reminded of this scene. We take off our clothes and pull on our swim suits, and tight fitting, white rubber swim caps. My pudgy body makes me a bit self-conscious in my old swimsuit, but these thoughts are soon lost in the thrill of water play.

We walk out on the pier. From the shore out two-thirds of the pier's length are rocks, the size of our heads. We must go down the ladder on the end of the pier to get beyond them. It is spooky, because I'm not sure what is on the bottom of the lake, and I hesitate to put my feet down. Maybe this is why I learn to stay afloat so quickly. In a short time I have so much fun, I hardly think about the bottom of the lake.

"Let's try to do some water ballet," I suggest. I remember seeing some water shows at the natatorium in Beloit.

"Okay, let's!" Barbie responds.

"Lock your legs around my waist, then we will both lay back and use our arms to float around," I instruct. When she complies, I pick up my feet from the bottom of the lake. We both flounder frantically around until we sink under water. We pull apart and come up coughing, sputtering and convulsed in laughter.

Grandpa comes part way down the stairs and calls us to lunch. Within an hour after lunch we are back in the lake. Once in awhile Grandpa comes down and sits on the step to watch us for a time, but not often. The days fly by as we spend hours in the water. Eventually I accomplish a side stroke that will take me several yards, and I can stay afloat to rest.

We can only go about six feet beyond the pier before the water is over our heads, so we swim to the neighbor's pier and back in both directions. I am more at ease in the water now, and we continue to try our ballet antics. We climb up the ladder and walk on the sun warmed boards of the pier leaving wet footprints on the dry wood.

"Look at our footprints," Barbie giggles. Her smaller prints have the nice little arch curve and toe prints of normal feet. My prints are long and straight with toe prints, reflecting my hopelessly flat feet. Again, we fall into gales of laughter.

In the back yard we each consume a bottle of grape soda and munch on potato chips. Our activity and the fresh lake air perk our appetites. We have consumed most of the case of pop. We will soon go home with browned bodies, and white rings around the outer edge of our foreheads and faces from the swimcaps.

Mother, Dad, Grandma and my siblings welcome me home. Mother is satisfied that I am all in one piece and have increased my knowledge through happy experiences. It is much easier to obtain consent to go the next time. We go to the lake often in the weeks and years to come, with their blessings.

* — * — *

"Oh, Mrs. Kissling, I can't believe that you could convince my mother to let me go with Barbara to Grandma and Grandpa Kissling's lake home by bus," I say. "I've never been up there in the winter before."

"Well, it wasn't easy, but she knows Grandpa will be at the bus depot in Stoughton to pick you up. This bus depot in Beloit, Wisconsin is not satisfactory. I promised I would see both of you get on the bus before I leave."

At eleven, I feel so grown up with my little 9-year-old friend at my side on this January afternoon, in 1947. Climbing the steps into the bus, we take a seat near the front. We wave goodby to Barbie's mom, and chat as we roll along. Our feet are cold and the windows are steamy. I rub a peep hole through the steam on the window with a tissue. The white countryside with snow flocked trees and fence posts fly by our window. It seems like no time, before we climb off the bus and find Grandpa Kissling ready to whisk us out to the lake home in his white Lincoln Continental.

Grandma Kissling welcomes us with open arms and her warm smile. She brushes a few stray strands of grey hair up under the green and white print cotton cap that matches her dress. She pushes a hanky into the pocket of her tan print apron. The tantalizing aroma of a pork roast dinner beckons us to get the table set for Grandma. Barbie and I tote dishes from the kitchen to the small dining room. We take silverware from the drawer in the little antique wash stand, and put knives and forks by each plate. The teaspoons are always in the glass spoon holder on the table.

On the wall is a plaque that reads "Eat, Drink and be Merry." Grandma Kissling tells us it is a verse from the Bible. It will be many years before I learn that Scriptural comparisons of this verse teach us to enjoy the good things that God has provided for us. But cautions us of the loss of eternal life if we leave Jesus, and His teachings out of our lives. We accept the joyful invitation on the plaque.

After an evening of games and conversation, Barb and I start upstairs to the attic double bedroom. As we go Grandma says, "Now remember girls, no giggling."

These are the magic words. There was nothing funny until now. We cover our mouths with our hands. We stumble, half crawling up the stairs. What is there to laugh at? Only the fact that Grandma told us not to laugh. Our repressed laughter continues to squeeze out as we prepare for bed.

Once in bed we scratch each others back. Then we decide to play our favorite mystery writing game. With my finger I draw letters on Barbie's back. Y O U "Get it?"

"You," Barbie replies.

I continue to draw the letters A R E "Got It?"

"Yeah, `are'," says Barbie.

I draw another S L E

"No. Do it again," Barbie requests.

I start again; S L E E P Y, I draw.

"I am not," says Barbie, and we go into gales of muffled laughter again.

We awaken to a chilly room, but the sun is shining through our window. I plunk Barbie on the head with my pillow. We scramble out of bed, pull on our clothes and make the bed.

"I smell toast and Grandma's coffee," I say.

"Let's hurry and eat so we can go out and play in the snow," says Barbie.

It's a winter wonderland. The woods behind the cottage that were green with summer foliage, now look bare and open. Every tree or blade is coated with ice or flocked in white fluff. Our summer hut no longer has its green cover.

"Let's make some trails in the woods," suggests Barbie.

Our heavy snowsuits are soon coated with snow over our knees. The hours fly by.

After lunch I ask, "Do you want to walk along the front yard above the lake?" Grandma and Grandpa's place is on the highest hill above Lake Kegonsa.

"Okay, let's" Barbie answers.

We make our way through snow drifts and over a few bare areas that are icy. We walk past several vacant cottages. At one place we discover a stairway coated with ice and covered with snow.

"I wonder if we could slide down these stairs?" I question.

"Oh, let's try it," responds Barbie.

I sit on the top step and give myself a little push. Bump, bump, bump - I'm on my way sliding down, and Barbie is right behind me. We screech and squeal in delight! It's difficult working our way back up the stairs. We hang on to the rail, slipping, pulling and tugging our way to the top. Immediately we sit and shoot right back down, bump, bump, bump, over each step, laughing and squealing all the way. How can the afternoon disappear so fast? We have a fantastic time and have bruises on our fannies to prove it!

* — * — *

Summer 1947, Barb and I are at the lake for several days. Her mother brings a car full of our neighborhood girlfriends, and other friends up, for a day, to celebrate Barbara's July tenth birthday. We have a great time swimming and playing in innertubes. Two or three girls try to get on an inner tube at once, and there is great merriment to see who wins the struggle. We throw a waterball around and it goes in places most difficult to retrieve. Mrs. Kissling observes our antics from the pier. "You can have another half hour down here. So keep an eye on your watch and then come up for dinner," she says, as she heads up the flights of stairs.

191

Amid the shouts, the splashes and the laughter, one girl announces that she has to use a toilet. Unfortunately, there is none down here. Now much energy can be expended in water play and swimming around, but no one seems to have enough energy to climb the flights of stairs. "I'll just go down here," she announces. The girls are all focused on her now, with giggles, whispers and disbelief.

"You aren't really going to go—there?" I ask, giggling.

"I can't wait. I've got to," she replies.

The need is urgent and she is not about to climb the stairs. She spies a four-inch gap between the cement foundation of the boathouse and the wood pier. As her audience looks on, she squats and pulls the crotch of her swimsuit to one side. Well, obviously this is not something she can do through her suit in the water. With reddened face and a little grunt, a small brown log floats in the lake. A few are embarrassed, but most of us are in gales of laughter, as she gets a long branch and tries to steer the intruder away from our swimming site. Some have lost the desire to swim and opt for sunning themselves on the pier. The more hardy of us stay in the water.

"Well, I suppose it's no worse than the fish going in the water," somebody says. But we wonder about that.

Up at the cottage we enjoy hamburgers, hot dogs, potato salad, baked beans, soda pop and birthday cake. After games and gifts and a rousing rendition of "Happy Birthday," Mrs. Kissling takes the other girls home.

Our days fly by with water play, exploring the woods and playing in the hut. Occasionally, I have a little wave of being homesick, especially if Grandma Kissling is out of sorts. One day as we come into the kitchen, Grandma is having a bad time peeling some hard-boiled eggs.

"Just look at these stupid eggs," she says, throwing an egg into a gallon jar, of what looks like beet juice. The egg lands ker-plop in the juice and splashes up toward the top of the large jar. Grandma is frustrated and angry.

"What's the matter, Grandma?" Barbara ventures.

"These dumb eggs are too fresh, I guess. The whites are all sticking to the shells," she says, slamming another bumpy white egg into the jar.

"What are you making?" I ask.

"I'm making `Red Beet Eggs'," she answers, starting to calm a little. "Haven't you ever had them?"

"No. What are they like?"

"It is pickled beets with hard-boiled eggs added. I store them in the refrigerator overnight, and the eggs turn rosy colored and take on the pickled beet flavor," she says, with her warm grin returning. "Pat, Grandpa brought a letter in from the mail box for you," she adds.

The letter from home eases my wave of homesickness, and after lunch we head back to the lake. In a few days, Barbara's mother comes after us.

I spend so much time playing at Barb's house or accompanying her to the Lake Kegonsa cottage that Mother misses me.

"Why don't you just move your bed over there?" she asks.

In late August we are at the lake again, down at the pier.

"Instead of getting into our swimsuits, let's hike around the lake for a ways," Barbara suggests.

I look at the edge of the lake with its rocky shoreline, weeds and overhanging trees and brush, at the foot of the hill.

"Are you serious?" I ask.

"Sure, let's see how far we can go," she says.

I'm not sure this is a good idea, but maybe it will be an adventure, so I follow her. It is most precarious trying to climb over the rocks and under the brush at the same time. In some spots Barbara seems to fit better than I do. I edge close behind her. Suddenly, a green, leafy branch snaps back, dips through the water and smacks me with black, mucky gluck. I scream. Barbara looks back and roars with laughter, as I attempt to wipe off the muck.

When we reach the neighbors, we have to go over their boathouse foundations and on along the rocky shore. At one point I climb over a rock, trying to fit under a low hanging limb, suddenly my foot slips. It plunges into the green and black muck at the shoreline. I scream, and bring my foot up with my leather, oxford shoe covered with crud. Barbara looks back.

"Oh, Pat," she squeals, drawing in her breath with her favorite little snicker. We are both laughing as we continue along.

I hear her scream, and I stretch my neck trying to see what is happening. She has climbed face first into a large spider web, and is frantically trying to remove it. It's my turn to laugh. "Are you ready to give up?" I ask. "We could cut through the back and work our way through the fields toward home."

"Sure. Let's try it," she answers.

We have come farther than we realize, and have a long trudge home. We get caught up in the burrs of some tall dock plants and have to stop to pull off big prickers. My shoe is beginning to dry, but our clothes are dirty. I'm not sure how we will explain this.

One morning as we come down to swim, we are horrified at the appearance of the lake. For several feet, out from shore, there are great light green globs of slimy stuff floating on top of the water.

"Oh, yuk. Are we going to swim in that?" I ask. I know the answer before I ask it.

"We can probably get beyond it," Barbara answers.

We climb down the ladder at the end of the pier. Going a couple feet farther out, we try to swish the junk away from us with our hands. Then we decide the innertubes will be a good idea today.

Suddenly, I look around and see how big the lake looks, and realize that we are in very deep water. My heart quickens, realizing that neither of us swims well.

"We should get back closer to the pier," I caution. We are in the tubes with our bottoms hanging through the hole, and our legs flopped over one side and our arms over the other. With our arms we paddle back to the pier.

In the boathouse we strip off our suits. Looking at each other, we burst into laughter. Our skin is totally covered with tiny green particles, making us resemble mermaids. We rub furiously with our towels, and then they are green, too.

Grandpa says the water is a mess because the government has been spraying the other end of the lake for weed control. Our parents become concerned about the lake being polluted, so our happy swimming days are over for this season.

Each new season has its own experiences to file in our treasure chests of memories to cherish for a lifetime. Rainy days find us sitting on a bed in the attic room playing with paper dolls, for hours. Occasionally, Grandpa takes us into Stoughton with him, while he pays bills or picks up some groceries. Barbara and I roam the shops, and especially enjoy Schultz's five and ten cent store.

Pat and Barb

There are some unpleasant times, too, like the occasions that Barbara has the terrible bouts with poison ivy. When she arises in the morning her eyes are swelled shut and have to be bathed before she can get them open. "Stay away from the far side of the

194

boathouse when you are playing," commands Grandpa. "Poison ivy grows there in abundance."

"Even the wind can carry it to her because she is so allergic to it," cautions Grandma.

The doctor advises shots to help protect her from the terrible allergy to poison ivy. Barbara is not at all receptive to the idea. She doesn't like the thought of the shots much better than having the reaction to the poison ivy. The needles are real toad stabbers, in fact, they look as though they were made for Paul Bunyan. However, the thought of the agony of the unbearable itching and swollen eyes helps convince her to take them.

Eventually, though we haven't become great swimmers, we learn to do some shallow diving from the end of the pier. Sometimes it is a belly flop and the sting of hitting the water, in a flat position, is the worst spanking we could ever receive.

One day we come out of the boathouse with our swimsuits on, and smile with surprise to see a good-looking boy laying on the next pier. We both dive into the water and start showing off to attract his attention. He watches us, but says nothing.

"I'll get the innertubes," exclaims Barbara, going after them. We are soon doing our acrobatics with them.

I have a new aqua blue, one-piece, skirted swimsuit with a drawstring at the top. I place the innertube behind me with both hands on it. Then I give one tremendous jump, with the idea of sitting in the center of the innertube. But as I go up, the suit comes down! I go down under the water and come up under the pier. Never do I want to show my face again, nor anything else!

Barbara comes around to the other side of the pier, where I am struggling to replace my suit. "Oh, Pat," she says through her rib tickling laughter.

Even my embarrassment can't suppress the laughter that emerges from deep within. We laugh until we are almost too weak to get out of the water. To my tremendous relief, when we retrieve the innertubes, the handsome boy on the next pier is gone.

* — * — *

Summer 1950 we are sitting on the pier. The sky is a blaze of reds and yellows as the sun slips low in the west. The lake still as glass, reflects the brilliance.

"Isn't it beautiful? We have had some wonderful times up here, Barb," I say. Somehow, I sense that these carefree days will change. High school has brought some new challenges to me, and created a small gap, with Barbie still in grade school.

"I'll never forget all the funny things we've done," says Barb. "We've been like sisters. Gram and Gramps are getting older. I don't know how much longer they can maintain this place."

Chapter 15
Serendipity
-1951-

My heart is full of the joy of spring as I walk north toward Joyce Field's home, this Good Friday evening in 1951. A red breasted robin lands in the green grass a few feet ahead of me as if to say, "Spring is here. This is a special day!" It is warm for the twenty third day of March.

This day when our Lord Jesus Christ suffered so much for the salvation of humanity, is not called Black Friday to commemorate His pain, though we grieve at the thought of it, but is called Good Friday to commemorate the great good that He has accomplished in saving a lost world. But it will be a long time before I understand the full impact of the Easter story.

My black, flared, taffeta skirt swishes as I walk along. Dark brown, medium length hair parted on the left and softly waved, accents my deep brown eyes. A touch of pink rouge, and lipstick adds bloom to my face. I have a deep pink rose pinned at the throat of my aqua blue blouse. At fifteen, the glow of youth flourishes.

I knock on Joyce's door, and am greeted by her mother. Mrs. Brooks says, "Joyce is next door, at Carol's."

"Oh," I say. I know who Carol Kniprath is. She is in the group of girls that often walk to school together, but I have never become well acquainted with her.

"Go on over and knock on the door. Several girls are over there. She will be happy to have you join them."

"Alright," I say. I have no idea why I am doing this. I have never been to this house before, in my life. I am really not accustomed to going to anyone's house with whom I am not well acquainted. I can't believe that I am walking boldly to the door and knocking.

Carol invites me in and introduces me to her mother, whom the girls call "Gracie." Joyce and Nancy Matthews are here. Nancy lives east of Carol, and is two years behind me in school. The other girls are a year behind me. All the girls are in blue jeans, sitting in chairs with their legs draped over the arms. Music is playing and they are visiting.

Soon someone knocks on the door, and Carol welcomes in a couple of boys. She introduces one as Dan and he introduces his friend, Dick Phillips. Dan is a fellow Carol is dating. I try not to stare, but my eyes are drawn to Dick, almost like a force beyond my control.

He is tall, with dark brown wavy hair, and extremely handsome. He wears dress slacks, a white shirt and tie. He appears older, business-like, and quiet. He stands at the oil burner looking through the funnies in a newspaper. His appearance is magnetic to me.

Patricia Ann Singletary, 1951

Richard Arthur Phillips, 1951

When the boys leave, we buzz like a hive of bees. I have already determined that I must see Dick again. No one here has met him before. Carol is cooperative, and her mom suggests that we could have a party at their house. Of course, Dick will be invited. My relationship with Carol begins to bloom.

I walk over to Carol's Saturday evening, April fourteenth. We had decorated the large kitchen with colorful balloons and streamers. The house is bustling with music and young folks.

One game we play is called "Winkum". Chairs are arranged in a large circle. The girls sit in the chairs with the boys standing behind them. There is one chair that is empty, with a fellow standing behind it. That fellow is "it". He looks around at all the girls and then quickly winks at one. That girl is to try to get up and run to his empty chair, but the guy behind her is supposed to grab her shoulders and keep her in his chair. The anticipation and chase create a lively time with much laughter.

We enjoy potato salad, jello, sandwiches and soft drinks.

Everyone has a fun time, and Dick asks to walk me home. It is the first time I wish my house is farther than a block away. He takes hold of my hand, and the current is almost visible.

The moon lights a soft path, as shadows dance along beside us. The stars of heaven have fallen into our eyes, where they glisten and twinkle. Is this the sweet scent of lilacs I smell? It can't be, they have not yet burst into bloom. Why does the sidewalk seem to float beneath my feet? Or have I ascended into the clouds of heaven? All too soon, we arrive at my home. We stand on the sidewalk near the back steps.

"What year high school are you in, Pat?"

"I'm finishing my sophomore year. When did you graduate?"

"I graduated last year. I am working at Beloit Iron Works."

"South Beloit High school is having their prom May fifth. Would you like to be my escort?" I ask.

"I would enjoy that, Pat," he says. "It was a nice party. We had a lot of fun. Good night."

"Good night, Dick," I say. I float up the steps.

Before I go to bed, I talk to God about Dick. I haven't studied God's Word, or established a church home, but God and I have regular conversations. I sense God's blessing.

Saturday, April twenty first I am at Carol's when Dan and Dick arrive. Carol and I go out and sit in Dan's car with them for awhile. Dick and I are visiting in the back seat.

"Next Friday there is a dance at Beloit High School. The theme is `Bali Hi'. Would you like to go with me?" Dick asks.

"It sounds wonderful," I say. His arm is up behind me on the back of the seat. He lowers it around my shoulder, and pulls me close to him. I look up at him and taste the sweetness of our first kiss.

He says, "That first night I met you. I was just pretending to read the funnies. I couldn't keep my eyes off you. You stood out special among the girls, like a flower blooming. Isn't it strange that neither of us had ever been to Carol's before?"

Dick is such a gentleman, his manners and appearance impress me. Was it God who brought us together, at this home neither of us had ever visited before? Is there a new horizon for us? Well, that is another story.

Author Pat with husband Richard in Hawaii-1994

Epilogue

Somewhere in the rush of feathering the nest, surviving a depression and sacrificing through the war years, Mama and Daddy drifted away from active involvement in their church.

They never abandoned the Christian principles with which they had been raised. Dad found it extremely difficult to speak the words, "I love you," but his actions expressed it throughout our lives. Mother's prayers protected us and kept us on the right track.

Dad was a reserved man with idiosyncrasies that tested those who dealt with him. Yet, after his death, we found hidden in his drawer a lifetime of greeting cards from his family, and small gifts that were never used, but treasured. Inside he was tender-hearted and sentimental. Dad carried a drive and devotion to provide for his children. Mend it, repair it, keep it forever was a way of life with him. His father's philosophy was, "Nothing ventured, nothing gained." Dad's philosophy was, "Waste not; want not," and "A penny saved is a penny earned."

Mother was high spirited and fun loving. You always knew where you stood with her. She was respected and loved by business acquaintances all over the area. Sometimes she barked, but her bark was always worse than her bite. She could be crisp on the outside, but soft as a marshmallow inside. Through the years Mother worked as hard as Dad but her philosophy was, "All work and no play, makes Jack a dull boy."

Dad chose plain attire and cared not how old it was. Mother was classy, liked baubles and everything that glittered. Their differences caused great chasms between them in their elder years, yet underlying it was the unconditional love that Jesus speaks of. They would have died for one another. Their sixty five year marriage proved that commitment.

They found their way back to God's house in later years, and all their children found their place in God's plan, too.

Last Family Picture Taken August 1992—Back Row—Tom, Pat, Dick, Bob, Gene—Center Row—Eleanor, Jackie, Ruth—Front—Mother (Della), Dad (Elton)

ORDER FORM

Whispering Pines Publications
3282 Yale Bridge Road
Rockton, Illinois 61072
Phone 815-624-7647

Name _____

Address _____

City _____

State _____ Zip Code _____

Life in Illisconsin (1927-1951)

Number of Copies _____@$9.95 each $ _____

In Wisconsin 5% sales tax ($.50 per book)   _____

In Illinois 6.25% sales tax ($.63 per book)   _____

Shipping and Handling ($1.50 per book)   _____

TOTAL ENCLOSED $ _____

ORDER FORM

Whispering Pines Publications
3282 Yale Bridge Road
Rockton, Illinois 61072
Phone 815-624-7647

Name _____

Address _____

City _____

State _____ Zip Code _____

Life in Illisconsin (1927-1951)

Number of Copies _____@$9.95 each $_____

In Wisconsin 5% sales tax ($.50 per book)   _____

In Illinois 6.25% sales tax ($.63 per book)   _____

Shipping and Handling ($1.50 per book)   _____

TOTAL ENCLOSED $_____